NORTHERN IRELAND —

(p 9)

JONATHAN TONGE

polity

First published in 2006 by Polity Press

Polity Press
65 Bridge Street
Cambridge CB2 1UR, UK.

Polity Press
350 Main Street
Malden, MA 02148, USA

ISBN: 0-7456-3140-1
ISBN: 0-7456-3141-X (pb)

A catalogue record for this book is available from the British Library.

Typeset in 10.5 on 12 pt Sabon
by Servis Filmsetting Ltd, Manchester
Printed and bound in Great Britain by T.J. International Ltd, Padstow Cornwall.

The publisher has used its best endeavours to ensure that the URLs for external websites referred to in this book are correct and active at the time of going to press. However, the publisher has no responsibility for the websites and can make no guarantee that a site will remain live or that the content is or will remain appropriate.

Every effort has been made to trace all copyright holders, but if any have been inadvertently overlooked the publishers will be pleased to include any necessary credits in any subsequent reprint or edition.

For further information on Polity, visit our website: www.polity.co.uk

Contents

To Maria

Acknowledgements

I wish to thank a number of people for their help in producing this book. Dr Louise Knight at Polity commissioned the work and proved a patient and helpful publisher, as did her colleague, Ellen McKinlay. The anonymous reviewers were also very supportive, and I am grateful for their constructive comments. Dr Catherine McGlynn helped with chapter 7 on loyalist paramilitaries. Professor James McAuley, Dr Jocelyn Evans, Dr Peter Shirlow, Professor Steven Fielding, Dr Kevin Bean, Dr Chris Gilligan, Andy Mycock, Jennie Coates, Anita Hopkins, Dermot Zafar, Stanley and Brenda Tonge all contributed in many different ways. Yvonne Murphy and Kris Brown were as helpful as ever in the Northern Ireland Political Collection in the Linenhall Library in Belfast. I am indebted to various officials at Sinn Fein, the SDLP, the Alliance Party, the Ulster Unionist Party and the Grand Orange Lodge of Ireland for facilitating interviews and/or membership surveys in recent years. The Economic and Social Research Council has financed three of these surveys, and their financial assistance is gratefully acknowledged. Thanks are due to the University of Salford for research sabbatical leave in 2004–5. I am grateful to all the political parties for permitting interviews with members over a prolonged period between 1999 and 2004. Garda Siochana detectives took an interest in research visits for chapter 6. My young son Connell has a knack of asking difficult but brilliant questions. The book is dedicated to Maria. Responsibility for its content is of course my own.

List of Tables ─────────────

List of Abbreviations

APNI	Alliance Party of Northern Ireland
CIRA	Continuity Irish Republican Army
CLMC	Combined Loyalist Military Command
DUP	Democratic Unionist Party
FRU	Force Research Unit
GFA	Good Friday Agreement
IICD	Independent International Commission on Decommissioning
IIP	Irish Independence Party
INLA	Irish National Liberation Army
IRA	Irish Republican Army
LVF	Loyalist Volunteer Force
MLA	Member of the Legislative Assembly
MRF	Military Reconnaissance Force
NIHRC	Northern Ireland Human Rights Commission
NILP	Northern Ireland Labour Party
NIO	Northern Ireland Office
NORAID	Irish Northern Aid Committee
NSMC	North–South Ministerial Council
NUPRG	New Ulster Political Research Group
OIRA	Official Irish Republican Army
PFI	Private Finance Initiatives
PIRA	Provisional Irish Republican Army
PSF	Provisional Sinn Fein
PSNI	Police Service of Northern Ireland
PUP	Progressive Unionist Party

RIRA	Real Irish Republican Army
RSF	Republican Sinn Fein
RUC	Royal Ulster Constabulary
SAS	Special Air Service
SDLP	Social Democratic and Labour Party
SEUPB	Special European Union Programmes Body
STV	Single Transferable Vote
UDA	Ulster Defence Association
UDR	Ulster Defence Regiment
UFF	Ulster Freedom Fighters
UKUP	United Kingdom Unionist Party
ULDP	Ulster Loyalist Democratic Party
UPRG	Ulster Political Research Group
UPV	Ulster Protestant Volunteers
UUC	Ulster Unionist Council
UUP	Ulster Unionist Party
UVF	Ulster Volunteer Force
UWC	Ulster Workers Council
32 CSM	32 County Sovereignty Movement

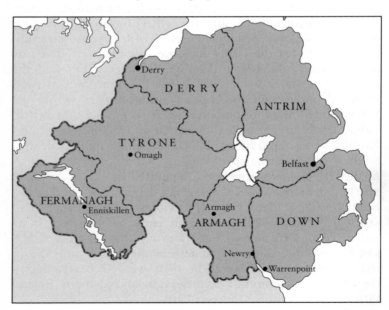

Introduction

Historical Background: Understanding Northern Ireland as a 'Hot Spot'

The conflict in Northern Ireland from 1969 until the beginning of the twenty-first century was by far the worst seen in Western Europe since the Second World War. Of the 3,665 deaths in the conflict up to 2002, republicans, fighting mainly within the Irish Republican Army (IRA) for an independent, united Ireland, were responsible for 2,148. Loyalist paramilitaries, mainly in the Ulster Defence Association (UDA), its 'killing wing', the Ulster Freedom Fighters (UFF) and the Ulster Volunteer Force (UVF) killed 1,071 in their avowed 'defence' of Northern Ireland's continued place within the United Kingdom. The combined 'security forces' of the British Army, Ulster Defence Regiment, Royal Irish Regiment and Royal Ulster Constabulary (RUC) accounted for 365 deaths, in their avowed role of combating paramilitary activity. A further 81 deaths were either committed by others or could not be attributed (McKittrick et al. 1999). The conflict has been subsiding, albeit unevenly (with some particularly bad years in the early 1990s), since the early 1970s, when, in its worst year, 497 were killed. During that decade, 2,176 lost their lives, compared to 891 in the 1980s and 553 in the 1990s. From 2000 to 2003, there were 46 deaths due to the security situation (Police Service of Northern Ireland 2003).

At the heart of the armed conflict was the campaign of the Provisional IRA (PIRA), effectively *the* IRA for most of the conflict, for the ending of the partition of Ireland, the removal of British rule in Northern Ireland, and the establishment of a thirty-two-county, independent Irish Republic. In pursuing this cause, the IRA targeted the British security forces, although a substantial minority of its victims were civilians. The PIRA's *raison d'être* may have been the territorial unity and independence of Ireland. However, after its inception in 1970, much of the PIRA's support from the minority Catholic population in Northern Ireland was on the basis that the IRA was that population's 'defender', rather than necessarily being the creator of a united Ireland, although the IRA proved incapable of fulfilling either role. Support for the IRA was fuelled by resentment of the British Army and the police force in Northern Ireland, seen as partisan entities oppressing nationalists. The IRA's armed struggle was not formally abandoned until 2005, but its campaign against British rule effectively ended in 1997, when it called its second cease-fire of the 1990s.

IRA violence prompted a strong backlash from loyalist paramilitary groups, the self-appointed 'cutting edge' of the resistance of the British population of Northern Ireland, as armed loyalists demonstrated that they would not be coerced into an independent Ireland. The polity of Northern Ireland was carved from a dubious but pragmatic sectarian head count in 1920, designed to allow the Protestant-unionist-British population concentrated mainly in the north-east corner of the island to retain their Britishness. Unionists, many supporting the heavily armed UVF formed in 1912, were determined to resist absorption into an independent Ireland; decades later, that resistance had not diminished and formed the basis of the revival of the UVF and other loyalist groups, even though, in the modern troubles, most unionists expressed their unionism in constitutional form. Although the post-1969 conflict did not descend into a civil war between loyalists and republicans, there were periods when such a scenario appeared possible.

The IRA based its case upon an interpretation of history which viewed Ireland as a colonial possession of the British, with 'armed struggle' necessary to remove the British govern-ment's claim to sovereignty. The IRA had rebelled against British rule in 1916, and the majority of the island's citizens had supported Sinn Fein, campaigning for an independent Irish state, in the last all-Ireland election ever held, in 1918. As such, there was a democratic mandate for the establishment of an independent Ireland. Unionists in the North declined to accept this result or the Home Rule (semi-independence) offered by the British government to the entire island. Instead, what became termed by republicans as the 'unionist veto' emerged, by which Ireland was partitioned. Six of the nine counties in north-east Ireland, those with the strongest Protestant-unionist-British majorities formed Northern Ireland, with its own devolved parliament under the sovereign Westminster parliament. The IRA in the other twenty-six counties of Ireland divided over whether to accept partition and only semi-independence under the Anglo-Irish Treaty and fought a civil war. However, these twenty-six counties eventually asserted their independence, no longer swearing allegiance to a British monarch and leaving the British Commonwealth in 1949. The parties in what eventually became the Irish Republic, notably *Fianna Fáil* (Soldiers of Destiny), the descendant of the original IRA which had resisted the Anglo-Irish Treaty, continued to oppose the partition of Ireland, but verbally, not physically.

Unionists based their case to be British upon a similar premiss as the IRA: the right to national self-determination. Regarding themselves as politically, religiously and culturally British, in addition to having developed the north-east part of the island economically, unionists argued that two nations existed on the same territory, and that partition was formal acceptance of an existing scenario. Sinn Fein had obtained relatively little support in the 1918 election in Ulster, where there was a narrow unionist majority, stronger when Ulster was redefined politically as Northern Ireland. Absorption of Protestant unionists, present on the island since the plantation of Ulster in the early 1600s, would have created a dissident minority within a disjointed Catholic Irish state in which Protestant political and religious freedoms could be threatened.

Despite rival historical interpretations and the unhappiness of the one-third Catholic-nationalist minority population in Northern Ireland, trapped in a Protestant-unionist-British entity in which they felt alien and second class, the northern state suffered only episodic violence during its first five decades, conflict being most substantial in the early years after the partition of Ireland and during an easily quashed rebellion by the IRA from 1956 to 1962. The tensions within the province were less easily suppressed on a long-term basis. Nationalist demands for reform of Northern Ireland were met by an insecure and at times hostile unionist response. Partly as a consequence of the failure to reform Northern Ireland, the IRA rose, phoenix-like, in 1970, to create what was supposed to be a 'final' outcome to the problem of Northern Ireland: its abolition and the establishment of an independent, united Ireland, free from British sovereign claims. Measured by its own objectives, that campaign ended in failure amid the watering down of republican demands in the peace process in the 1990s. After the 'peace deal' of the 1998 Good Friday Agreement, Northern Ireland moved initially into perhaps its more common form, with the following elements apparent: sporadic, low-level violence; paramilitary criminality; distrust between (Irish Catholic) nationalists and (British Protestant) unionists; malfunctioning political institutions; sectarianism and a dependency culture. However, with the Provisional IRA eventually 'going out of business', the possibility of a durable political settlement, based upon power sharing between unionists and nationalists, appeared stronger than at any previous period in the history of the province.

The violence that characterized the three decades after 1969 looks dated. Global Islamic extremist 'jihad' now claims much greater attention than any lingering Irish republican militancy. The IRA pledged to fight until British rule in Northern Ireland was ended, but ended its campaign with its political wing, Sinn Fein, attempting to manage British rule in a Northern Ireland Assembly at Stormont, a parliament which the IRA had destroyed in 1972. Almost nine out of ten supporters of Sinn Fein, now the main nationalist party in Northern Ireland, state that they 'could accept' or 'could live with' Northern Ireland remaining in the United Kingdom if its population never voted to join a united Ireland (Bric and Coakley 2004b: 3).

The question begged, therefore, is what has been the purpose of political violence in Northern Ireland, given grudging nationalist acquiescence to the constitutional *status quo*. For many, the answer may be that violence has served no purpose. Given how the IRA campaign atrophied, this may be true, although it is perhaps to overlook the extent to which Northern Ireland has been formed and reshaped through political violence, or, perhaps more accurately, the threat of violence. For all the pious incantations throughout the Troubles about the need to defeat terrorists, Northern Ireland was a statelet formed partially through the threat of violence and, in the south, the Irish Free State, later the Irish Republic, was at least partly a product of British miscalculations in dealing with the 1916 Irish rebellion. The presence of the UVF prevented Home Rule for the entire island, and forced partition upon a reluctant British government and an opposed Irish population. After 1969, reborn loyalist paramilitaries reminded the British government of its supposed duty in respect of Northern Ireland, and served warning to the British government of civil war should it attempt to disengage from Northern Ireland. As a result, British 'policy' towards Northern Ireland has been 'residual colonial'. Britain exercises a reluctant sovereign claim over a territory in which it acknowledges it has 'no selfish strategic or economic interest'. The persistent underestimation of the impact of armed loyalism upon the British government created within the IRA 'fantasy politics and poor history', as the potential consequences of rapid withdrawal were too severe (Cusack and McDonald 2000: 1). Equally poor history, however, is the notion that constitutional arrangements in Ireland have been shaped merely by politics.

In an oft-quoted passage, Winston Churchill remarked after the First World War how 'we see the dreary steeples of Fermanagh and Tyrone emerging once again. The integrity of their quarrel is one of the few institutions that have been left unaltered in the cataclysm that is the modern world' (cited in Cusack and McDonald 2000: 39). The Good

Friday Agreement reshaped that quarrel by downgrading Irish historical territorial claims and attempting to replace their integrity with more abstract notions of 'identity'. It began to eradicate key questions of national sovereignty and self-determination. The IRA and Sinn Fein, having acted as the supposed will of the Irish people, now begged for recognition of their mandate on equal terms with all the other parties in Northern Ireland. Having insisted for decades that its existence was based upon opposition to Britain's colonial presence in Ireland, the IRA adopted pluralist notions of equality and parity of esteem for nationalists in a Northern Ireland still part of the United Kingdom.

By relegating questions of who governs to a more minor spot, the Good Friday Agreement climaxed a peace process of long gestation. Although historical evidence discourages such a conclusion (and historical determinism motivates some violent republicans), it is possible that serious violence in Northern Ireland is over permanently. The political conflict may not have ended, but the violence of the dispute has largely subsided, unlikely to return. Few Catholics in Northern Ireland care passionately about a united Ireland; few loyalists might fight to stay exclusively British. The possible difficulty with this argument is that few ever did feel passionately in these respects. Certainly on the Catholic side, support for armed struggle to achieve a united Ireland was only ever a minority taste, but this did not stop the descent into serious conflict. A political fault line remains apparent. According to survey evidence, variation in attitudes towards Northern Ireland's constitutional future according to religious denomination remains stark, as table 1.1 shows.

There remains a diminishing Protestant majority in Northern Ireland, 45 per cent of the population belonging to a Protestant denomination according to the 2001 census, compared to 42 per cent Catholics and 13 per cent of no religion. When the overwhelming support for the Union among Protestants is added to the 21 per cent of Catholics backing the Union and the 45 per cent of those of no religion, it is apparent that the Union is safe for the foreseeable future if the 'consent within Northern Ireland' principle is applied to constitutional change. A united Ireland remains the most popular option among Catholics in

Table I.1 Long-term constitutional preferences in Northern Ireland, according to religion

Long-term preference	Religion (per cent)		
	Protestant	Roman Catholic	None
Remain part of the United Kingdom	82	21	45
Reunify with rest of Ireland	5	49	27
Independent state	5	10	10
Other	1	2	4
Don't know	7	18	14

Source: Northern Ireland Life and Times Survey 2003

Northern Ireland and is almost certainly favoured across the island, but Catholic constitutional preferences in respect of Irish unity would need to be even more overwhelming than those among Protestants in favour of the Union for a demographic political time bomb – a rising Catholic population capable of voting Northern Ireland out of the Union – to confront unionists. Should the unlikely happen and a pro-united Ireland majority emerge, over half of Protestants could live with the scenario, but 19 per cent would find it 'almost impossible to accept' (Northern Ireland Life and Times Survey 2003).

Overall, only 24 per cent of Northern Ireland's population support Irish unity (Northern Ireland Life and Times Survey 2003). This figure would rise only to just over 30 per cent if Catholic 'don't knows', possibly reluctant to advocate Irish unity because of its past association with violence and confrontation, were included.

The IRA's campaign was of course built upon the perceived illegitimacy of Northern Ireland, an entity contrived against the expressed wishes of the majority of Irish people. Yet, by 2003, only one-third of Catholics rated the prospect of a united Ireland an even chance or better in the next 20 years, fewer than the 38 per cent of Protestants who rated similarly the prospects for Irish unity (Northern Ireland Life and Times Survey 2003).

Although described as a hope against history, the Good

Friday Agreement, and any similarly framed successor, is likely to consolidate peace and develop political stability in a polity acknowledged hitherto by supporters as insecure and seen until recently by opponents as illegitimate. The constitutional contest has diminished markedly in ferocity, and Northern Ireland is barely a contested state, given the willingness of Sinn Fein to serve in its political institutions. The new politics of Northern Ireland might still be competitive between unionists and nationalists, but tends to concern the spoils of the settlement rather than the immediate future of the state. Seventy per cent of Protestants believe that nationalists 'benefited a lot more than unionists from the Good Friday Agreement', none believing the reverse (Northern Ireland Life and Times Survey 2003). Despite having to shelve their constitutional ambitions, nationalists believe that both communities benefited equally. The messages from these ostensibly paradoxical findings are that territorial ambitions and constitutional futures are less important for nationalists than equality, whilst, for unionists, the defence of the constitutional *status quo* was either not apparent, or overshadowed by concessions to nationalists elsewhere.

This book examines the reasons why Northern Ireland has long been a political hot spot. It explores the rationale for violence on the Irish republican and Ulster/British loyalist sides and assesses how the propensity for violence has shaped mainstream party politics and the attitudes of the British and Irish governments. Despite highlighting the contradictions within Northern Ireland as a political entity, the book indicates why a return to previous levels of violence is unlikely in a polity that may gradually become depoliticized. Nearly a century after Churchill's exasperation, there are indications that the quarrel between British unionism and Irish nationalism has been ended by newer forms of politics than the old certainties of anti-colonial struggle versus British sovereign claim.

The Plan of the Book

The main aims of the book are to examine the bases of division which led to political violence; explore the nature of that violence; assess the roles of the key perpetrators of that violence, and discuss whether the causes of conflict and the paramilitary actors have finally been removed. Chapter 1 examines rival theories of the conflict. It explores the contention that Northern Ireland is a site of ethno-national rivalry between two national groups, Irish and British, with distinctive characteristics and political ambitions. It assesses the validity of the claim that the essence of the conflict is ethno-religious, a claim normally made when particular attention is given to unionist perspectives. Colonial explanations, rare these days but deserving of attention, are explored, whilst economic disparities, important but perhaps not crucial in mobilizing nationalist discontent at the start of the conflict, are assessed.

Chapter 2 assesses the aims, objectives and methods of the PIRA. It examines the extent to which the organization represented continuity from the 'old IRA' of the early twentieth century, and outlines the structural and political differences. The chapter analyses whether the IRA was the sectarian organization claimed by its critics or whether it represented the physical force tradition of 'liberating' Ireland and creating unity of Catholic, Protestant and Dissenter, envisaged by the 'first' Irish republican, Wolfe Tone, in the late eighteenth century. The IRA's avowed aims and the failure to fulfil its territorial demands are assessed, as is the utility of violence in achieving a united Ireland or creating a better deal for nationalists within Northern Ireland. The chapter traces the reasons behind the IRA's 'full circle' movement, from violence seen as necessary and just towards the decommissioning of its weapons.

Chapters 3 and 4 examine the different means used to prosecute the war against the IRA. First, there was the overt action taken by the British Army, the UDR, the Royal Irish Regiment and the RUC, assessed in chapter three, which made Northern Ireland easily the most heavily policed area of Europe. At the height of the conflict, more than 30,000 British troops were based in the province, many in front line duties, with the remainder acting as policing support. Although many mistakes were made in the early years of the conflict, the coercive policy eventually contained an IRA which had developed as a result of those early blunders. Secondly, and detailed in chapter 4, behind the public 'war' against the IRA lay a secretive 'dirty' war in which elements of the British security forces conspired with loyalist paramilitaries for part of the conflict to defeat the IRA. Operating beyond legal parameters, the full details of these operations are only now being revealed.

With the IRA under such pressure, republicans were obliged to develop their political strength to survive and did so successfully, a process examined in chapter 5 on Sinn Fein. The need to enlarge electoral appeal has led to Sinn Fein's growth as the dominant force within Northern Irish nationalism. Among a small section of republicans, however, the electoral concerns of Sinn Fein have eclipsed traditional republican principles and tactics. Chapter 6 assesses the views and methods of die-hard republicans, still committed to a physical force 'struggle'. Chapter 7 examines the logic of loyalist violence, and considers whether it was based on naked sectarianism or a rational defence of the Union. Chapter 8 explores the party system in Northern Ireland, as the old moderate parties of the Ulster Unionist Party (UUP) and nationalist Social Democratic and Labour Party (SDLP) have been eclipsed by, respectively, the DUP and Sinn Fein. Chapter 9 examines the implementation deficit of the Good Friday Agreement (GFA), a deal designed to manage conflict through elite accommodation, but one which has been unstable and prone to substitution by direct rule from Westminster. The necessary ambiguities of the GFA have permitted a residual culture of low-level paramilitarism and organized criminality. Concurrently, political instability has increased cynicism over whether the deal can move Northern Ireland towards a fully functioning democracy.

The book ends by assessing whether ongoing political rivalries will continue to destabilize Northern Ireland, or whether it is likely to move from being an insecure post-conflict entity towards a durable, secure and peaceful polity in which political violence and, eventually, sectarianism will be seen as historic relics of a distant era.

1   Theories of the Conflict ——

Part of the problem in resolving the Northern Ireland conflict was that for years those involved or interested, whether 'combatants' or analysts, disagreed on its basis. Republicans offered a beguilingly simple colonial analysis, which found much sympathy outside the narrow confines of unionism, in which Northern Ireland was seen as one of Britain's last colonies, a relic of Empire from which it had rapidly retreated elsewhere. This analysis was not confined to the militant republicans of Sinn Fein and the IRA. Northern Ireland was described as a 'failed political entity' by a *Taoiseach* (Prime Minister) of the Irish Republic, Charles Haughey. Constitutional republicans within Fianna Fail, often the governing party in the Irish Republic, denounced the partition of Ireland, suggesting that unionist-British rule in the North had been disastrous. It had been sectarian majority rule, followed by descent into violence and failed political initiatives.

Non-republicans offered a variety of alternative explanations, although the most common unionist complaint was the 'irredentist' claim to Northern Ireland held, if not pursued, under the 1937 constitution of the Irish Republic. Within academia, accounts of the conflict were often partisan unionist (e.g. Wilson 1955, 1989) or nationalist-oriented accounts (e.g. Farrell 1976). Given that academic inquiry was often coloured by background, the lack of consensus among political representatives and paramilitary actors was unsurprising. None the less, academics did acknowledge that the conflict was a product of a multiplicity of factors. In his assessment of rival academic works, John Whyte noted that 'while there is agreement that the conflict results from a mixture of religious, economic, political and psychological factors, there is no agreement on their relative importance. In particular there is a divergence on how much stress to put on religion' (Whyte 1991: 245).

Ethno-national Explanations and Solutions

The most orthodox modern explanation of the Northern Ireland problem is that it is ethno-national in nature, a contest between two peoples who want their 'state to be ruled by their nation' (McGarry and O'Leary 1995: 354). The armed conflict from 1970 until the end of the century was based primarily around the violent attempt of Irish republicans to coerce the unionist population into a state to which they felt they did not belong. Unionists believe themselves to be 'simply British' (Ulster Unionist Party 2003). Nationalists regard themselves as Irish, and both populations desire political expression of their identity. Unionists, an overwhelming majority of whom want Northern Ireland to remain in the United Kingdom, defend the constitutional *status quo*, whilst conceding a modest all-Ireland dimension to political arrangements. Nationalist desires for an independent, united Ireland are not as extensive or as intense as unionist demands for Northern Ireland to remain out of an independent Ireland, according to successive Northern Ireland Life and Times Surveys (see also Bric and Coakley 2004a: 2–4). Nationalists have been prepared to settle for an Irish dimension, rather than Irish unity and independence, accepting, however reluctantly, Northern Ireland's location within the United Kingdom. The violent struggle of armed republicans to achieve a united, independent Ireland ended in failure, although the compromise reached by republicans, the 1998 Good Friday Agreement (GFA), offered power sharing for nationalists within Northern Ireland, allied to the establishment of six new cross-border bodies, creating all-island economic activity.

Ethno-national explanations offer a number of advantages. They acknowledge the polarity of identity and aspiration in Northern Ireland. Palpably, most individuals from a Protestant-unionist tradition are likely to support Northern Ireland's continued place in the United Kingdom and regard themselves as British. Equally, the sense of Irishness felt by a Catholic nationalist is unlikely to wither. Ethno-national explanations legitimize the political aspirations of both communities, whilst allowing the diversion of such aspirations into the identity politics which began to displace territorial politics during the Northern Ireland peace process. Territorial politics are more dangerous, being based upon the assertion, by force on occasion, of national self-determination within boundaries which may be contested. Identity politics are less threatening, in that the recognition of unionists and nationalists as British and Irish respectively does not threaten the state.

Colonial Explanations

The IRA's armed struggle had impetus from a range of perceived grievances, including the illegitimacy of partition, the mistreatment of nationalists by the unionist population, economic inequality and religious sectarianism (Bishop and Mallie 1988; Buckland 1981; Coogan 1996; English 2003; Farrell 1976; McIntyre 1995, 2001; M. Smith 1995; Tonge 2002, 2005). Supposedly at the core of IRA activity, however, was a desire to end Ireland's connection with Britain, the source of 'all our evils' according to one of the 'fathers' of republicanism, Wolfe Tone, who led a rebellion against British rule in 1798.

According to colonial interpretations, Ireland was colonized by Britain, a subordination codified by the Act of Union of 1800. This colonization involved a series of crimes against the Irish people, who were denied nationhood: discrimination, evidenced by a series of anti-Catholic laws during the nineteenth century; maltreatment and neglect, demonstrated by the Irish famine; and subordination, epitomized by the brutal quelling of rebellions and execution of rebels, most notably after the 1916 Easter Rising against British rule. Under pressure from the native population, the British government retreated from twenty-six of the thirty-two counties of the colony it held. The 'war in the North' against British rule, episodic after partition but sustained from 1970 until the mid-1990s, was justified as 'unfinished business' – a struggle for national liberation against a foreign occupying force. The IRA believed that Britain would withdraw from one of its remaining colonies in the same manner as it had retreated from Empire elsewhere. Republicans of different hues shared the colonial analysis of Britain's occupation of Northern Ireland. There were marked differences concerning the morality and utility of force as a means to end that occupation, but republicanism was the 'dominant dream' on the island (Bowyer Bell 2000: 36, 98).

Under traditional colonial interpretations, the assertion of the 'principle of consent' for constitutional change, the basis of British policy towards Northern Ireland for decades, was unacceptable. It referred only to consent within the six counties which created the artificial statelet of Northern Ireland, against the will of the majority of Irish people. In the last – perhaps final – all-Ireland general election of 1918, a majority of Ireland's voters supported Sinn Fein, campaigning for an independent Ireland. Instead, they got partition, formally chosen by no voters. Since that election, the option of a sovereign independent and united Ireland has never been laid before the inhabitants of the island. Whilst it could be claimed that the Irish people voted *de facto* for partition by supporting the GFA in the referendums North and South in 1998, this was not a true act of Irish self-determination, as the colonial power determined which constitutional options were laid before the electorate. Only 50 per cent of the Irish electorate registered support for the removal of Articles Two and Three of the constitution of the Irish Republic, laying claim to Northern Ireland, in the 1998 referendum. Had the option of registering support for a united Ireland appeared on the ballot paper, the outcome might have been different, even though the practical possibility of its rapid implementation appeared to be zero. Although results depend on whether the prospect of Irish unity is posed as an aspiration or an imperative, up to two-thirds of the citizens on the island of Ireland support a united Ireland

(W. H. Cox 1985; Hayes and McAllister 1996; Tonge 2005). The colonial analysis of Britain's supposed 'lack of interest' highlights the willingness of successive Westminster governments to commit thousands of troops to defend the territorial integrity of a statelet created against the will of the majority of Irish people.

The colonial interpretation has not necessarily been diminished by Britain's insistence that it has no 'selfish, strategic or economic interest' in Northern Ireland. British withdrawal would have been humiliating for a British government, and its continuing claim to sovereignty is at least a partial consequence of aversion to such a reverse. The British sovereign claim, under the no 'selfish interest' mantra, has been portrayed as an altruistic act which prevented the Irish and British on the island from engaging in civil war. There may be some truth in this analysis, but it was unclear why *British* forces were required to maintain order when they were clearly not neutral brokers. Indeed, British security forces sometimes colluded with loyalist paramilitaries to quell insurgency. Although the level of suppression of the native population was minor compared to several other global conflicts, the state apparatus deployed to stop the secession of Britain's 'last colony' was hardly a paradigm of liberal democracy. It included (the list is far from exhaustive) internment without trial, state-sponsored killing and collusion, direct state killings, inhuman and degrading treatment of prisoners, the arrest of thousands of Irish people under the Prevention of Terrorism Act, only a small minority of whom were ever charged, the construction of a plethora of security installations, extensive stop and search powers, and the abolition of trial by jury. If these were the actions of a government without 'selfish strategic or economic interest', it is tempting to ask what would have happened if such altruism and selflessness had been replaced by partisanship?

The Weaknesses in Colonial Arguments

The flaws in colonial arguments include three principal items; the extent of the mandate for British withdrawal, the status of unionists, and the role of the British government. The 1918 all-Ireland referendum result produced an aggregate majority for British withdrawal, given that nationalists won 70 per cent of the votes in contested seats (McGarry and O'Leary 1995: 36). In four of the six counties – Antrim, Armagh, Derry and Down – that were to comprise Northern Ireland, unionists none the less won a majority of votes (O'Leary and McGarry 1996). It could be argued that what was wrong was not partition *per se*, but the border drawn on the map, which had little political, geographic or historic logic. Although Fermanagh and Tyrone contained nationalist majorities, they were included in the new statelet, often erroneously referred to as Ulster, despite Northern Ireland being a deliberately emaciated version of the historic province. The border's contours have become increasingly absurd given that demographic change (a rising number of Catholic nationalists) indicates that only Down and Antrim continue to have pro-Union majorities. 'Self-determination' for two counties appears preposterous.

None the less, it is apparent that, at the time of partition, the majority of the population in the north-east corner of the island did not want Ireland to secede from the British state, of which, after the 1800 Act of Union, it was an integral part. The intensity of British unionism exceeded that of Irish nationalism on several indicators. Many Irish nationalists fought for Britain in the First World War; the Sinn Fein vote in 1918 was partly a sympathy vote due to the execution of Irish rebels after the 1916 Easter Rising, and 471,000 unionists signed a solemn covenant to resist even the semi-independence of Home Rule for Ireland. The plea of the democrat that unionists should not have been permitted to opt out of the people's verdict was unpersuasive to those affected. Disagreement over the unit of self-determination has been central to the 'problem of Ireland'. What emerged was a contrived and unsatisfactory unit in the North (although few states have natural boundaries), one which displeased the majority population on the island, but satisfied those to whom self-determination perhaps mattered more.

Under orthodox colonial interpretations, unionists are

reduced to the status of neo-colonial agents of the British, duped into holding a British identity when they are merely deluded Irish people suffering from a false national consciousness. Leaving aside arguments over who was on the island first (one unionist account claims that settlers from Scotland were there first (Adamson 1982)), the claim that Protestant-British-unionists were simply Irish hardly resonated with a population whose national and political identities were essentially British. Adherents of colonial arguments could claim, with validity, that the 'Britishness' of unionists was something of a post-partition flag of convenience; indeed, until the collapse of Northern Ireland's devolved parliament in 1972, a sizeable percentage adopted either an Ulster or an Irish identity (Rose 1971). None the less, unionists have always argued that their political identity is British, and that unionism is an ideology based upon defence of their Britishness. The classic colonial view was that, following British withdrawal, unionists would abandon attachment to the dissolved Union and recognize their status as Irish people. In such an unlikely scenario, it would indeed be possible that some unionists would acquiesce in a unification process, in the way that many nationalists accepted partition. Equally, the chance of an entirely peaceful unionist acceptance of such change, or their redefinition as Irish, is slim. By the 1990s, even republicans acknowledged the difficulty of Irish unification via coercion. Sinn Fein's policy document, *Towards a Lasting Peace in Ireland*, conceded that unionism was not merely a deluded tradition, and that unionists would have to be persuaded by the British government that a united Ireland could work in their interests, as a precursor to Irish unity (Sinn Fein 1992). This amounted to acceptance of the existence of two national populations on the island of Ireland, rather than the previous 'we are all Irish' republican approach.

The final weakness of colonial arguments lies in the perception of the role of the British government. The traditional republican view was based upon a critique of the 'denial of national sovereignty to the Irish people through British occupation of part of the national territory' (32 County Sovereignty Movement constitution, cited in Coakley 2002: 135). The

British government insists that its 'occupation' represents nothing more than the will of the majority of the citizens of Northern Ireland. Although Britain was culpable in the partition of Ireland, that division was a consequence of existing ethnic rivalries, rather than a cunning plot by the British government, which desired Home Rule for the entire island. Far from being a colonial aggressor, the British government has long been anxious to divest itself of its 'Irish problem'. The Westminster government draws no economic benefit from involvement in a Northern Ireland economy largely devoid of industrial capacity. Any geo-strategic value of Northern Ireland as an Atlantic outpost evaporated with the end of the Cold War. Indeed, it has been claimed that the end of the Cold War allowed a peace process to develop in which Britain could more credibly plead neutrality (M. Cox 1998; M. Cox et al. 2001). The British government has indicated that it will legislate to withdraw should there be sufficient demand within the 'occupied' territory.

Structural Explanations

Structural explanations of the Northern Ireland conflict suggest that much of the antagonism that developed in the late 1960s was a nationalist response to a disadvantaged economic position, exacerbated by second-class political status, rather than a demand for a united Ireland. Civil rights marches in the 1960s, attended overwhelmingly by nationalists, were demands for 'British rights for British citizens'. Catholics began to demand a stake in the polity they had previously rejected, demanding 'one man [sic] one vote' (non-ratepayers were denied the franchise in local elections), economic equality and impartial policing. The structural argument suggests that nationalist demands were reformist. They were mishandled by a divided unionist government in the late 1960s, unsure how to deal with the challenge to its authority and vulnerable to reactionary forces within and outside the Ulster Unionist Party (UUP). In response to unionism's hardline reaction, backed by the British Army from late 1969 onwards, nationalists divided into two broad categories: participatory constitutional forces within the SDLP, formed in 1970, and militant paramilitary forces, represented mainly by the PIRA. The responses of nationalists were conditioned by their conditions of oppression: long-standing political and economic inequality and then the crude responses of unionism and the British state to their subordinate position. As such, although economic issues have been 'subsidiary themes' in Northern Ireland, they may have been highly significant (Rose 1976: 36; Wichert 1999).

Protests against structural inequalities fuelled the rebirth of republicanism, providing it with modern meaning, in which the British government and its devolved unionist state could be blamed for oppressing Irish people. Significantly, the revival of militant republicanism was largely confined to the downtrodden Catholic working class, or poorer rural workers, in Northern Ireland and did not become an island-wide phenomenon. As McIntyre (2001: 209) notes, 'partition in itself was insufficient to nourish, let alone sustain, a thirty-two countrywide nationalist ideology articulating the necessity of completing the "unfinished business" of 1921'.

Catholics were under-represented in political institutions, the police and civil service, also suffering economically in the 'Orange state' from 1921 until 1972. Various pleas of mitigation have been offered for the unionist regime. Discrimination was exaggerated for political ends, and was a product partly of Catholic inferiority according to accounts which engaged in cultural stereotyping (Wilson 1955, 1989). Nationalist abstention from state institutions worsened their plight (Buckland 1981). Sectarianism was practised to mask divisions within a unionist government less united than popularly supposed (Bew, Gibbon and Patterson 2002). Moreover, the unionist 'Protestant state for a Protestant people' (Northern Ireland's Prime Minister notoriously referred to the legislature as being a 'Protestant parliament for a Protestant people') was created partly in response to the way in which the initially non-confessional Irish Free State increasingly became a Catholic state for a Catholic people. The twenty-six-county state in the South embodied laws derived from Catholic social teaching and enshrined the special position of the Roman Catholic Church in its 1937 constitution. That constitution laid claim to Northern Ireland in Articles 2 and 3, heightening the siege mentality of unionists, a mind-set hardly assuaged by the IRA's 1956–62 border campaign of violence, even though the IRA's revival met with little Catholic enthusiasm.

Despite the extenuating circumstances, the unionist government was palpably guilty of sectarian discrimination. The regime was condemned by the words of its own leaders. A future Prime Minister, Basil Brooke, recommended 'those people who are Loyalists not to employ Roman Catholics, 99 per cent of whom are disloyal', sentiments endorsed by the Prime Minister, James Craig, who insisted that 'there is not one of my colleagues who does not entirely agree with him' (cited in Ryder and Kearney 2001: 43). Brooke boasted that he had 'not a Catholic about his place', insisting that 'Catholics are out to destroy Ulster [sic] with all their might and power', and later confirming that his remarks were made 'after careful consideration' (*Irish News*, 1 December 1935). Clientelist relationships developed in which Protestant workers were rewarded for support of the regime by preferential economic treatment (more jobs). Proportional representation was abolished for all forms of election by the end of the 1920s, to deny nationalist representation and solidify the unionist party bloc. Protestant supporters of the unionist government on local councils were allowed to create self-perpetuating fiefdoms through the gerrymandering of electoral boundaries. The extent of gerrymandering, blatant in cities such as Derry, allowed unionists, two-thirds of the population, to control 85 per cent of councils. The requirement for district election voters to be home-owners disproportionately disadvantaged Catholics, as did multiple business votes, given that homes and businesses were more likely to be owned by Protestants.

Economic discrimination was rife, with Catholic rates of unemployment more than double those of Protestants, one of the few differentials that has remained despite a plethora of fair employment legislation since the collapse of the unionist government in 1972. Catholics were largely excluded from the labour aristocracy of skilled manual workers, and rarely held engineering positions. A disproportionately high number of Catholics were found in the ranks of the unskilled, vulnerable to periodic unemployment in a declining economy which endured rates of joblessness exceeding the United Kingdom average. Catholics endured relative deprivation compared to the Protestant working class, itself poor, but more likely to find work whilst indigenous industry remained in Protestant hands. As a British government minister conceded:

> the type of work done by Catholics was on average more menial, more temporary, less interesting and less rewarding. There was a problem and the nationalist community was right to demand the injustices be addressed. Many unionist leaders had refused to accept the problem's existence. A number of superficial and sometimes almost racist anecdotes were often trotted out in support of insupportable arguments.
>
> (Needham 1998: 302)

Catholics were, however, beneficiaries of the British welfare state, reluctantly introduced by the unionist government, which largely eradicated absolute poverty and allowed academically gifted Catholics to attend grammar school and eventually form part of a small but growing Catholic middle class, which helped organize the civil rights campaign.

The economic plight of Catholics was accompanied by political exclusion, based predominantly upon the fear of nationalist insurgency, but with an added theological distrust of the supposed expansionism of the Roman Catholic Church (Kennedy-Pipe 1997: 11–12). The UUP governed alone from 1921 to 1972, insulated from challenge by the in-built majoritarianism established via partition and effectively forcing confrontation 'onto the streets'. The Nationalist Party, clergy-dominated and ineffectual, did not bother to become the official opposition until 1965, such was its impotent position.

These political and economic deprivations were necessary but insufficient conditions for armed nationalist rebellion against the state. It was their conjunction with the inability of the unionist government to head off reactionary forces that provided the motivation for militancy. When the British Army arrived in August 1969, it was initially welcomed as a neutral force, replacing the loathed Protestant B Specials, the reserve police force. Amid little political progress, the British Army soon came to be seen as an element of the forces propping up the unionist government, shoring up a discriminatory regime and, by late 1970, becoming a target for attack by a reborn IRA.

Structural explanations offer a plausible rationale for the rise and fall of the conflict. Nationalists rebelled due to their subordinate position in Northern Ireland, second-class citizens in a state from which they felt alienated. They felt no great allegiance to the Irish Republic, under whose lesser welfare state they might have fared worse, but resented unionist and British governments which presided over their derogatory treatment. The gradual eradication of differentials between the two communities during the conflict, under direct rule from the Westminster government from 1972 onwards, allied to the moderation of the Catholic middle class, limited the scope of that rebellion, preventing Sinn Fein and the IRA from gaining majority backing from the Catholic community. By 1998, nationalists were happy to support the Good Friday Agreement, offering economic equality, parity of esteem, policing changes and inclusive government, rather than a united Ireland. From this, it can be concluded that structural change, rather than territorial unity, was the primary goal of nationalists.

Sinn Fein recognized the plateau in its support created not merely by the continuing armed struggle of the IRA (although this was crucial) but also by the emergence of a prosperous Catholic class for whom partition had not provided a barrier to progress. Sinn Fein's support remains predominantly within the working class, especially among the young (McAllister 2004). None the less, the party had to re-pitch its appeal to those who have prospered under the Union (Coulter 1999). As such, Sinn Fein embarked on a 'process of de-ghettoization' (Shirlow 2002: 67). Discrimination against Catholics has largely disappeared (as have many of the industries in which it was exercised), as successive Westminster governments, Conservative and Labour, have legislated towards its eradication (Cunningham 2001). Entry to the police service, which Catholics have been reluctant to join, is now on a statutory 50/50, Catholic/non-Catholic basis. Catholics form a higher percentage of the work-force holding degrees, to cite one indicator of progress (Black 2004: 70).

The main criticism of structural arguments is that they amount to economic reductionism. The aspiration to a united Ireland remains the most popular option amongst Catholics in Northern Ireland, at around 50–60 per cent according to recent Northern Ireland Life and Times surveys. Economic progress for the Catholic community has not been accompanied by greater loyalty to the United Kingdom. Economic parity, achieved within a Northern Ireland forming part of the United Kingdom, has failed to reshape identity, as Catholics overwhelmingly declare themselves Irish, not British. Political representatives of the nationalist community have always rejected purely internal solutions to the Northern Ireland problem, demanding, as a minimum, an Irish dimension. Throughout its campaign, the IRA waged violence to achieve British withdrawal, settling, via Sinn Fein, for equality within Northern Ireland only when it accepted that Irish reunification was not attainable.

Ethno-religious Explanations and Criticisms

Attempts at political solutions in Northern Ireland have been predicated upon the assumption that the conflict is ethnonational in nature. None the less, some have attributed the problem mainly to its religious dimension (cf. Harris 1972; Hickey 1984; Bruce 1986; Crawford 1987). This view is expressed most straightforwardly by Bruce (1986: 249) in an oft-quoted passage:

> The Northern Ireland conflict is a religious conflict. Economic and social differences are also crucial, but it was the fact that the competing populations in Northern Ireland adhered and

still adhere to competing religious traditions which has given the conflict its enduring and intractable quality.

The argument that the conflict is essentially religious can be constructed in the following ways. First, religion has been a historical dividing point between the native Catholic Irish and the 'immigrant' Scottish Presbyterians, however absurd it may seem to describe the latter, 400-year-old tradition on the island as immigrant. Secondly, partition was enacted largely because of Protestant hostility to the prospect of 'Rome rule' via Dublin, and the defence of 'Protestant Ulster' has been a key part of unionist discourse. Thirdly, the main unionist parties have been closely linked to Protestant organizations. The UUP was linked formally to the Orange Order, and the Democratic Unionist Party (DUP) is connected informally to Ian Paisley's Free Presbyterian Church. The DUP pledges to be at the forefront of the 'battle to defend the way of life for the Protestant, loyalist, unionist and British people of Ulster' (DUP 1996). Fourthly, the four main parties in Northern Ireland have religiously near-exclusive support bases and memberships. Finally, as the ethno-national conflict subsided during the peace process, with republicans in Sinn Fein tacitly accepting the existence of Northern Ireland, the facet of the Troubles that endured was religious sectarianism. This 'religious aspect' was reflected in increased residential segregation and a plethora of sectarian pipe bombings and shootings. Hundreds of such incidents occurred annually in the years immediately after the 1998 Good Friday Agreement, a deal which accommodated the territorial issues upon which the conflict was supposed to have been based. Thus, whilst no serious commentator claims the Northern Ireland conflict to be a theological war between Protestants and Roman Catholics (although theological divisions excite religious fundamentalists), the pre-existence of communal divisions based upon religious identity, and their perpetuation after peace and political processes, indicate the durability of the strong religious aspect of the problem. Religion may be a label more than a badge of practised faith, and Northern Ireland has not been immune to secularism. None the less, the overwhelming,

albeit slightly diminishing, majority of the population
tinue to identify themselves as Protestant or Roman Catholic,
evidenced in the 2001 census. Religious labels may be more
accurate than political badges, as Catholics are diverse in their
constitutional preferences.

The difficulty with the religious argument is that none of the
protagonists in the conflict espoused religious causes. Loyalist
paramilitaries offered the slogan 'For God and Ulster', but it is
doubtful whether many were aware of the essential components of Protestantism. Most members joined to stop Northern
Ireland being forced from the United Kingdom, a mainly territorial and political argument. The DUP has often been identi-
fied with the religious aspect of the problem, but it dropped the
label of Protestant Unionist Party and became the DUP in 1971
to hold a secular appeal stronger than its religious association.
For the leader of the DUP, the Reverend Ian Paisley, the Pope
was the Antichrist, and the papacy was seen as having a 'political constitution', one based upon the ambition for global
dominance (O'Malley 1983: 174). However, Paisley was
joined by several more moderate and less religious acolytes,
not all members of his Free Presbyterian Church, who came to
wield influence in the party.

On the republican side, the notion of a relationship
between the IRA and the Catholic Church ignored most of the
available evidence, notwithstanding the Church's support for
Irish unity. Although local relationships with individual
priests were occasionally fairly cordial, republicans were often
critical of the Catholic Church. Despite the religious exclusiv-
ity of their support bases and memberships, neither of the
principal nationalist representatives, Sinn Fein and the SDLP,
has any link to the Catholic Church; nor do they espouse
Catholic social teaching, with the possible exception of the
parties' views on the unacceptability of abortion.

Although religious segregation of the two communities has
increased over recent decades, separation should not be
equated with conflict causation. Rather, separation was a
logical security step for many as an ethno-national conflict
developed. The conflict was never a civil war between
Protestant and Catholic communities, although there were

occasional sectarian massacres by republicans and loyalists. Had the IRA wished to precipitate a civil war, it could have targeted Protestant religious leaders such as Paisley, actions which would have plunged the province into deeper conflict. The killing of the UUP MP, the Reverend Robert Bradford, by the IRA in the 1980s *was* seen by many as sectarian, and threatened to escalate the conflict into a sectarian war, but, despite the high level of civilian deaths, this did not materialize.

The Solution to Ethno-national Conflict: Consociational Power Sharing?

Ethno-national explanations of the conflict may be accompanied by consociational proposals for redress, although linkage is not automatic. The classic features of consociationalism are designed to harness ethno-national rivalries within a co-operative framework which recognizes the equal validity of ethnic traditions, rather than attempting their dilution. These features are power sharing, proportionality in government; mutual vetoes and bloc autonomy (Lijphart 1975; O'Leary 1999, 2001; McGarry and O'Leary 2004). These ideas have informed the two main attempts at resolving the Northern Ireland conflict: the failed 1973 Sunningdale Agreement and the more successful, but still uncertain, 1998 Good Friday Agreement. The power-sharing executive introduced in January 1974 under the Sunningdale deal collapsed in May that year. The backdrop, of continuing violence and popular opposition to the agreement, augured poorly for its implementation. Sunningdale brought together a section of the UUP, led by Brian Faulkner (many within the UUP did not support the deal), the centrist Alliance Party and the nationalist SDLP in a power-sharing coalition. Consociational features were also apparent via proportionality in government and veto rights, the cross-community executive having to act unanimously. There was, however, little in the way of self-government for either the unionist or nationalist communities. Moreover, attached to the power-sharing executive was a Council for Ireland, designed to give a voice to the Irish government in the hitherto internal affairs of Northern Ireland, a role that, although minimal, antagonized unionists. If consociationalism was designed to foster a basic loyalty to the state, it was unclear that Sunningdale fulfilled this condition, as nationalists were also encouraged to look to the Irish government as their protector, through the Council for Ireland and other proposed measures such as an all-island policing authority.

Sunningdale represented a form of 'consociationalism plus', a term applied to its successor, the Good Friday Agreement (GFA), both agreements containing an Irish dimension, in addition to the power-sharing arrangements for the internal governance of Northern Ireland (O'Leary 1999, 2001). The GFA was famously, and appositely, described as 'Sunningdale for slow learners' by the SDLP's Seamus Mallon, an aside reflecting how the constitutional and institutional architecture of the 1998 deal bore marked similarities to its predecessor (Tonge 2000b). Both agreements kept Northern Ireland in the United Kingdom on the basis of the consent of the citizens of the province. Each brought together unionists and nationalists to share power within an executive, and the two deals also attached a modest all-island dimension. The differences between the two agreements were of nuance, with the important exception that the 1998 version contained far more end-of-conflict measures and attempted to incorporate paramilitary groups within the political process, rather than strive towards their marginalization. In this respect, the 1998 deal was assisted by a greatly changed backdrop, the IRA abandoning its 'Brits out' mantra in favour of vaguer and softer Sinn Fein aspirations for an 'Ireland of Equals'. The new measures included the release of paramilitary prisoners and the promise of a revamped police force, under the independent commission established by the GFA. With equality and human rights commissions also established under the 1998 deal, the GFA promised to end any lingering notion of second-class citizenry held by nationalists. An equality, rather than a unification agenda, was ample for this community, evidenced by the 99 per cent support for the deal among nationalists in the referendum on the GFA in May 1998 (Hayes and McAllister 2001).

Is the Consociational Approach Apposite?

The critique of consociational solutions to the Northern Ireland problem has come mainly from those who believe it enshrines ethnic division (Taylor 2001; Wilford 2001; see also Little 2004). Critics may offer a republican perspective, believing that internal enforced power sharing in Northern Ireland reinforces sectarian division in a sectarian state (e.g. Rooney 1997). Alternatively, such critics may be unionists who prefer the full integration of Northern Ireland within the United Kingdom rather than the more risky approach of sharing devolved power with historic enemies. Integrationists such as the UUP leader from 1979 to 1995, James Molyneaux, and the UKUP leader, Robert McCartney, have supported full incorporation of Northern Ireland within the United Kingdom, a view which continues to attract sympathy among a section of the unionist community, however untenable in a devolved United Kingdom. Intellectual criticisms of consociationalism are less concerned with a cost–benefit analysis of its value to unionism or nationalism. Instead, sceptics are critical of what they see as the lack of transformative possibilities offered by consociational solutions. Consociationalism is criticized for its lack of optimism over the human condition, with society divided into seemingly permanent ethnic blocs from where individuals do not escape. According to detractors, it fails to create societal or institutional dynamics. Instead, it is associated with rigidity and polarization rather than democratic norms (Wilford 2001). Accommodation among elites fails to change society and hardens, rather than diminishes, the ethnic division which formed the basis of conflict. Such critics point to the empirical evidence concerning consociationalism, which is not encouraging globally (Horowitz 2001) or in Northern Ireland, where the experiments in consociational power sharing lasted five months (1974) and three years (1999–2002) respectively (Gillespie 1998).

Opponents of consociationalism view its 'deployment' as a guarantor of permanent instability, under which the particular interests of one community demand attention as much as mutually beneficial shared governance. In respect of the

Northern Ireland executive created immediately after the GFA, which sat from 1999 until 2002, such critics had a point. The DUP participated in the governing executive, whilst undermining the agreement under which it was established. The requirement that executive ministers participate in Strand Two of the GFA, the all-island North–South Ministerial Council, was ignored by the DUP, which also regularly rotated its ministers to undermine the executive. The DUP played to its unionist constituency, discouraging support for the GFA as unionists shared power with Sinn Fein amid prisoner releasers, policing changes and continued, albeit modest, IRA activity. Whilst many of the items in the GFA that enraged unionists were 'add-ons' to its consociational aspects, they emphasized how a deal straddling two rival ethnic blocs was vulnerable to zero-sum game perceptions, in which aspects of the deal were interpreted as victories for the 'other' community.

Consociationalism's critics argue that it breaches ideas of liberal democracy (Little 2004). The statutory requirement for mutual power sharing means that a system of government and opposition does not emerge, sacrificed to the need for an inclusive executive to remain stable. Scrutiny of the executive is performed by an assembly, a feat possible if assembly members are prepared to criticize the leaders of their ethnic parties in the executive. Such a scenario is unlikely in respect of Sinn Fein and the DUP, both of which are tightly run, top-down parties. Indeed, the members of the 1999–2002 executive were insulated from criticism and could take decisions against the advice of their departmental committees.

Criticizing the Critics? Consociationalism Assessed

As the most popular parties in Northern Ireland, the DUP and Sinn Fein, inched towards a reformed, GFA-type, consociational settlement, it appeared that the doom-mongers who argued that consociationalism would never work might be silenced. The shift from conflict to (imperfect) peace produced conditions in which power sharing between rivals no longer looked like an outside bet, but instead appeared as an item which could not be removed from the agenda. It was difficult to assess the degree to which consociational ideas or exponents could take the credit. Such ideas could not have worked had Sinn Fein and the IRA remained true to traditional republican ideas of absentionism or armed struggle, rather than pursuing an equality agenda within Northern Ireland. None the less, the enticement of Sinn Fein into consociational arrangements, under which the party acted as the custodian of the interests of the community it represented, indicated that consociational ideas had much to offer. The siren voices arguing that consociationalism could never work were unconvincing; it had never been attempted in a peaceful Northern Ireland. The relatively peaceful Northern Ireland of 1921 to 1968 laboured under a majoritarian perversion of democracy which alienated the minority nationalist community. Direct rule from 1972 was interrupted briefly in 1974 by an ill-timed and inappropriate consociational experiment, whilst the post-1998 problems associated with the GFA could be seen as 'teething' problems, to be overcome when the more strident representatives of nationalism and unionism, Sinn Fein and the DUP, emerged as the strongest parties and cut a deal.

The GFA was not a pure version of consociationalism. Its adherents described it as 'consociationalism plus', given its external linkages to other states; to the Irish Republic, in Strand Two, and to Britain and the Irish Republic in the confederal dimension of Strand Three (O'Leary 2001). Sceptics questioned whether the deal was consociational, or whether this was a loose form of power sharing for which consociational exponents were determined to take the credit. Of the four core elements, community autonomy was largely absent, but the other three pillars were apparent: power sharing, although power tended to be divided into individual ministerial or party fiefdoms in the first post-GFA executive; proportionality in government, exemplified by the allocation of executive places under the D'Hondt formula, according to party strength in the assembly; and rights of veto, with controversial legislation requiring either the parallel consent of both communities or a minimum of 40 per cent support in each.

Dixon (2001) suggests that consociationalists have been too

willing to claim vindication of their ideas, arguing instead that the GFA was not really consociational. It did not establish an inclusive coalition, as the DUP often remained an outsider; self-government was not evident for each community, and the executive was not strictly proportional, excluding the Alliance Party. The thrust of his argument is that there has been broad British policy continuity since the 1970s, based largely upon expediency – a desire to minimize the cost to the British state of the problem. This contrasts with the alternative view that British policy has been characterized by variability and some-what clumsy and belated policy learning (O'Leary 1997). The argument that British policy has generally been consistent is persuasive. It has always been about protecting the constitu-tional *status quo* and reducing violence. Dixon may also be correct in asserting that British policy has never been condi-tioned by one particular theoretical approach. Indeed, it is possible to speculate as to whether several secretaries of state, neither theoretically nor politically attuned to Northern Ireland politics, have even heard of consociationalism, let alone applied the theory. Power sharing has been, for the British government, a useful aspect of policy, but never an essential component. However, to claim that the GFA was not consociational was surely stretching a point? The core features of executive power sharing and mutual veto were clearly apparent, and although the bi-national dimension of the GFA represented a substantial modification to classic consocia-tional ideas, it did not necessarily negate them, if it helped build loyalty to political institutions.

Alternatives to a Consociational Deal?

The assumption of British policy towards Northern Ireland has long been that the political parties will eventually manage their differences sufficiently amicably to create a durable power-sharing deal. In this respect, direct rule from Westminster, introduced in March 1972 when the majoritarian unionist government was suspended, was seen as a temporary expedient. The collapse of the Sunningdale Agreement in May

1974 none the less cooled such enthusiasm, to the extent that intergovernmental arrangements were introduced in 1985, with the Anglo-Irish Agreement providing consultative rights for the Irish government on Northern Ireland. Despite vehement unionist protests, the deal was hardly a slippery slope to a united Ireland. Yielding basic rights of consultation to the Irish government did not fundamentally alter British policy towards Northern Ireland; yet it netted improved cross-border security arrangements for the British government, crucial given its vulnerability in defending its only land frontier. The bi-national approach to Northern Ireland has remained; the difference since 1998, however, has been that it has attempted to oversee power sharing between political parties, rather than operate as the basis of governance. Intergovernmentalism remains the default position in the event of the failure of a consociational deal, but such bi-nationalism has never been a partnership of equals. Instead, the British government remains dominant, merely adopting direct rule with a green tinge (Aughey 1989).

Direct rule from Westminster, with Irish consultative rights, remains the most likely option in the unlikely event of a permanent failure of power sharing. The failure to achieve a united Ireland has been recognized by republicans, one declaring that the 'war is over and the good guys lost', and noting how the IRA was reduced to a bargaining tool for equality gains within Northern Ireland (Bernadette McAliskey, cited in McIntyre 2004). Such a reverse cannot, for obvious reasons, be acknowledged by the party itself, which believes all-Ireland electoral gains can produce a dynamic for change. One alternative to a consociational deal, joint British–Irish authority, has not been supported actively by Sinn Fein, even though it could give far more transitional status to Irish unity than a largely internal consociational deal like the Good Friday Agreement. Whilst the imposition of joint authority would be strongly opposed by unionists and would be difficult to implement practically, it might command the support of a sizeable percentage of the island-wide population, given the continuing aggregate desire for Irish unity. Whilst supporting the expansion of all-island economic bodies, currently far short of anything tantamount to joint authority, Sinn Fein's disinterest stems from its removal from executive positions in Northern Ireland if joint authority is imposed by a London–Dublin axis. With no takers for joint authority and all 'republicans' on the island, outside a small band of ultras, seemingly having given up on a united Ireland in the short term, a consociational settlement 'wins' not merely because of intrinsic merit, but because no sizeable organization is advocating an alternative. The 'only show in town' may not be much good, but it attracts support because any show is better than none.

External Assistance to Conflict Resolution

One of the problems in producing agreement to end the conflict was the lack of an honest broker. The British government was not seen as a neutral actor by republicans, and the Irish government was viewed as irredentist by unionists. Any United Nations involvement, a prospect briefly raised in the early years of the Troubles, was seen as unacceptable by the British government and unionists, for whom Northern Ireland was an internal matter, although the British government softened its position from 1973 onwards, conceding a bi-national dimension to the problem.

The view that Northern Ireland was a 'domestic' issue for the British government to sort out held sway in the United States under the pro-British Reagan and Bush presidencies of the 1980s and early 1990s. The lobbying efforts of Irish-American groups were mainly directed towards redressing discrimination in Northern Ireland, the big exception being the pro-IRA Irish Northern Aid (NORAID) organization. The involvement of the United States increased markedly in economic terms after the 1985 Anglo-Irish Agreement, through extensive reconstruction aid, which enjoyed high visibility among the population of Northern Ireland (Irvin and Byrne 2002). From 1992 until 2000, the US administration took a more pro-active political brokerage role under the Clinton presidency. This shift was facilitated by the triumph of the National Security Council over the more cautious and pro-British State Department in a 'turf war' within the admin-istration (Arthur 2000: 158–9).

Recognizing the desire of the republican leadership to end the IRA's campaign, Clinton provided the Sinn Fein presi-dent, Gerry Adams, with an entry visa to the USA and appointed Senator George Mitchell to assist in the formulation of principles of non-violence and to broker the Good Friday Agreement. Clinton was directly involved in brokering the Good Friday Agreement at difficult moments, although accounts of the significance of his role vary from the sceptical (Riddell 2003) to the eulogistic (O'Cleary, 1997; Clinton 2004). Clinton described his role as 'giving a positive impact, psychologically' for what was 'a crucial issue not only for per-sonal and emotional reasons but also for the future of European peace' (BBC Northern Ireland, *The Politics Show*, 18 July 2004). Two perceptive elements of Clinton's approach were evident. First, he aligned the Northern Ireland peace process with other European ethnic disputes, seeing such matters as resolvable. Thus, for Clinton, 'old divides give meaning and order to people's lives, but they are ultimately self-defeating' (ibid.). Secondly, he recognized that the GFA was a 'big step for the republican movement', a realistic assess-ment amid the mantras of unionist critics concerning the peace process being based upon concessions to nationalists (ibid.). American involvement diminished during the following years, but George Bush did intervene personally to encourage a deal between the DUP and Sinn Fein.

The second external agent in Northern Ireland, the European Union, has had a minimal role politically, but, pending the embedding of a durable multi-stranded deal, remains a key agent of all-island economic activity. There are three key dimensions of EU input, not always direct, into con-flict resolution in Northern Ireland. First, the EU may facilitate economic and political cross-border co-operation, by shaping bi-national agreements and institutional structures in a manner designed to elicit maximum EU support. The EU thus provides a structural influence upon conflict resolution. Secondly, the EU may play a role in withering contentious borders by placing demands upon previously competing user groups in civil society to co-operate across borders and civil society divides to maximize financial support. As such, contestatory rivalries between ethno-national groups are displaced by common clientelistic relationships with the EU. Thirdly, the EU may provide a changed context for political parties to address questions of national sovereignty, evidenced in this paper by the considerable change in Sinn Fein policy towards the EU.

Historically, the EU eschewed direct political input into the conflict in Northern Ireland. None the less, to claim that the EU was inactive is erroneous, as the European Parliament (EP) did take an interest in conflict resolution in the province. The EP established a working party to examine modes of conflict resolution in Northern Ireland in 1981. The Haagerup Report (1984) advocated power sharing and increased intergovernmental co-operation. The report condemned violence and acknowledged that the EU had no role to play in respect of Northern Ireland's constitution. It nevertheless advocated European Community involvement in social and economic reconstruction. In 1985, the EP backed the Anglo-Irish Agreement by 150 votes to 28, a symbolic gesture of support, and in 1992 the EP launched an investigation into anti-Catholic discrimination in Northern Ireland. Direct input into Northern Ireland's affairs came with the arrival of substantial peace funds in the 1990s.

During the early 1990s, Northern Ireland benefited from EU funding awarded as a result of its Objective One status, entitling the region to maximum EU structural funds. This was not renewed for 2000–6, but substantial compensatory transitional aid was awarded. Institutional links have grown, with the European Commission holding a permanent office in Belfast and the Northern Ireland executive operating a Brussels office. The implementation of EU programmes will become increasingly a matter for a sustained devolved Northern Ireland executive.

EU funding for Northern Ireland is provided via the Community Support Framework. This is based around two programmes: the Programme for Building Sustainable Prosperity, which accounts for two-thirds of funding, and the Programme for Peace and Reconciliation, which provides the remaining one-third. The EU has provided a plethora of funds for reconciliation, regional development and cross-border co-operation, notably via the PEACE, INTERREG, LEADER, EQUAL and URBAN programmes. The PEACE and INTER-REG programmes provided 1.33 billion euros (£830 million) of funds across the island between 1995 and 2006. (<www.northsouthministerialcouncil.org/communiques/spjc091002.htm>). The PEACE I programme (Special Support for Peace and Reconciliation in Northern Ireland and the Border Counties) ran from 1995 to 1999, followed by a PEACE II programme with an even larger budget. The PEACE II programme finance is distributed mainly via twenty-six Local Strategy Partnerships, six county council border task forces, and fifteen intermediary funding bodies.

The GFA made provision for the consideration of the implementation of EU programmes by the North–South Ministerial Council (NSMC). The most important cross-border organization established under the GFA, the Special European Union Programmes Body (SEUPB) is the paying and managing agent for the PEACE II programme, as it is for INTERREG IIIA, the cross-border element of the INTERREG programme. The establishment of the SEUPB as an all-island implementation body gave extra impetus to the European dimension of trans-national co-operation. The downside is the tendency towards 'recognition of the EU as a cash cow', rather than its acceptance as a governing entity (McGowan and O'Connor 2004).

The placement of EU all-island activity under the auspices of the NSMC and an executive cross-border body is of more than mere symbolic importance. It represented the most substantial movement towards cross-border activity apparent under the GFA. The political impacts of cross-border EU activity have been to reduce economic problems in areas of former republican militancy, to promote cross-community co-operation among EU funding recipients, and to diminish unionist suspicion of all-island activity. As in other policy areas, Sinn Fein has undergone transformation in respect of its attitude towards the EU, moving from demands for withdrawal in the 1970s and 1980s to 'critical engagement' by the late 1990s and support for the extension of the euro from the Irish Republic to Northern Ireland, as part of an all-island economic approach, from 2003 onwards (Sinn Fein 1999, 2003).

Conclusion

External economic aid aside, the Northern Ireland problem has been addressed within a British–Irish framework designed to uphold the principle of consent within Northern Ireland and to foster all-party institutional co-operation. The willingness of Sinn Fein to adhere to the principle of consent within Northern Ireland, anathema to republicans for so long; the standing down of the PIRA; and the implementation of a cross-community political deal, all beg the question of whether a conflict remains, even if its legacy of societal division endures. A war over sovereignty and territory has been displaced by politics 'more concerned with equity issues' (Arthur 2000: 249). Under an equality agenda, parity of esteem and respect for different identities have displaced the old argument over partition. The demand for equality was of course how an age-old conflict was revived in the late 1960s. After 3,600 deaths in that conflict, republicans shelved territorial demands for equality in a state that the IRA sought to dismantle.

Northern Ireland remains a contested polity, in that a significant minority of its citizens, a majority on the entire island, desire the eventual ending of partition and the reunification of the island under a single Irish government. Yet the fierce assertion of this demand, tagged to a desire for the ending of second-class citizenry, has subsided among republicans. Sinn Fein has moved from the position of republican militants to become another constitutional nationalist party. The party's growing political strength across the island may yet serve to highlight the minority position and isolation of a minority unionist community in the North. In the meantime, however, the peace and political processes have served to lessen the party's stridency.

The 1998 Good Friday Agreement was a consociational deal, based upon an ethno-national interpretation of the problem, that of two communities demanding expression and recognition of their national identity. It could be argued that joint British–Irish authority over Northern Ireland would provide a more balanced means for this, although there is a broad consensus amongst the political parties over the desirability of devolution. The advantage of the application of consociational ideas, to which were added limited all-Ireland economic initiatives, was that they gave local political parties a bigger stake in the deal by allowing them to share power in a devolved assembly and executive. This approach, although risky, given historic enmities, could forge a more permanent *rapprochement* between rival parties, with a 'spill-over' effect in society.

2

The Provisional IRA

The Physical Force 'Tradition'

From 1970 until its second and final cease-fire in 1997, the PIRA represented the physical force tradition which had always existed in Irish republicanism. That tradition was rarely dominant in the movement and was often ineffective, yet its existence helped shape Irish politics, North and South. The PIRA's campaign probably represented the last gasp of physical force republicanism on the island. None the less, obituaries for the IRA have been written several times. A mere eight years after it appeared that the IRA was redundant, following its failed 1956–62 border campaign, the organization revived to become the most formidable paramilitary group in Europe. Despite giving the IRA credibility as a fighting force that it had not enjoyed since 1922, the PIRA's campaign, like all other physical force attempts since partition, ended in failure in terms of its declared objective of achieving a united independent Ireland. Instead, as the main parties in the southern Irish state emerged from the IRA, so Sinn Fein in the North emerged as a strong political party as the PIRA's campaign subsided.

Successive IRAs have placed themselves in the tradition of Wolfe Tone's United Irishmen. The United Irishmen launched a failed rebellion against British rule in 1798, pledging to end the connection with the colonial power, the 'source of all evil', and replace it with an independent Ireland with equal respect for Catholic, Protestant and Dissenter. Although Tone was a Protestant, Irish republicanism tended to become associated with Catholicism in the 1800s, partly as a consequence of anti-Catholic laws introduced by the colonial power. The Irish Republican Brotherhood emerged as the forerunner of the IRA after 1858, whilst the Fenians, also Irish rebels, launched attacks in Britain in 1867. The revival of physical force in the 1900s arose as a result of the unsatisfactory nature of Home Rule, with the promised level of self-government inadequate and the Home Rule Bills failing, due to Unionist opposition. The physical force section of republicanism remained weak; the majority of Irish Volunteers pledged to achieve self-government fought for Britain in the First World War. However, the dedicated band of rebels who launched the Easter Rising in 1916, declaring an Irish republic, enshrined the role of physical force within the republican tradition. Although the Rising was a failure, like so many armed actions before and afterwards, the harsh British response (a mistake to be repeated decades later) engendered sympathy for the rebels to the extent that Sinn Fein, the IRA's political wing, won a landslide victory in the 1918 all-Ireland elections.

The failure of the British government to implement the will of the majority of the Irish people, as expressed in the 1918 election, by withdrawing from Ireland, provided physical force republicans with a justification for subsequent violence. The messy compromise of an Anglo-Irish Treaty, which created a partitioned island under British rule in the North, was rejected by republicans, even though the twenty-six-county state in the South achieved full independence by 1949. The physical force republican wing has attempted to maintain an armed struggle against overwhelming odds since partition, beginning with a crushing defeat in the Irish Civil War of 1922–3, when the pro-Treaty IRA, bolstered by the acceptance of the deal by the majority of Irish people, used more repressive methods than the British to defeat erstwhile comrades. Many of the defeated IRA entered parliamentary politics after the formation of Fianna Fail under Eamon De Valera in 1926. Fianna Fail formed a government in 1932, and often thereafter, as an avowedly republican party.

For die-hards in the IRA, entry into any partitionist parliament which presided over only part of the island was betrayal. This section of republicanism has maintained a belief that armed struggle, rather than parliamentary politics, is the best means of ending Britain's claim to Northern Ireland. None the less, the physical force tradition revived only briefly thereafter until 1970. A short-lived campaign in England in 1939–40 was easily contained. Misled into thinking that there was mass support for armed struggle by Sinn Fein's 152,000 votes in the 1955 Westminster election, the IRA launched a border campaign from 1956 to 1962, which after modest early success became an abject failure. The campaign was called off, with the IRA claiming that the Irish had 'been deliberately distracted from the supreme issue facing the Irish people – the unity and freedom of Ireland' (*United Irishman*, March 1962). With arms dumped and its volunteers reluctant to rejoin upon release from jail, it appeared that the physical force tradition of the IRA had expired.

The Growth of the Provisional IRA

The rebirth of the IRA in 1970 was portrayed by its leaders as a continuation of hundreds of years of armed struggle by republicans against a colonial aggressor. Grounded in historical determinism, such a view perceived the existence of the IRA as an inevitable response to Britain's sovereign claim over Northern Ireland. As such, the IRA would not disappear until the indivisible island was restored and a thirty-two-county united, independent sovereign Ireland was in place. Yet among those who joined the Provisionals, there were few such republican theologians. Rather, the PIRA grew through a combination of civil unrest, social agitation, religious sectarianism and inappropriate military action by the unionist and British governments. The leadership of the PIRA proclaimed allegiance to the proclamation of 1916 declaring an Irish republic, yet its adherents tended to join the organization partly in response to the sectarian attacks they faced from loyalists, the 'Unionist' police force and the British military. For the first time, the IRA became a Northern creature, albeit one still led in the 1970s from Dublin and partly financed by sympathetic sources in the Irish Republic. Most of its members were based in Northern Ireland and joined due to the street combat of 1969, rather than the Holy Grail of the Republic of 1916. Of course, the politics of 1969 were shaped ultimately by partition; as such, the emergence of the PIRA can be seen as a consequence of the belief that the division of Ireland was illegitimate and unsustainable.

The IRA's left turn of the 1960s led to its involvement in civil rights campaigns, as nationalists demanded more equitable treatment from the unionist government. The presence of even a moribund, peaceful IRA within the civil rights movement and the lack of Protestant participation led to the denunciation of such agitation by suspicious unionists, such as the Stormont Home Affairs Minister, William Craig, as 'Republican Nationalist' (Mulholland 2000: 159). The physical response to the civil rights campaign by the police and loyalists fuelled Catholic grievances, and disorder broke out in 1968–9. The failure of the unionist government to complete reforms added to violence which, although far from one-sided, was often targeted against Catholics, allowing the IRA an opportunity to revive in 1970, when the newly arrived 'oppressors', the British Army, also began to alienate the Catholic population. The IRA split, its non-Marxist element angered at the failure of the organization to defend Catholic areas, whereas the leftist IRA leadership of the time feared that such defence would be seen as sectarian. One of the few IRA members prepared to engage in Northern defenderism, Sean McStiofain, was told to 'do nothing and if I was doing anything already, I was to stop' (McStiofain 1975: 125). Having remained in favour with the Belfast IRA through his rejection of the Marxist theorizing of the IRA leadership, McStiofain emerged as the first Chief of Staff of the PIRA, a militarist who, whilst not averse to politics in certain circumstances, was 'visibly bored by the arguments for the need of a political campaign' according to one PIRA member (McGuire 1973: 32).

Although emerging from the structural conditions of the time, the newly formed Provisional IRA was anxious to stress its adherence to republican orthodoxy, detailing the reasons why it felt it necessary to emerge. The PIRA was scathing of what became known as the 'Official IRA' (OIRA) due to the latter's ending of abstention from twenty-six and six-county parliaments and the Westminster parliament, arguing instead that Stormont was illegitimate and could not be reformed. The PIRA also condemned the IRA's move towards communism, the irregularities in voting at the IRA convention on abstentionism, and the abandonment of nationalists in the North (Horgan and Taylor 1997). In pledging fidelity to the Irish Republic declared in 1916–19 and invoking the memory of the 1916 rebel Padraig Pearse, the PIRA leadership reasserted the old republican belief in the necessity of blood sacrifice, insisting 'we know of no way by which freedom can be obtained and when obtained, maintained except by armed men' (*An Phoblacht*, February 1970: 8, 'The Rock of the Republic').

The PIRA positioned itself along the historical continuum of physical force republicanism. A former member, Anthony McIntyre (1995: 100), is critical of conventional accounts of the IRA and Sinn Fein which ascribe 'continuity to republicanism which does not in fact exist, or at least is so fractured by periodization that continuity as a concept is seriously compromised'. Instead, McIntyre (1995: 99) locates the shifts in the IRA's strategy within a 'dialectic of republican/British state conflict', in which the British generally held the upper hand. These tactical shifts may indeed be explained by this dialectic, but the birth of the PIRA and the longevity of a militaristic IRA, in its various forms, were consequences of the willingness of its leadership to adhere to republican ideals of enforcing British withdrawal, refusing to recognize partition and asserting Irish self-determination. Should the leadership not hold these ideals, there is no purpose to an IRA. In assessing the formation of the PIRA, there is a need, however, to disaggregate the perceptions of local volunteers from those of the more fundamentalist leadership. Abstentionism and militarism *were* restated as core republican principles by the Provisionals' leadership. For such principles to survive long term, however, there needed to be an effective military campaign, capable of ending British rule in Ireland. For the traditionalists of the Provisionals' leadership, the IRA had 'resumed the war where it had been interrupted half a century earlier, with the truce of July 1921' (Laffan 1999: 455).

The PIRA had little interest in the stageist theories of the OIRA, which saw the unity of the unionist and nationalist working classes as a prerequisite to Irish unity. For the OIRA, only a united working class would have the power to end imperialism in the six-county and twenty-six-county states. For the PIRA, working-class unity would be a consequence of British withdrawal; until the British withdrew, it could not occur. According to an early PIRA leader, Daithi O'Connaill, loyalists were merely 'a settler class that arose out of partition' (quoted in Walsh 1994: 250).

Initial Success: PIRA Gains, 1970–2

The initial tasks of the PIRA in 1970 were to restore the reputation of the IRA and to sour relations between the local population and the 'colonial occupier', the British Army. Given the initial welcome afforded to the Army, the tiny IRA might have floundered in either task, had it not been for a fortuitous combination of events. The Orange Order's marching season, beginning in April 1970, saw Catholic hostility dealt with firmly by the Army, which began to be seen as the oppressor of Catholics from then on. A combination of ignorance, abuse, curfews and arms searches soon wrecked the relationship between nationalists and the Army, a growing hostility nurtured by the IRA, which discouraged 'fraternization' in an increasingly brutal manner. Although the PIRA were the chief critics of the British Army, the OIRA were also hostile, and warned locals in Derry not to co-operate with British forces before the Provisionals had issued such strictures (O'Dochartaigh 1997).

As the security-oriented policy demanded by unionists reached its nadir, with internment of Catholics (mainly non-republicans, due to poor intelligence) in 1971 and the killing of thirteen innocent civilians by the British Army on 'Bloody

Sunday' in Derry in January 1972, the alienation of the nationalist community was complete. Applicants for the PIRA had already 'formed a queue' after the British Army killed two people in the same city in summer 1971 (McCann 1980: 146), and in the Irish Republic, rioters burnt the British Embassy. Yet, despite the insistence of the Taoiseach, Jack Lynch, that his government 'cannot stand by' as rioting erupted in the North in 1969, material support was confined to small-scale, unofficial assistance from republicans in Lynch's Fianna Fail party, including the creation of a sympathetic newspaper, *Voice of the North*. The extent of Fianna Fail support for the IRA remains disputed. Members of Lynch's government did offer guns and money. Ironically, some of this was granted to the neo-Marxist IRA leadership, which declined the offer, rather than given to the green nationalists of the PIRA, to whom Fianna Fail were ideologically closer and whose emergence several members of Fianna Fail were keen to encourage (Bishop and Mallie 1988; Walsh 1994).

The latent sympathy for the PIRA meant that detention without trial, used successfully against the IRA in the Irish Republic in its 1950s border campaign, was not reintroduced by the Irish government. The IRA found it relatively easy to train in the Irish Republic, and in Northern Ireland the PIRA was not short of volunteers. In Derry alone, it was estimated that 'up to 1,000 people were imprisoned for PIRA activities, which, in a town of only 50,000 Catholics, was a strikingly high level of paramilitary activity' (O'Dochartaigh 1997: 285). Emboldened by its capacity to recruit, and encouraged by the rapidity of disaffection with the British Army, the PIRA changed tactics regularly during the early 1970s. Initially, it assumed a defensive posture, one never matched by reality, as subsequent events proved that the IRA was incapable of defending the community from the loyalist attacks it partly provoked. The defensive role of the IRA was helpful in terms of community image, rather than substance. Thus the sight of IRA men defending St Matthew's Catholic Church from a loyalist mob in the Catholic enclave of Short Strand in June 1970 was a public relations triumph in linking the IRA to its community base.

In 1970, the IRA needed to engage in a process of legitimation. This achieved, the organization went on the offensive in February 1971, killing the first British soldier, an event followed one month later by the killing of three Scottish soldiers. At this stage, the PIRA, although already organized into three 'battalions' across Belfast, still lacked sufficient confidence to claim responsibility for the killing and issued a denial. The loyalist backlash that followed, added to an ever-stiffening and often inept security policy, enhanced the PIRA's status within the nationalist community. In arming itself, the PIRA drew upon an eclectic range of friends, establishing a weapons supply line and financial support from Irish-Americans, acquiring Russian-made weaponry and securing funding, and later weaponry, from Libya.

The PIRA offensive produced dramatic results, yielding, within eighteen months, the collapse of fifty years of Protestant ascendancy, as the unionist government at Stormont collapsed, suspended by the Westminster government in March 1972. The PIRA's leadership were invited to talks by the British government in July that year. After almost fifty years of failure, the IRA had revived as a major player in the Irish question, in a manner astonishing to those who had witnessed the state of the organization during the 1960s. Arguably, however, July 1972 represented the high-water mark of PIRA's influence. Having ended Orange rule at Stormont and reduced the conflict to one of beguiling simplicity – the respective might of the British Army versus the IRA – the PIRA expected to complete its victory within the next few years. Its core aim, of enforcing British withdrawal from Ireland within a single term of a Westminster parliament, was non-negotiable. The question begged from here on was what would happen should the British government refuse to concede this stance? The omnipotent threat of loyalist violence was discounted by the PIRA, which believed that loyalists would 'come quietly' once their British imperial masters removed their prop. As such, the onus was upon the British government to begin withdrawal. The favoured analogy was Algeria, from which the French had withdrawn under pressure from anti-colonial forces, even though the Algerians could not inflict outright military defeat

upon the colonial power. The PIRA preferred not to dwe
differences between the situations. The settler colonial p
French population, at 8 per cent, was only one-third of the pe
centage of 'settler-colonial' Ulster unionists resident on the
island of Ireland, whilst French Algeria had much greater
impact upon French domestic politics than Northern Ireland
would ever make upon Westminster politics (O'Malley 1983:
299). Given British disinterest in Northern Ireland and the
level of PIRA success up to this point, republican optimism
may have been justified, but it proved misplaced. Ultimately,
the PIRA, via Sinn Fein, ended up putting back the Northern
Ireland parliament they had destroyed. 'New Stormont', post-
1998, was a very different version from the unionist one-party
rule of old, but it none the less involved Sinn Fein, in the words
of one of its senior members, Francie Molloy, 'administering
British rule for the foreseeable future' (*Sunday Times*, 28
March 2003).

From Years of Victory to 'Long War'

Even prior to talks with the British government, the PIRA had
proclaimed 1972 the 'Year of Victory', with Britain 'on its
knees' (*Republican News*, 2 January 1972: 1). Such claims were
to become annual features. At the beginning of 1974, the PIRA
again claimed that this would be 'Victory Year' (*Republican
News*, 4 January 1974: 1). Amid the propaganda, some within
the republican movement began to have doubts. The 'negotiations' with the British government in July 1972 proved nothing
of the sort, the British Home Secretary, William Whitelaw,
explaining that British withdrawal was not on the agenda. The
PIRA response was to end a temporary truce and heighten its
campaign, leading to increased civilian casualties. Although the
PIRA was built upon a historical rather than a modern
mandate, it needed support, a feature undermined by events
such as Bloody Friday, when nine civilians were killed as
the IRA detonated more than twenty bombs in Belfast city
centre on a single afternoon in July 1972. Shortly afterwards,
the IRA's 'safe havens', the 'no-go' areas in 'Free Derry' and

d by the British Army, and from then on
y on the defensive. The IRA countered by
England, mainly in London, episodically
. Its initial operations were compromised
olice intelligence, allowing the perpetrators
en operations were not compromised, there
sastrous impact, twenty-two civilians being killed
ombings in Birmingham in 1974. Indeed, it has been
ed that the entire English campaign was, like its predecessors, an unmitigated failure, even though such actions
achieved far greater media coverage for the IRA than its activity in Northern Ireland (McGladdery 2004). Such a view needs
some qualification; the sheer scale of IRA bombings during the
1990s obliged the British government to negotiate.

As support dwindled, so did the PIRA's military campaign,
under mounting pressure from the security forces. Duped by
the British government that withdrawal might be on the
agenda, the PIRA leadership called a cease-fire in 1974–5.
Without an effective political outlet as a back-up, Sinn Fein
being a moribund adjunct to the PIRA, the republican
project was in serious difficulty. Despite protestations of non-
sectarianism, the PIRA was sucked into a tit-for-tat sectarian
assassination during its supposed cease-fire, killing more than
forty Protestant civilians in two months in 1975, using pseu-
donyms to veil slaughters such as that of ten Protestant
workers at Kingsmill in South Armagh (Walsh 1994: 149). In
1976, the Irish government began to take a tougher line
against the PIRA, introducing emergency legislation which
reduced the extent to which the Irish Republic could be
regarded as a relatively safe haven.

From this crisis, PIRA's long war strategy emerged.
Incarcerated for a period in the mid-1970s, having operated as
an IRA leader in Belfast, Gerry Adams began to articulate the
need for a strategy broader than militarism. Writing under the
pseudonym Brownie, Adams stressed that a one-dimensional
approach, resting solely upon PIRA's armed struggle and confined to the North, was insufficient to sustain a republican
campaign. Outside the jails, the new approach was articulated
by the hard-liner, Jimmy Drumm, in the 1977 Bodenstown

Wolfe Tone oration, using a speech drafted by Adams and his associate, Danny Morrison. Urging the forging of a broader set of alliances with the working class throughout the island, Drumm argued:

> We find that a successful war of liberation cannot be fought exclusively on the backs of the oppressed in the six counties, nor around the physical presence of the British Army. Hatred and resentment of this army cannot sustain the war, and the isolation of socialist republicans around the armed struggle is dangerous and has produced, at least in some circles, the dangerous notion that 'Ulster' is the issue, which can be somehow resolved without the mobilization of the working class in the twenty-six counties.

(Cited in English 2003: 217)

The Bodenstown oration marked the end of the short war, based upon militarism, and the beginning of a more political approach to the 'republican struggle'. Adams desired a 'complete fusing of the military and political strategy' (*Republican News*, 29 November 1975: 6, 'The Republican Reality'). However, the weakness of Sinn Fein, which was to be reorganized under direct IRA control, abstention from political institutions, and frequent reluctance to contest elections, meant that the overhaul from a military-oriented approach would take some years.

Meanwhile, the fusion of violence and politics was accompanied by a leftward shift in the movement, instigated by the increasingly influential Northern element of the movement. The PIRA was once viewed (by a left-wing non-member) as the 'vanguard of the anti-imperialist struggle' in Ireland (McCann 1980: 176), a claim which perhaps overstates the case. The PIRA was, however, an important force against non-economic colonialism (British imperial interests ended in the Second World War) under which Britain held part of Ireland against the will of the majority of Irish citizens. The leftward shift led to the assassination of businessmen by the PIRA in the late 1970s, partly because they were an easier target than the military, but also because republicans began to embrace left-wing revolution as much as green nationalism. Adopting with increasing regularity the language of 'anti-imperialism', the

PIRA insisted that 'the war is not merely a conflict between Republican and British forces; it is also a conflict between the interests which those forces represent' (*Irish Times*, 23 March 1977). Neither the left turn nor the killing of businessmen endeared the PIRA to most Irish citizens, and Gerry Adams, then vice-president of Sinn Fein, made clear the limits to any left-wing shift in the Provisional movement, insisting 'there is no Marxist influence within Sinn Fein. I know of no-one in Sinn Fein who is a Marxist or who would be influenced by Marxism' (*Hibernia*, 25 October 1979).

Aside from the internal debates concerning its left turn, the PIRA was also confronted by the problem that its level of support was regularly contained by accidents which killed civilians, one of the most grotesque being the fire-bombing of La Mon restaurant in 1978, in which twelve died. Yet, with the PIRA not yet having developed a political wing willing or capable of contesting elections, the extent of public support was a peripheral issue. By the end of the 1970s, the IRA had reorganized into tighter cell structures, replacing the looser battalions, and had survived the stringencies of the mid-1970s, emerging stronger despite the tough security policy of the Secretary of State for Northern Ireland, Roy Mason, from 1976 to 1979. The killing of eighteen British soldiers by the IRA in two bombings at Warrenpoint in August 1979 emphazised that the PIRA was not beaten, even if the episode was overshadowed by the absurd killing of Lord Mountbatten by the PIRA in the Irish Republic on the same day. The IRA's move leftwards took it into ideological space already occupied by a violent offshoot of the old Official IRA, the Irish National Liberation Army (INLA). Spouting revolutionary anti-imperialism, the INLA killed the Conservative Shadow Northern Ireland Secretary, Airey Neave, at the beginning of the 1979 general election campaign.

Violence and Politics

The equality of armed and political struggle which came about in the 1980s can be attributed partly to the strategic planning of Adams and his associates, but also owes much to the emotion associated with the protests for political status undertaken by republican prisoners. The tactic of a hunger strike was not new, but it proved highly effective in mobilizing support. It was employed by IRA and INLA prisoners in 1980–1 as the climax of a campaign for recognition as political prisoners, in contrast to their treatment as common criminals. Until this point, prisoners had engaged in a dirty protest, refusing to wash and smearing excrement on their cell walls, with the result that the sympathetic Catholic Cardinal of Ireland, Thomas O'Fiaich, condemned the conditions in which prisoners lived. O'Fiaich's highlighting of the prisoners' plight proved valuable in mobilizing support from a broader constituency than that normally enjoyed by the PIRA and Sinn Fein, and for the first time, unconditional support was not a requirement for participation in PIRA-led activity (Adams 1995).

Support among the electorate was demonstrated by the by-election of the lead hunger striker, Bobby Sands, as a Westminster MP, shortly before his death in May 1981, the nationalist population of Fermanagh and South Tyrone rallying to the cause to defeat the rival unionist candidate. This republican victory was followed by the triumph of Sands's election agent, Owen Carron, at the by-election necessitated by the death of Sands. The surge of support led to the election of hunger strikers in the hitherto electorally barren Irish Republic. There remains a debate over how the hunger strike was maintained. Conventional accounts indicate that it was organized by the prisoners, against the wishes of a reluctant IRA leadership (Beresford 1987). Republican prisoners stayed on strike for a long period due to suspicion over any 'deal' from the British government, having been duped into accepting an offer in 1980. This version has been challenged by an IRA member imprisoned at the time, who claims that the strike was prolonged by the IRA Army Council, beyond an agreement, for electoral gain (O'Rawe 2005).

Even allowing for the emotion of the hunger strike campaign, it was evident that there was sympathy for republicans, which required conversion through a more active electoral stance to complement armed struggle. For the remainder of the 1980s, therefore, the republican strategy was that the movement would take power through the 'armalite and ballot-box', an approach first articulated by Sinn Fein's director of publicity, Danny Morrison, at the Sinn Fein *ard fheis* (annual conference) in October 1981. IRA violence would continue whilst Sinn Fein would contest elections. The IRA continued to claim the more prominent role in the struggle, asserting in 1982:

> Only through armed struggle will we be listened to, only through the struggle waged by the men and women of the IRA can we win national freedom and end division in Ireland. Before and since 1916 armed struggle remains the only option and the only means by which the demand for a British withdrawal can be pressed upon the British government.
>
> (*An Phoblacht/Republican News*, 15 April 1982: 3)

Privately, Morrison doubted whether the ballot and bullet strategy was sustainable in the long term. It relied upon a precision to the IRA's campaign often lacking, exemplified by the huge unpopularity of the killing of civilians. Incidents like the bombing of Harrods in December 1983, killing eight, alienated public opinion and failed to advance the IRA's military cause or Sinn Fein's electoral base. The IRA none the less enjoyed substantial support within the nationalist community for what Gerry Adams (1995: 65) defended as a 'terrible but necessary form of resistance which is engaged in as a means towards an independent Ireland'. Exasperated by the negative impact of civilian casualties, Adams nevertheless warned the IRA in 1989 to be 'careful and careful again' (McKittrick and McVea 2001: 175). The IRA's volunteers enjoyed a measure of respect and admiration from many working-class nationalists for their sacrifices. Moreover, even the British Army offered grudging admiration of the IRA's volunteers as politically motivated, suggesting, in a 1978 report publicized by the IRA, that 'our evidence of the calibre of rank and file terrorists does not support the view that they are merely mindless hooligans drawn from the unemployed and unemployable' (Brigadier J. M. Glover, quoted in Adams 1995: 66).

A vote for Sinn Fein during the 1980s could readily be interpreted as a vote of sympathy for the IRA, given that Sinn Fein's electoral candidates were mandated by the party to provide unequivocal support for the armed struggle; one-third of nationalists consistently offered such support. The problem for the republican movement was extending this support beyond the one-third, as support for Sinn Fein reached a plateau by the mid-1980s. Whilst 'successful' attacks, such as the mortar bombing of an RUC station in Newry in 1985, did not harm the republican base, 'accidents' ensured that the republican campaign attracted widespread opprobrium, by no means confined to the unionist community.

Military Stalemate

During the 1980s, the IRA showed a deadly capacity in some of its operations, but also suffered serious reverses. Bombings such as those in London's Hyde and Regent's Parks in 1982, killing eight soldiers, achieved global publicity, but the most notable of all the PIRA attacks occurred at the Conservative Party Conference in Brighton in 1984. The bombing of the Grand Hotel came close to killing Prime Minister Margaret Thatcher and many of her cabinet, but instead caused the deaths of five party activists. Its impact helped produce the Anglo-Irish Agreement during the following year, a London–Dublin accord based partly upon counter-insurgency, but which also gave the government of the Irish Republic formal consultative rights over British policy in Northern Ireland. Unionist protests were overblown, creating the illusion of serious nationalist gains. For the IRA and Sinn Fein, the popularity of the Agreement created problems. The deal was anything but a republican one; indeed, it copper-fastened partition according to the leader of Fianna Fail, Charles Haughey, and was the brain-child of the 'collaborationist' SDLP, Sinn Fein's moderate rival. Accordingly, the PIRA and Sinn Fein were dismissive of the Anglo-Irish Agreement, yet were anxious to claim that its 'concessions' to nationalists were a product of IRA 'fire-power', which the SDLP exploited for its gains.

The avowed role of IRA violence during the 1980s was to 'sicken the Brits' into eventual withdrawal, rather than attempt outright military victory. A member of the IRA's Army Council declared: 'We can't be beaten: there is no question of us winning in the sense of driving the British Army into the sea. But we always maintain the capacity to bring the situation to a crisis at some stage' (quoted in Coogan 1989: 650). Despite periodic spectaculars, the IRA's capacity to sustain its war against the security forces diminished during the 1980s. Between 1981 and 1986 the number of security force personnel killed by the IRA diminished annually, apart from a marginal increase in 1985, with twenty-four members killed in 1986, compared to forty-four in 1981 (Bishop and Mallie 1988: 416). The death toll for the security forces in urban areas dropped dramatically, IRA actions becoming increasingly confined to rural locations. The INLA killed more people than the IRA in 1982, before going into decline. The PIRA broadened the battle front, attacking British forces in Western Europe.

During the 1980s, the PIRA line on loyalists hardened. Sinn Fein's proposal for a federal Ireland, conceding unionists a majority in an Ulster parliament, was replaced by a 'no concessions to loyalists' policy. The unionist MP, the Reverend Robert Bradford, was killed by the IRA in 1981, which, added to the bitterness of the hunger strikes during that year, emphasized the extent of division between the two communities. The republican leadership insisted that it 'cannot and should not ever tolerate or compromise with Loyalism' (*An Phoblacht*, 5 November 1981: 1). Having once described unionists merely as the deluded Irish, the IRA appeared prepared to fight the unionist community, declaring: 'If a civil war is to be the consequence of the execution of a British MP then it must be an inevitable consequence of any struggle for a United Ireland' (*An Phoblacht*, 19 November 1981: 1).

Civilian casualties continued to harm a movement increasingly aware of the need to harness contemporary political support, rather than rely upon historic mandate. In this respect, the IRA bombing of a Remembrance Sunday parade at Enniskillen in 1987, killing those paying respects to the dead of two world wars, was a disaster for republicans.

The IRA eventually conceded that the bombing was a mistake, whilst its political representatives were incandescent. Sinn Fein's political support, which had grown rapidly during the first half of the 1980s, now stalled. Meanwhile, the IRA was penetrated by informers, exemplified by the killing of seven of its members in an SAS ambush at Loughgall in 1987. Hopes of a revival of the military campaign rested upon the arrival of significant amounts of weaponry from Libya. The supply line from the United States had been broken by the seizure of weapons sent by sea from the Eastern seaboard in 1984. Three significant consignments of weaponry arrived from Libya in the mid-1980s, enough to arm the IRA for at least another decade. However, the largest consignment, one designed to allow the PIRA to launch a 'Tet offensive' and render parts of rural Northern Ireland entirely 'no-go' for the security forces (already operating largely by air in South Armagh), was intercepted after a tip-off from an IRA informer (Moloney 2002). The passing of such information had decimated the capacity of the IRA outside South Armagh by the mid-1990s, notwithstanding its capacity to mount the occasional devastating operation.

The overall failure of the Libyan operation did not prevent the IRA's involvement in incidents which gave the organization unprecedented publicity. In 1988, an IRA team of three was assassinated by the SAS in Gibraltar, sparking not merely controversy but a dramatic chain of events. Mourners at the subsequent funerals came under fire from the loyalist gunman Michael Stone, leading to three more deaths. At the subsequent funerals, two off-duty British soldiers drove into the path of the funeral cortège and were dragged from their vehicle and killed. The IRA's tactics became even more brutal by 1990, as 'collaborators' with the British 'forces of occupation' were targeted. Patsy Gillespie, an individual who risked contract work for the British Army, was obliged to act as a 'human bomb', driving a primed vehicle into an Army checkpoint, killing him and several soldiers. Two years later, at Teebane, a bus carrying workmen from a British Army base was blown up, killing eight. The savage attack was portrayed as sectarian, although, had Catholics been aboard, they would have met the same fate; this was not 1975–6. The IRA policy of 'dealing' with all those 'collaborating' with the colonial power was designed to further isolate the British Army and make its presence in Northern Ireland even more problematic. The irony was that the republican leadership, having sanctioned the killing of such 'collaborators' with British rule in the early 1990s, managed such rule by the end of the decade.

Informal Dialogue and Ceasefire

Although offering a mantra of 'not talking to terrorists', the British government had always kept open lines of communication with the IRA. In the early 1990s, representatives of MI5 and MI6 each had indirect contact with Martin McGuinness, a member of PIRA's Army Council (P. Taylor 1997). Whilst clandestine, due to the political fallout, such meetings had become public knowledge, but the indirect dialogue did not amount to much more than a restatement of British constitutional policy on Northern Ireland, although it did provide an indication of the type of imaginative steps the British government might engage in if an IRA cease-fire were to be called. Contact between British government intermediaries and the IRA was placed on a sounder footing, but one still officially denied, through the establishment of the Back Channel in 1990 (Mallie and McKittrick 1996).

Documents from the British government underwent detailed, often tortuous scrutiny, within the republican leadership, the IRA Army Council passing its commentary to the Sinn Fein leadership (there was considerable overlap, but the formal distinctions were maintained), and often discussed at Sinn Fein's *ard chomhairle* before a formal position was put to the British government.

A combination of forces led to the 1994 IRA cease-fire. The organization was hardly on its knees, having launched the most devastating attacks upon England during the 1990s. It was short of recruits, although fewer operatives were needed. Increasingly, its effective operations were launched by its units in South Armagh, traditionally the most militant and the element least riddled by informers (Harnden 1999). The South Armagh IRA and the units south of the border were less vulnerable to reprisals from loyalist paramilitaries in the Ulster Freedom Fighters (UFF) (a cover name for the Ulster Defence Association) and the Ulster Volunteer Force (UVF), which were proving a major problem for the IRA in Belfast. As IRA members, Sinn Fein councillors and random Catholics were targeted, the IRA was drawn increasingly into attacks upon loyalists in 1993 and 1994, which normally were viewed as an unwelcome distraction from its war against the British security forces. The bombing of a fish shop on the Shankill Road in 1993 was an attempt to kill loyalist paramilitary leaders which went disastrously wrong, instead killing nine Protestant civilians and one of the bombers. The surviving Shankill bomber, Sean Kelly, defended the bombing thus: 'From 1990 Ardoyne had suffered an awful lot: the UFF/UDA were slaughtering Catholics an awful lot and it was time for us to take the people responsible out of circulation' (Ardoyne Commemoration Project 2002: 490).

Despite regular claims to the contrary from opponents, the PIRA did not think in particularly sectarian terms. Despite some shift by Sinn Fein, republicans tended not to think about Protestants and their identity at all. Sean Kelly highlighted the lack of PIRA acknowledgement of Protestants in Northern Ireland as the British presence when he insisted: 'I have nothing whatsoever against the Protestant community. To me the conflict is not based on Protestants against Catholics or Catholics against Protestants: this conflict is based on the British presence in our country' (Ardoyne Commemoration Project 2002: 490). The real significance of the Shankill Road bombing was that it highlighted how the IRA's war against the British had been driven instead towards a civil war against loyalist paramilitaries, a conflict it stood no chance of winning outright, and one which merely highlighted the real barrier to Irish unity.

In Britain, the IRA undertook some disastrous operations, such as the bombing of Warrington in 1993, which killed two young boys and prompted significant protests in England and Ireland. Yet the IRA also succeeded in mounting effective operations in London. A mortar attack on Downing Street in 1991 nearly wiped out the British cabinet. A huge bomb at the Baltic Exchange was detonated within 24 hours of the Conservative Party's 1992 election victory, and an ever bigger operation reduced Bishopsgate to rubble in April 1993. These operations were very expensive in insurance terms, Bishopsgate alone costing £500m (Dillon 1994: 292). They led to the creation of 'ring of steel' security operations involving regular road blocks and extensive disruption to traffic. These attacks were designed to force the British government to enter into peace negotiations with the IRA, the outcome of which could not be certain, but which would not yield a united Ireland. The bombings highlighted the inadequacy of a security-oriented strategy, which failed to accept that Sinn Fein enjoyed significant, albeit dipping, support and appeared reluctant to concede that the IRA could not be defeated outright.

Having proved these points, the IRA began a cessation of its operations at the end of August 1994, designed to facilitate Sinn Fein's entry into negotiations with the British government. Devoid of a parliamentary majority and reliant upon unionist parliamentary votes to remain in office, the Conservative government stalled on inclusive negotiations, leading to a breakdown in the IRA cease-fire in February 1996, with the bombing of Canary Wharf in London. Adams was aware of the breakdown, and, as the IRA telephoned its warnings, the Sinn Fein president was acting similarly in informing the US administration. According to the United States president, Bill Clinton, 'it was evident from his tone that Adams disagreed with the decision' to return to war (interview on BBC Northern Ireland, *The Politics Show*, 18 July 2004). Clinton was correct in his perception, although Adams had been obliged to support the IRA Army Council's decision to protect the unity of the movement and avert a damaging split. Four months later, the IRA detonated its largest bomb ever, demolishing a considerable part of Manchester city centre. Yet the bombs had different meanings to different people within the IRA Army Council and the IRA executive. For some, it was back to business as usual, part of an ongoing war against the 'Brits', whose lack of good faith had been highlighted by the failure to negotiate. For the Adams-led majority, however, two factors necessitated a restatement of the cease-fire. First, the newly elected Labour government, with a large parliamentary majority, would admit Sinn Fein to negotiations if the cease-fire revived and would drop the Conservatives' insistence on some form of prior decommissioning of IRA weapons. Secondly, the successful demolitions of Canary Wharf and Manchester masked the underlying weakness of the IRA. Both the 1996 'spectaculars' were undertaken by the South Armagh PIRA, effectively the 'last shot' of the PIRA, which elsewhere in Ireland was weakening rapidly due to penetration by the security forces. With such penetration likely to be extended to South Armagh, there was scant utility to an IRA campaign which could achieve the short-term goal of Sinn Fein's inclusion in negotiations within months.

Not all within PIRA accepted Adams's arguments, and a heated IRA convention in 1996 sharply criticized the initial cease-fire as undermining the organization and failing to produce results (Moloney 2002). These militarists within the movement objected to the principles of non-violence introduced in 1996 by Senator George Mitchell, the United States envoy to Northern Ireland, requiring all participants in the peace and political process to adhere to non-violence in a manner which spelt the end of the IRA. Sinn Fein declared support for the Mitchell principles, but the IRA's executive opposed Adams's peace strategy and a renewal of the IRA cease-fire, also insisting that there should be no decommissioning of IRA weapons prior to achievement of a united Ireland. Given that the achievement of Irish unity was the *raison d'être* of the IRA, the contention was logical, but the demand was overridden by Adams's supporters, who viewed decisions on cease-fires and weapons as the preserve of the IRA's Army Council.

The IRA Army Council remained dominated by Adams's supporters after new elections at the 1997 cease-fire convention, and the cease-fire was duly restored in July 1997, leading to a split in the movement and the formation of the Real IRA

(RIRA). Given that the IRA had done what it had always said it would not do, enter a cease-fire without pre-conditions on the establishment of unity, the emergence of the dissenting RIRA, committed to traditional republican methods and principles did not surprise. From 1997 onwards, the PIRA remained intact, but its role as a movement designed to achieve a united Ireland was redundant. Instead, it operated as a policing force within the nationalist community, dealing with local criminals and 'dissident' republicans, whilst engaging in slow, staged acts of decommissioning designed to yield maximum concessions for Sinn Fein. The policing role attracted particular scorn from dissidents, Sinn Fein and PIRA leaders ensuring safe passage for the British Army amid a riot after the passing of an Orange parade and its supporters in July 2004. None the less, PIRA, its members now engaged almost entirely in Sinn Fein business, remained popular within its working-class base, and the continued electoral successes of Sinn Fein conveyed an image of a vibrant republicanism which had salvaged tangible items from an IRA campaign, a conclusion lacking at the closure of IRA campaigns in the 1940s and 1960s.

For the PIRA, the war was clearly over, yet, by 2001, 82 per cent of Protestants declined to believe the evidence, instead expecting that the organization would return to war (Irwin 2002: 242). As a senior Sinn Fein figure in Belfast, Dennis Donaldson, explained, the three items which the IRA considered in terms of the utility of armed struggle were 'whether or not the support is there, and the political conditions are there, and whether they can sustain an armed campaign' (Pardoe 1998: 59). All three questions yielded negative answers, and the IRA had thus supported the Good Friday Agreement in 1998, which, on any objective consideration, was incapable of yielding a united Ireland for at least a generation, and possibly permanently. The Agreement offered a two-state solution, and ended the Irish government's constitutional claim to the North. This claim had never been of practical value to the IRA. As the PIRA declared in the 1980s, 'these territorial claims mean nothing to the nationalist people of the North, have never given any protection to the nationalist people and do not even relate to the motivation or zeal of the IRA'

(*An Phoblacht/Republican News*, 17 October 1981: 1). None the less, the existence of the territorial claim meant that the difference within the 'republican family' concerned methods of goal attainment, given that the entire family agreed that Northern Ireland was an illegitimate entity. The Good Friday Agreement endorsed the six-county state, taking Irish republicanism in a fundamentally different direction and ending the IRA's purpose.

Summary

Ultimately, PIRA violence did not achieve its goal of reuniting Ireland. One architect of the PIRA, Joe Cahill, its chief of staff for a time in the 1970s, declared before his death in 2004: 'I was born in a united Ireland and want to die in a united Ireland' (BBC Northern Ireland, *Newsline*, 27 July 2004). As a Belfast citizen, Cahill spent his life as an Irish republican under British jurisdiction. The PIRA campaign was a determined effort to end British sovereignty in Northern Ireland, one ultimately defeated by three elements: first, the ever-improving military and intelligence capability of the British Army and its associates, which meant that the PIRA's onslaught was ultimately a war contained; secondly, the threat of loyalist violence and civil war, which remained a calculation in the British government's deliberations; and thirdly, the lack of passion for a united Ireland among sections of the nationalist population, which favoured the moderate SDLP to Sinn Fein for most of the conflict, and often resented the IRA in the Irish Republic, resulting in the marginalization of the PIRA outside its northern urban working-class or rural strongholds. This is not to say that the IRA did not achieve gains for the nationalist population. To suggest that the huge changes that have occurred in Northern Ireland would have happened anyway is to assume a generosity within the one-party Unionist regime, or interest and reformist zeal within the British government, not easily detected prior to the 1970s. It is doubtful that the SDLP could alone have achieved the equality gains evident for nationalists in recent times. For a time, the PIRA highlighted the undemocratic and illegitimate basis of partition and its consequences for the nationalist population in the North. Ultimately, however, Cahill's claim, in his final speech to a Sinn Fein *ard fheis* in 2004, that 'we [PIRA] won the war' reduced the organization to a reformist or defender organization, not the republican army whose stated purpose was to achieve an indivisible island. When selling the Good Friday Agreement to Sinn Fein and the IRA, Gerry Adams had insisted that republicans 'cannot and will not ever recognize as legitimate the six-county statelet' (presidential address to Sinn Fein *ard fheis*, April 1998). With the IRA decommissioned and Sinn Fein in government in the North, it was unclear how Provisional republicans were failing to recognize the legitimacy of the state.

By the early part of the twenty-first century, the PIRA was effectively subsumed into Sinn Fein, the organization which had acted as a mere cheer-leader and welfare adjunct in the early 1970s. The PIRA's formal winding-up, other than as a comrades' association, and the decommissioning of its weapons, the climax of the Adams-initiated peace process, was duly announced in 2005. Adams became increasingly explicit concerning the prospect of a future without the IRA, offering the prospect of disbandment of the organization in talks with the British and Irish governments at Leeds Castle in 2004. However, episodic IRA activity, including the largest bank robbery in British and Irish history in 2004, led to continued unionist scepticism. Adams accepted the view articulated by Tony Blair that the IRA was now an impediment to political progress. The republican assumption had been that it was the British presence and the unionist veto which were the creators of Ireland's political problems. If the political progress envisaged by Adams was likely to lead to the united Ireland fought for by the IRA, the organization's removal might be seen as consistent with republican ideas. However, no such outcome was waiting. In previous eras, the IRA had dumped arms, but awaited more favourable times; at the end of the PIRA's conflict, Provisional republicans had, through decommissioning, de-legitimized armed struggle as a tactic, let alone a principle. An IRA-free Northern Ireland, with unbridled nationalist political participation, meant a normal Northern Ireland, in which the old issue of partition and the longer history of British involvement in Ireland would no longer be seriously contested.

3

The Overt War against the IRA

From Honeymoon to War

The arrival of British troops in Northern Ireland in August 1969 quelled temporarily the disturbances between Protestants and Catholics that had erupted during the civil rights campaign. The role óf the British Army as protector ensured that the soldiers were warmly received by besieged Catholics, but the Army's arrival dismayed many Protestants, who saw it as a usurping of 'their' security forces. The disturbances of August revived in October in Belfast, when the disarming of the RUC and the dismantling of the B Specials was proposed in the Hunt Report (1969). Protestants felt betrayed and again attempted to attack Catholic areas, even killing a member of the RUC, which they were purportedly defending. The role of the British Army in defending Catholics produced remarkable scenes, given what happened during the following thirty years. In Ardoyne, an area of north Belfast which became a PIRA stronghold and endured more deaths than any other part of Northern Ireland, a British Army major was made an honorary member of the local Shamrock Club, whilst soldiers were fed and watered by the local population (P. Taylor 2001). The reception afforded the British Army was indicative of the lack of republican sentiment among the Catholic population in 1969. Its main concern was with defending the streets, with ready acceptance of the British Army as the organization best equipped to perform this task. The IRA of 1969 had proved

utterly incapable of such a role, and the revival of its legitimacy, under the PIRA banner, began when it started to defend
Catholic property.

The General Officer Commanding in Northern Ireland, Sir
Ian Freeland, was not fooled by the initial cordial welcome
given to his troops. From the outset, he insisted that it was
necessary to find political accommodation. Moreover, the
British government did not believe that a quick fix to the
problem was likely. With the split in the republican movement
confirmed at the turn of the year, the newly born PIRA busied
itself in local defence committees, initially co-operating with
the British Army, but preparing to sour relations. Early in
1970, the first PIRA calls to the local population not to frat-
ernize with the Army did not have much impact, but from
April 1970, relations between the Catholic population and the
British forces collapsed. The catalyst was the commencement
of the Orange marching season, rather than PIRA activity, a
parade through mainly Catholic Ballymurphy being followed
by a riot. As the British Army quelled the disturbance, the
Catholic population began to see the Army as a surrogate
RUC, used to suppress protest. Amid a political vacuum, with
the unionist government retaining one-party power and controlling security issues, the situation deteriorated sharply,
allowing the PIRA to assume the status of nationalist defender
against the old enemy of British forces.

The Early Years: Crisis in Security Policy

The souring of relations between the British Army and the
Catholic population continued apace throughout the remainder of 1970. The Army's imposition of a curfew upon the Falls
in Belfast, as part of an arms search operation, alienated the
local population. During the searches, the Official IRA opened
fire on the British Army, which returned fire, often indiscrim-
inately, killing three civilians, before imposing a 'restriction on
public movement' against its own preferred approach and
under pressure from unionists (Sunday Times Insight Team
1972: 218–19).

An important feature of security policy in the previous IRA campaign of 1956–62 had been the use of internment. Given its success, it was unsurprising that unionists soon demanded its reintroduction. By the early 1970s, the UUP leadership was coming under increasing internal pressure from hard-liners and from outside the party, from the newly formed DUP, for even tougher security measures. The British Army cautioned against the move on three grounds: first, its intelligence was inadequate; second, the Irish government would not reciprocate, undermining the value of the policy in defending the United Kingdom's only land frontier; third, the policy would further alienate an increasingly disaffected Catholic community. Despite these protests, internment was reintroduced in August 1971. Its operation was never even-handed; during its life span from 1971 to 1975, 2,060 republicans were detained, compared to only 109 loyalists (O'Leary and McGarry 1996: 197). The outdated intelligence upon which internment was based led to swoops which defied credibility; 105 of the 342 people arrested on the first day of internment were released within 48 hours (M. Smith 1995: 105). None the less, internment had its defenders, most senior among them Major-General Anthony Farrar-Hockley, who, whilst preferring more selective netting, none the less argued that the operation yielded important intelligence and forced the IRA leadership into hiding (P. Taylor 2001). As O'Malley (1983: 209) put it: 'the Army's strategy – break the IRA and bring a halt to its operations by arresting as many IRA officers as possible and putting them behind bars – not only was fallacious in conception, it actually spawned a new generation of IRA leaders who revitalised the movement in the late 1970s.' Yet the Army was confronted with a classical problem of a neo-colonial rule; how to eliminate a guerrilla army rebellion without alienating the population from which it might draw support. The prospect of undertaking this task successfully was dependent upon political change accompanying military incursion, but the political agenda of the unionist government from 1969 to 1971 was not primarily concerned with reform. Instead, the British Army drew upon previous experience of anti-colonial insurgency in non-urban locations and in different circumstances. The results ranged from clumsy to brutal, with the legacy that over one-third of the population believe that the Army was either 'very responsible' or 'responsible' for the Troubles with a further one in five believing that it was partly responsible, and less than one-quarter believing that it was 'not responsible' (Morrisey and Smyth 2002).

The approach of the security forces during this period, aided and abetted by the unionist government, was that the IRA could be defeated through a tough approach. The nadir of the resulting operations, the shooting dead of thirteen unarmed civilians on a civil rights march in Derry in January 1972 by the Parachute Regiment, led to widespread support for the IRA. The Parachute Regiment claimed that it had been fired upon first. The claim and the near-exoneration of the Army in the subsequent Widgery Report (1972) merely heightened animosity. A second inquiry, under Lord Saville, was initiated by the Labour government elected in 1997. With memories fading and only a limited amount of new evidence, it was unlikely that the expensive inquiry would settle matters, and the impact of that day upon recruitment for the IRA was already known. It was already in the public domain, pre-Saville inquiry, that the 'removal' of rioters, known as the Derry Young Hooligans, was one of several options outlined by the Commander of Land Forces, Major-General Robert Ford, although he ruled out the option, despite a personal preference, due to a risk of the 'slaughter of the innocent' (quoted in P. Taylor 2001: 85).

There were elements within the British Army who recognized that insufficient attention was paid to winning respect among the local community. Brigadier Frank Kitson, a brigade commander in Belfast, held a reputation as a hard-liner, but drew upon overseas experience to implement local civilian representatives who could liaise between the locals and the Army and organize some services. Given the deterioration in relations after 1970, Kitson's ideas were too little, too late. Moreover, as Kennedy-Pipe (1997: 70) argues, following the decline in violence after 1972, the worst year of the conflict, with 467 killed, 'many believed that a hard-line approach backed up by special legislation was working'.

The competence of the security forces gradually improved, and two IRA blunders in summer 1972 allowed the security forces to regain control. First, its Chief of Staff, Sean McStiofain, overplayed his hand in talks with British government, behaving, in the words of the head of MI6, Frank Steele, 'like the representative of an army that had fought the British to a standstill' (quoted in P. Taylor 2001: 123). Second, the IRA failed to shore up its support, instead bombing civilian areas in Belfast on 'Bloody Friday' with inadequate warnings. Whilst the period from Easter 1970 until July 1972 was calamitous, the Army regained the initiative with Operation Motorman at the end of July 1972, just ten days after Bloody Friday, removing the IRA's no-go areas in Derry and Belfast. The operation, involving 12,000 troops, was the biggest mounted by the British Army since Suez in 1956 (P. Taylor 2001). Violence peaked in summer 1972 with an extraordinary 2,778 shootings in July alone. Although the IRA was on the defensive from then on, violence in the second half of 1972 was considerable, with almost 300 soldiers wounded (Fields 1989).

Legal Frameworks

A draconian legal framework pre-dated the conflict that erupted in 1969, the Special Powers Act having been introduced shortly after partition and surviving, in modified form, until the collapse of the unionist government in 1972. It had been accompanied by petty restrictions, such as the 1954 Flags and Emblems Act, which prohibited the display of the Irish national flag. The 1973 Emergency Provisions Act, updated in 1978, and the 1974 Prevention of Terrorism Act, updated in 1976, more than replaced the Special Powers Act. The British Army was given wide powers of search, arrest and detention, searching over 75,000 homes in 1973 alone (Boyle, Hadden and Hillyard 1980: 27). The rhetoric from the authorities concerning the need to uphold the rule of law overlooked the abnormality of the law in the province. Aside from detention without trial from 1971 to 1975, there were many stark examples. One was the creation of juryless courts following the 1972 Diplock Report, from which much of the Emergency Provisions Act originated. Another was the widening of admissible evidence following the 1975 Gardiner Report, which facilitated the use of uncorroborated testimonies of 'supergrass' police and Army informers, allowing the mass conviction of terrorists. A further element in the abnormal legal framework was the ending of a defendant's right to silence from 1988, which from then on could be construed as an indication of guilt. From 1988 until the IRA's cease-fire in 1994, the security framework also involved a denial of political voice; media outlets were acting illegally if they broadcast directly the utterances of the political affiliates of paramilitary groups, a prohibition which also existed in the Irish Republic under Section 31 of its Broadcasting Act.

The flexibility afforded to the security forces and judges under these acts allowed normal rules of justice to be circumvented, a scenario defended by the authorities as a reflection of the abnormal circumstances in which they operated. The Prevention of Terrorism Act resulted in trawling by the police, who were allowed to hold suspects for up to seven days with the approval (invariably forthcoming) of magistrates. The net effect, as it could be labelled, was that 93 per cent of individuals detained under the Act were released without charge during the 1970s and 1980s (Scorer and Hewitt 1981: 66; Colville Report 1989: 4). The use of the Prevention of Terrorism Act also led to some spectacular miscarriages of justice.

Those in custody sometimes sustained ill-treatment. The 1979 Bennett Report upheld allegations of ill-treatment at RUC interrogation centres, although there remained dispute over its extent, the British government claiming that only 0.5 per cent of detainees had been injured in police custody during the final year prior to the investigation (Elliott and Flackes 1999: 178). The European Court of Human Rights cleared the British government of torture, but stated that it had allowed 'inhumane and degrading' treatment of prisoners. Meanwhile the British government did not introduce a Bill of Rights, despite the recommendation of the Gardiner Committee, preferring instead to establish merely a Standing Advisory Commission on Human Rights. Those not in jail could be made subjects of 'banning orders' from the British mainland, effectively a bizarre form of 'internal exile' within the United Kingdom (O'Duffy 1993: 139).

The Containment of the PIRA

With a tough legal framework in place, the security forces, like the IRA itself, settled down to a prolonged battle. A private assessment of the IRA in 1979 by Brigadier James Glover, *Northern Ireland, Future Terrorist Trends*, discovered by the PIRA, acknowledged that the organization 'has the dedication and the sinews of war to raise violence . . . at least for the foreseeable future . . . The Provisionals' campaign of violence is likely to continue while the British remain in Northern Ireland' (quoted in Coogan 1989: 581–2). The report continued: 'The Provisionals have not the large number of active terrorists they had in 1972–73. But they no longer need them . . . though PIRA may be hard hit by security force attention from time to time, they will probably continue to have the manpower they need to sustain violence during the next five years' (quoted in Cronin 1980: 342).

As neither side envisaged outright victory in the immediate future, the two protagonists developed realistic ambitions of what was attainable. For the IRA, the killing of members of the security forces would eventually disillusion the British government to such an extent as to place withdrawal on the agenda. For the British Army, the IRA would eventually be hemmed in to such an extent that the dividends of an armed campaign would be so minimal as to make its continuation pointless. The IRA enjoyed substantial support among working-class Catholics, but was never a majority taste among the Catholic community in its entirety, which preferred to support the non-violent approach of the SDLP. Even more importantly, the IRA did not have the weaponry to inflict defeat upon the British. Supply lines of weaponry were vulnerable to British intelligence and informers. In 1973, the IRA's route from Libya was intercepted. In 1986, the action of an informer curtailed a much larger supply route from Libya, ending the IRA's hopes of 'liberating' border counties of

Northern Ireland (Moloney 2002). Although three substantial shipments had already arrived via this route, the seizure of the next, much vaster, cargo of weaponry was a turning-point in the conflict, ensuring that the British would remain able to contain IRA violence.

The concentration upon restraining the IRA resulted in a highly security-oriented policy. After the collapse of the Sunningdale power-sharing agreement in 1974, there was a clear 'fragility of commitment to political initiatives' for a decade (Rolston 1991: 170). Instead, the government proceeded with Ulsterization, placing local security forces in the front line of policing wherever possible, and criminalization, treating paramilitary prisoners as common criminals rather than awarding them special category status which effectively recognized them as prisoners of war. The primary use of the RUC and Ulster Defence Regiment (UDR) was in part for pragmatic reasons, as they knew local areas well, but also for political purposes, diminishing the appearance that the IRA was at war with another army and portraying its battle as a local sectarian contest. This did not unduly concern the IRA, who targeted all 'Crown forces' and responded by killing RUC and UDR personnel at a rate of almost eight to one compared to British Army soldiers by the mid-1980s (Mallie and McKittrick 2001: 62). From 1976 until 1990, two-thirds of security force deaths were suffered by local forces, compared to less than one-third from 1971 to 1975 (O'Duffy, 1993: 139).

The security policy involved saturation policing throughout the 1980s, with Northern Ireland having 8.4 security personnel per 1,000 of its population, compared to, for example, a figure of 1.6 in France (Baldy 1987: 12). In the four years following eruption of the conflict in 1969, the combined security force personnel of the RUC, the UDR (which replaced the B Specials) and the British Army almost tripled, from 11,600 to 33,000, and averaged more than 30,000 until the IRA's 1994 cease-fire (Hillyard 1997: 105). There was a temporary reduction in the strength of the British Army, from 13,000 to 9,000, in the early 1980s, but the number rose again after the upsurge of violence following the Anglo-Irish Agreement.

At the time of the IRA cease-fire in 1994, Army numbers were at a record high of 18,000, although this figure includes the Royal Irish Regiment, into which the UDR was merged.

By the close of the 1980s, the security forces had been responsible for 310 deaths in the conflict. The number of republican paramilitaries killed, at 123, greatly exceeded the death toll of loyalist paramilitaries at the same hands, only thirteen, and the security forces had killed almost six times as many Catholic civilians as Protestants, an obvious factor in explaining continued Catholic alienation (O'Leary and McGarry 1996: 25, 149; McGarry and O'Leary 1995: 25, 36). The containment strategy worked in preventing an expansion of IRA violence. The number of killings by republicans never reached three figures in any year during the 1980s, and averaged fifty-six annually, representing a vicious conflict with episodic acute crises, but one on which the British had perhaps 'kept the lid'. This containment meant that the purpose of the IRA's war, begun in the expectation of victory, was less apparent by the 1990s, and in that context, a peace process was developed.

Special Forces, Special Methods

The particular difficulties of dealing with the IRA led the British Army to adopt a host of strategies to combat its enemy. In the early years, both sides used unsophisticated methods to try and outwit their opponents. The British Army was obliged to adapt the methods used in Aden and Kenya in the 1950s to the hostile urban environments of Belfast and Derry and the rural PIRA strongholds near the border. Recognizing that it needed to penetrate hostile urban communities, the British Army embarked on covert operations that brought it into close contact with local people, establishing a Military Reconnaissance Force (MRF) to tour the streets in plain clothes and unmarked vehicles. The success of the group is difficult to quantify, but a series of shootings in 1972 exposed the work of the MRF, work which ended with the discovery of one of its key intelligence-gathering operations in Belfast. The MRF established a laundry collection service, run by an established clearing firm but controlled by the Army, to run forensic tests on clothes for traces of explosives and also to place the local population under surveillance. An IRA man, Seamus Wright, was initially 'turned' by the security forces, but then informed the IRA of the operation in an unsuccessful attempt to save his own life. After the IRA had killed the laundry van driver and ended the surveillance operation, the MRF was abolished.

Despite the demise of the MRF, the British Army was still keen to gather intelligence beyond that provided by informers. The 14 Intelligence Company, known as the 'Det' from 1973 onwards, placed members of the Army on intelligence-gathering operations within republican areas. Their role was not merely to trawl such areas looking for possible clues to IRA operations and monitor lists of suspects provided by RUC Special Branch; increasingly, the 'Det' became involved in applying the Army's developing technology such as bugging and tracing equipment. The surveillance techniques of 14 Intelligence Company quickly paid dividends, with the arrests of the Belfast IRA leaders Gerry Adams and Brendan Hughes in 1973.

The spate of sectarian killings in the mid-1970s, as the IRA's cease-fire collapsed, led to the announcement by the British government that the Special Air Service (SAS) was to be sent to Northern Ireland in January 1976. The announcement was partly one of political expediency, given that there had been SAS members operating in Northern Ireland, attached to regiments, from the outset of the Troubles. The SAS recognized that the most vulnerable aspect of British security policy was that the IRA enjoyed a relatively safe haven on the Republic side of the Irish border. Although IRA operatives were liable to arrest by the Garda Siochana, the border was not particularly heavily policed on the Republic's side, and sentences in the event of conviction tended to be light. Moreover, the IRA enjoyed considerable support in the border counties of Louth and Monaghan. The response of the SAS on occasions during the 1970s was to engage in incursions across the border. Such an approach enraged an Irish government which, naturally, regarded these incidents as a breach of sovereign territory. In May 1976, eight armed British soldiers were arrested in the Irish Republic for an incursion, and tried and convicted, albeit on a minor charge. The Irish government was sometimes suspected of ambiguity in terms of its fight against the IRA, although in some internal respects it was tougher, introducing measures such as the broadcasting ban on republicans before the British government. Prior to the 1985 Anglo-Irish Agreement, it was less keen to help the British government deal with the IRA, and it allowed those suspected of committing terrorist crimes to lodge a 'political offence' justification, prohibiting extradition, until 1987.

Different perceptions of the SAS emerged. For the Irish government and for critics of British security policy generally, the SAS was regarded as the unacceptable face of British security (Murray 1990). The IRA feared the SAS, labelling it the 'Special Assassination Squad' (P. Taylor 2001: 194), given its reluctance to make arrests and take prisoners. Yet, initially at least, the existing covert operational forces in Northern Ireland of 14 Intelligence Company did not rate the SAS highly, regarding them as unsubtle operators, although such criticisms diminished with the interchange of personnel between the two bodies. The deployment of the SAS indicated that notions of 'police primacy' were shallow. Indeed, the British Prime Minister Margaret Thatcher did not really believe in such a policy, given the need to fight the IRA (Thatcher 1993; Kennedy-Pipe 1997). Instead, the war on the IRA was increasingly being won by elite armed forces and through ever-growing intelligence, assembled largely through a network of informers.

Inevitably, the SAS was involved in some of the other most controversial incidents of the war. It killed seven members of the IRA's East Tyrone brigade at Loughgall in 1987. This marked the beginning of a sustained onslaught against the IRA's hard-line units in the area, in which twenty-eight members of the IRA were killed during the next five years, twenty-one by the SAS, killed through a combination of information passed by an informer in Northern Command and expert surveillance by the SAS (Moloney 2002). In 1988 the SAS killed three members of an IRA active service unit in Gibraltar. The movements of the IRA team had been monitored from the beginning of each operation in both cases. For many (including some republicans), such killings were part of the fortunes of war, although they belied the notion often proffered by the government that the IRA was merely a criminal conspiracy, to be dealt with by normal legal processes.

Allegations of 'shoot to kill' were not confined to the SAS. The RUC was accused of this tactic after two INLA activists were shot in Armagh by an RUC team which included officers from Belfast who had never served in the county (Holland and McDonald 1994). The Catholic priests of Armagh condemned what they perceived as 'a policy of summary execution without trial' (*Irish News*, 14 December 1982). The subsequent investigation by the Deputy Chief Constable of Manchester, John Stalker, was routed down a long cul-de-sac, the main substantiated allegation in respect of his character being the heinous crime of once using a police vehicle to take his son to watch Manchester United (Stalker 1988). Stalker was aware that a unit of the RUC had engaged in what appeared to be premeditated killings by a specialist unit trained in firearms at RUC headquarters. The RUC's E4 anti-terrorist unit had already engaged in extensive surveillance of the IRA suspects, using mainly bugs and phone tapping, in addition to human covert operations. When the RUC shot two men in a hay shed in November 1982, killing one, the shed was bugged, sending signals to a nearby Army base, and the event was secretly tape-recorded. Stalker, however, was denied access to the tape, despite frequent requests. The RUC anti-terrorist unit also shot dead three IRA men in Armagh in 1982, having bugged their car. The use of tracker devices on equipment became increasingly common. Meanwhile, patrols became increasingly sophisticated, with computers recording the whereabouts of cars, coded if they had travelled through 'high-risk' republican areas. Districts where the PIRA enjoyed support were under constant surveillance, through infra-red devices and thermal imagery for viewing and photography. Phone tapping was much more common than elsewhere in the United Kingdom. All this surveillance was in addition to elaborate and detailed storage of information on paramilitary suspects.

In the same way that the IRA valued its propaganda war, British forces were keen to discredit their opponents. The Army maintained an Information Policy Unit, designed to disseminate analysis and information on how the Army was (successfully) responding to the IRA. The unit provided such details to journalists, some of whom were overtly sympathetic to the British forces and would readily report such information, irrespective of its veracity. The Information Policy Unit was designed to add to the psychological pressure upon the IRA, depicting the organization as comprising psychopaths, devoid of legitimacy within the community. The planting of fictitious stories was common, and at times the unit also engaged in internal 'dirty tricks', briefing against other elements of the security forces, due to ongoing disputes between MI5 and MI6 and between regular Army units and special units (Dillon 1988).

The Toughest Nut: South Armagh

In common with other units of the British Army, the SAS found South Armagh a difficult place to penetrate. The IRA inflicted its greatest 'successes' there, killing eighteen soldiers with two bombs at Warrenpoint in August 1979. The IRA operated semi-autonomously within the area. It mistrusted the Belfast leadership, and did not refer many operations to Northern Command – suspicions often reciprocated, despite the respect held by the leadership for the South Armagh IRA's combative skills. The level of secrecy within the South Armagh IRA held particular advantages, as the IRA's Northern structure had been penetrated by the British, who ran several informers, including the head of IRA security, 'Stakeknife'. The attempts of the SAS to gather intelligence in South Armagh were less successful than elsewhere. In 1979, one of its captains, Robert Nairac, was killed by the local IRA, when they discovered that he had been gathering intelligence and running informers in the local area. The IRA gathered little information from

Nairac prior to his death, but the episode highlighted the limit to 'close-quarters' work that could be undertaken by British forces in the area. Instead, the British Army concentrated much of its effort on spying on the local population through its watch-towers and listening devices.

Improved surveillance restricted the IRA's movements, and was increased systematically from the 1980s onwards, allowing the security forces eventually to gain the upper hand in this area, although the effect was to divert South Armagh units towards the IRA's campaign in England during the 1990s. The scale of security force operations was enormous; Operation Rectify, the rebuilding of the Crossmaglen security force base, was the largest British air-mobile operation since D-Day, involving more than 1,000 troops and 1,400 tonnes of building supplies (Harnden 1999: 253). The timing of the rebuilding in May 1994, amid much talk of the imminent IRA cease-fire, indicated distrust among the security forces that South Armagh could ever be fully 'tamed' by the republican leadership. The British Army maintained control of the skies, and could thus operate in border areas in helicopters equipped with cameras, despite the attempts of the IRA to secure surface-to-air missiles. A number were imported as part of the IRA's Libyan arms cache of the 1980s, but the Army's observation techniques meant that undetected operation was difficult. The Army was also capable of jamming the IRA's radio-controlled bombs. The Army was forced to operate covertly on the ground, in addition to deploying watch-tower surveillance, in attempting to end the revival of the IRA's single-shot sniping in South Armagh during the 1990s. The tactic had been used successfully by the IRA in the 1970s, reducing the risk of capture that followed a prolonged gun battle. Only after the IRA cease-fire in 1994, opposed by many within South Armagh, was the Army able to achieve the upper hand, by bugging weapons and vehicles involved in such actions.

Even outside South Armagh, the British Army found large parts of Northern Ireland inhospitable, with normal activity outside the confines of their military base discouraged. In 1982, eleven soldiers and six civilians were killed by an INLA bomb at the Dropping Well pub near Derry. The INLA was aware that the pub was frequented by soldiers from the Ballykelly Army base. Following the bombing, contact between the Army and the local population became almost impossible, and the two-year tours of duty for soldiers became largely devoid of the normal social pleasures. This formed part of the republican plan, to isolate the British Army as a force of occupation with no remit from the local population.

After the IRA: Is There a Consensus on Security Policy?

During the 1990s, the focus of security force activity remained the IRA, even though it was often not the largest killer from 1991 onwards. From 1991 to 1994, loyalists were responsible for 124 deaths caused by paramilitary groups, 56 per cent of the total, compared to 96 caused by republican paramilitaries (44 per cent). Yet there was little change in security policy, and the increased 'success' rate of loyalists was at least partly derived from the earlier passing of information on republicans by elements within the security forces. The temporary breakdown of the IRA cease-fire in 1996 was followed by the bombing of Thiepval Army barracks in Lisburn in October that year, killing one. In April 1997, the shooting of Stephen Restorick at Brookeborough marked the final British Army fatality of the conflict. The IRA was less interested in targeting the security forces during the 1990s, partly because such attacks often failed. It was calculated that in the 1980s, the IRA had to undertake an average of eighteen attacks to kill a member of the security forces, and the RUC claimed that four out of five IRA operations were intercepted (Elliott and Flackes 1999: 650–5).

The peace process offered the prospect of the demilitarization of Northern Ireland, but there remained a community divide on the importance of security issues. In 1998, the year the Good Friday Agreement was reached, the highest Protestant priority for peace, alongside the disbandment of all paramilitary groups, was for 'stronger and effective anti-terrorist measures', at 70 per cent (Irwin 2002: 168). However, 61 per cent of Catholics declared that the return of the Army to their barracks was essential, and only 40 per cent believed that stronger and effective anti-terrorist measures were essential (ibid.). Security policy was framed in a non-consensual atmosphere, in which the defeat of terrorism has been an overriding concern for unionists, whereas the need for internal reform has preoccupied nationalists.

Nationalist hostility to the security forces is diminishing. The decision of the SDLP to join the Policing Board in 2001 reflects how a section of the nationalist population accepted that the Patten reforms of policing had in effect disbanded the mistrusted RUC (Patten Report 1999). Sinn Fein's initial reluctance to join reflected internal disquiet and a demand for full implementation of Patten', but the party was set to play a role in policing.

Demilitarization

Old habits died hard during the peace process. The vehicles and homes of Sinn Fein personnel were bugged, two devices being found. Transcripts of conversations between the Sinn Fein leadership and the Secretary of State for Northern Ireland from 1997 to 1999, Mo Mowlam, appeared in the press, the recordings indicating the cosiness of personal relationships that had developed between supposed opposing forces. The controversies over the war against the IRA continued. In July 2004 the Ministry of Defence obtained a court injunction preventing a former soldier from making further allegations that the shooting of Stephen Restorick by the IRA in 1997 was permitted in order to protect an informer. It was also alleged in respect of this case that the vehicle used by the IRA's team in South Armagh had been fitted with a tracking device. Whatever the status of such claims, it is apparent that the security forces increasingly had the upper hand, albeit not an entirely controlling one, over the IRA.

Demilitarization began immediately upon announcement of the IRA's cease-fire in 1994, but the pace of change was grindingly slow during the early years of relative peace. The run-up to the cease-fire had been marked by experimental change in Derry, with the Army increasingly adhering to a highly informal code of conduct in its operations. The first few years after the cease-fire saw symbolic changes, such as the replacement of soldiers' helmets by berets, and more substantive change, such as the ending of street patrols in Belfast, other than in exceptional circumstances. In 2003 the British government outlined its proposals for demilitarization in the event of 'acts of completion', government-speak for the demise of the IRA. These included reduction in the size of the Army to 5,000, confined to a maximum of fourteen locations, with an annual programme of closures of bases and observation posts. The Army would no longer be housed with the police service. Counter-terrorist legislation specific to Northern Ireland would also be repealed, and a new legislative framework, based upon human rights, would be established under a Criminal Justice Bill.

Republicans none the less complained about the supposedly slow pace of change. Although the label 'securocrats' was classic Sinn Fein-speak, there was evidence that some within the security and intelligence services were reluctant to let go of the certainties of 'war'. A much-trumpeted IRA 'spy ring' at Stormont led to the collapse of the 1999–2002 Northern Ireland Assembly established under the Good Friday Agreement, but the allegations did not result in any successful prosecutions. Similarly, the mysterious break-in at Castlereagh police station during this period, blamed on republicans, failed to yield anything in the courts. Abroad, however, the 'Colombia Three' trial of suspected IRA members accused of aiding FARC guerrillas ended in convictions. In late 2004 the IRA was blamed for the largest bank robbery in UK history, after the theft of £26.5 million from the Northern Bank in Belfast. Robberies apart, the PIRA remained intact in the immediate post-GFA era, but its main activities consisted of dealing with 'dissident' republicans, local suspected criminals, or, in the killing of Robert McCartney from Belfast's Short Strand, having members involved in a murder far removed from any political cause.

Despite claims of slow change, there were substantial moves towards demilitarization and policing change. The peace 'dividend' in the first five years after the GFA was considerable. Half of the British Army's military spy towers were demolished; the number of bases was reduced from thirty-two to twenty-four and of these twenty-four, only twelve continued to house British troops (Independent Monitoring Commission 2004). None the less, even at the height of the Iraq conflict in 2003–4, the British Army had more troops stationed in Northern Ireland than in any other region.

The Patten Report (1999) promised a community-based police service to replace a unionist-oriented police force. The key proposals in the report promised a reduction in size to 7,500 full-time officers; 50/50, Roman Catholic/non-Roman Catholic recruitment; removal of the oath of allegiance to the Queen; neutral symbols; declaration of affiliations, such as those to the Orange Order; and enhanced accountability through the creation of an overseeing Policing Board and District Policing Boards. Previous abuses by the police would be prevented by these new arrangements and the recommendation that all police officers 'should be trained (and updated) in the fundamental principles and standards of human rights and the practical implications for policing' (Patten Report 1999: 20). These plans were reinforced by a government commitment, supported by the police, to de-fortify police stations, to replace armoured land-rovers with normal police vehicles, and remove army support for policing.

Resistance to implementation of the Patten Report was also evident, but a second wave of legislation under the Police Act 2003 ensured that most of the proposals emanating from the report found their way in to the statute-book. The key area of resistance was in the establishment of District Policing Boards, which were diluted to District Policing Partnerships, the size of which would be determined by the Chief Constable and which would have less control over local policing than originally envisaged. Unionists had feared Sinn Fein domination and a paramilitary presence on such boards in nationalist areas, but the latter fear was overcome by a ban on former paramilitary prisoners taking seats on the boards. The new oath of allegiance had to be sworn only by new officers, a curious dilution given that the claims of bias had been made against serving officers. There were also some areas of the report that were modest in proposals for change. Despite the emphasis upon community policing, Patten made no attempt to disarm the new police service, although the British government declared this a 'desired objective' (HM Government 2003: annex 1, para. 6). One-third of Catholics believed the disarmament of the police to be essential; 65 per cent viewed it as essential or desirable, compared to only 22 per cent of Protestants (Irwin 2002: 175). Policing remained very much an internal Northern Ireland matter, proposed links with the Garda Siochana merely routine. The Good Friday Agreement was less radical than the Sunningdale Agreement, in failing to offer an all-Ireland authority on policing.

Conclusion

The changes to policing and security represented the new dispensation, in which the IRA no longer posed a threat to Northern Ireland. Demilitarization came after the British security forces had won the long war, despite suffering thousands of casualties. The crude initial responses of the security forces to legitimate civil rights protests had partly created that war, but it was also the subsequent physical force response, albeit only when aided by intelligence, that had defeated the most sustained IRA campaign since partition. The IRA's defeat was not total in military terms, as the organization's ability to reduce parts of London and Manchester to rubble as late as 1996 had demonstrated. None the less the IRA's inability to inflict a decisive defeat upon the security forces led to its eventual channelling down political routes and a shelving of historic objectives. As the long war ended, the eventual devolution of control of policing to a Northern Ireland Assembly at Stormont was placed on the political agenda. A new Policing and Justice Department was likely to emerge to deal with security issues. In a new co-operative framework, Sinn Fein leaders would attempt to manage the security forces which their colleagues in the IRA had targeted during previous decades.

4   The Covert War against the IRA

How should collusion be defined? Synonyms that are frequently given for the verb to collude include: to conspire; to connive; to collaborate; to plot and to scheme. The verb connive is defined as to deliberately ignore; to overlook; to disregard; to pass over; to take no notice of; to turn a blind eye; to wink; to excuse; to condone; to look the other way; to let something ride.

(Cory Collusion Inquiry Report 2004c:71, paras 4. 199–200)

Non-consensual Policing: The Background

Dealing with the conflict in Northern Ireland made particular demands upon the security forces. The RUC, the British Army and the UDR all suffered grievously during the conflict. Given this, the propensity of these organizations to dispense with the normal rules of policing and justice might be seen as understandable, if not condonable. An abnormal situation demanded abnormal policing methods, and it was natural that the security forces recruited agents within paramilitary organizations, prepared to pass on information concerning activity within their group. As the Commanding Officer of the 3rd Battalion Royal Green Jackets, Robin Eveleigh (1978: 151) declared: 'the key to smashing a terrorist organisation is the development of inside informers and the infiltration of their ranks'. Given that the penalty if discovered was almost certainly death at the hands of their paramilitary group, such agents ran considerable risks. They tended to be motivated by a combination of money, the risk of long jail sentences if they did not agree to act as informant, and disillusionment with the paramilitary group they had joined. All the paramilitary groups were riddled with agents, and their penetration helped to bring about an end to the conflict. Whatever the controversies engendered, the use of agents and informers might thus be seen as a case of ends justifying means.

The running of agents needs to be seen in the context of a war-like situation in Northern Ireland, even if parts of the province, particularly middle-class areas, remained fairly serene. The British Army was targeted by the IRA because it represented a colonial force of occupation. The RUC and the UDR were seen by nationalists as the 'armed wing of unionism'. Having replaced the B Specials, seen by Catholics as little more than a Protestant sectarian militia, the UDR soon became the target of an IRA offensive. Its title indicated a political role, and the force became associated with partisan policing by its critics. Some evidence of links with loyalist paramilitaries emerged among members of the force, with weapons passed to loyalist groups. The UDR initially enjoyed a reasonable relationship with the legal UDA, and joint membership was permitted, although the UDR saw itself as a respectable vehicle of the state, rather than one linked to paramilitarism. It did not accept applicants convicted of arms offences.

Catholics were reluctant to join the RUC, an aversion which pre-dated the IRA's terror campaign, although undoubtedly that was a major contributory factor. At the time of its transition to the Police Service of Northern Ireland in 2000, the RUC was more than 88 per cent Protestant, appearing to critics as a Protestant force for a Protestant people. The hostility to the RUC felt by Catholics and the security-oriented nature of policing meant that, effectively, one community policed the other (McGarry and O'Leary 1999). The RUC lacked accountability, its supposedly independent overseer, the Police Authority, never daring to utter anything beyond the mildest criticism, and its internal 'investigations' producing a remarkable record of exoneration of officers, exemplified by non-upholding all 1,019 complaints of assault against the force from 1988 to 1991 (Tonge 2005: 220). The RUC's task was indeed difficult in a polity so divided that nationalists of different hues never offered full support, thus restricting Catholic recruitment; but the problem was exacerbated by the force's (unsurprising) willingness to defend the state vigorously against even hints of challenge (Ellison and Smyth 1999; Ni Aolain 2000).

In straining to defeat the IRA, elements within the British Army, the RUC and the UDR engaged in illegal activity, which blurred supposed distinctions between legitimate state forces and paramilitary armies. Most notorious of these dubious activities was the collusion between loyalist paramilitaries and the security forces. Although ostensibly on the same side, the British government's official approach was to treat paramilitaries in identical, criminal fashion, irrespective of their source and cause. Three reports concerning collusion by the senior police officer, Sir John Stevens, unearthed evidence of covert use of loyalist paramilitaries by the security forces in the targeting of suspected republicans. The Stevens Reports were complemented by six investigations by Judge Peter Cory, established following negotiations between the political parties and the British and Irish governments in 2001, which also covered other possible incidents of collusion, including between members of the Garda Siochana and the Provisional IRA in the killing of two RUC officers. The governments promised to establish independent inquiries in the event of any such recommendation by Cory. Further information on collusion might also have been obtained via the British Army's Force Research Unit (FRU) created within Military Intelligence in 1982, or through Special Branch 'whistle-blowers'. The FRU reported its work weekly to the Joint Intelligence Committee, which in turn reported to the Prime Minister and the Secretary of State for Northern Ireland. Special Branch reported to the RUC Chief Constable who also briefed the Joint Intelligence Committee and Secretary of State. The Ministry of Defence has been anxious to prevent such disclosures regarding the FRU, and has issued a series of preventative injunctions, and a critical former member of the RUC, Johnston Brown, has been the subject of intimidation and threats from erstwhile colleagues.

Given the rejection of the security forces by republicans, subsequent complaints of inadequate police protection, which form much of the substance of the collusion debate, might be seen as hypocritical. Furthermore, it would be naive to assume the possibility of normal policing amid the backdrop of the most savage ethno-colonial conflict in Western Europe since the Second World War. Against this, it is apparent that the 'rule of law' during the conflict was, on a charitable assessment, pushed to its outer limits. The extent of collusion and its necessity remain areas of dispute, but its existence is beyond doubt. The clearest cases occurred in respect of the handling of agents within the UVF and the UDA by the FRU and the RUC Special Branch. These were the key intelligence-gathering agencies and the most controversial elements within a 'dirty war', although they were supported by other units, such as the Army's 14th Intelligence Company, the RUC's Special Support Unit, and MI5 and MI6. Most agents run by the FRU (which had approximately 100 agents) and Special Branch operated within the IRA, and details are still emerging of their pivotal role; but it was the work of agents run within loyalist paramilitary groups that attracted greater controversy (See, for example, *Sunday Telegraph*, 22 March 1998: 8 'Army Set up Ulster Murders'). The secretive nature of work with agents meant that in such cases, one wing of the security forces could be unaware of the handling of an agent by another. Moreover, ordinary soldiers or police officers were subservient to the needs of the intelligence agencies.

Rivalries between the intelligence services, army and police were endemic, and agents were jealously guarded, to the point where in many instances the priority seemed to be the protection of informers (Dillon 1994). Given that a leading member of the IRA, 'Stakeknife', who at one time commanded the IRA's own intelligence and disciplinary units, was an agent, the emphasis upon the need to protect key sources was perhaps understandable. In 1992 MI5, no longer preoccupied with the Cold War, assumed overall control of intelligence. Dillon (1994) suggests that the clandestine role of MI5 extended to encouraging loyalist paramilitaries to reveal the extent of collusion by highlighting how they had been passed files by military intelligence and the UDR. The FRU agent Brian Nelson claimed that 90 per cent of his intelligence material on republicans, from which 'personality cards of potential victims were constructed, was passed by the UDR' (Cory Collusion Inquiry Report 2004a: 27). Such revelations would embarrass the security forces and harm their future intelligence capability. Indeed, the exposures proved a deadly blow for the UDR, which was merged with the Royal Irish Regiment. It was not merely nationalists who loathed the UDR; MI5 claimed that the regiment 'had been so deeply penetrated by both military intelligence and loyalist paramilitaries that the level of collusion would be obstructive in the event of moves towards a political settlement' (Dillon 1994: 246). MI5 also encouraged the establishment of an enquiry into the RUC, although its claim that this would 'exonerate the RUC' always looked optimistic (Dillon 1994: 249). Through a divide-and-rule policy, therefore, MI5 asserted itself as the controller of intelligence.

Later appointed as Commissioner of the Metropolitan Police, John Stevens produced a series of damning reports on collusion, whilst acknowledging the scale of the challenge confronting the security forces. During the main period covered by his investigation, 1987–89, 261 people died, and over 3,000 acts of political violence occurred (Stevens Report 2003: 4, para. 1.7). In total, the three inquiries produced more than 9,000 statements and more than 10,000 documents, leading to 144 arrests between 1989 and 2003 and 94 convictions. The first Stevens Inquiry, concluded in April 1990, led to several arrests and a number of recommendations, not all of them implemented (Stevens Report 1990). A second report, concentrating upon the handling of Brian Nelson by the security services, was issued four years later (Stevens Report 1994), followed by a more comprehensive third report (although investigations continued) in April 2003.

Although Stevens concentrated his investigation upon the late 1980s, links between the security forces and loyalist paramilitaries preceded this period. Indeed, it has been claimed that 'as late as 1975 policemen in the Shankill area were drinking in pubs which were the haunts of UDA and UVF units' (Dillon 1988: 253). Initially resented by loyalists, who preferred 'their' B Specials, the British Army established a reasonable relationship with the UDA before relations soured by the mid-1970s. UVF files on the IRA in 1973 were detailed documents drawn up by the British Army for its patrols, whilst the UDA was the recipient of files from Army HQ in Lisburn (Dillon 1988: 276). The British Army also displayed initial reluctance to attribute bombings of Catholic pubs, notably those at McGurk's Bar and Kelly's Bar, in 1971 and 1972 respectively, to loyalist paramilitaries. Whilst the relationship was never symbiotic, loyalists and the official security forces had a mutual interest in eliminating the IRA. In the frenzied climate of the time, with more than 1,000 deaths from 1972 to 1974, this common interest meant a willingness to share information on suspected republicans. The passing of information was distinct, however, from the running of agents within organizations, which followed in the 1980s.

Collusion Exposed: The Finucane Case

The third Stevens Inquiry indicated that there was collusion between loyalist paramilitaries and the 'official' security forces in the murders of Brian Lambert in 1987 and Patrick Finucane in 1989 (Stevens Report 2003). Lambert was a Protestant mistaken for a Catholic; Finucane was a Catholic solicitor, disliked by many within the security forces for the robustness of his legal defence of IRA suspects and regarded, erroneously, by the UDA as a leading member of the PIRA. At the inquest into Finucane's murder, the RUC confirmed that they did not regard him as a member of the IRA. Several years earlier, the investigations undertaken by John Stalker into the RUC revealed how officers sometimes linked solicitors defending IRA members in the course of their duties with the republican cause (Stalker 1988). Finucane was killed by a member of the UDA who was also working as a RUC Special Branch informant, and the planning of his assassination involved the FRU agent, Brian Nelson, named as an agent and murder suspect in each of the Stevens Reports. Nelson, promoted to the head of the UDA's intelligence-gathering unit during his double life, was eventually charged with thirty-five serious terrorist offences and received a sentence of ten years. In court, he was backed by a testimonial from a colonel in military intelligence, who paid tribute to his work as an agent, claiming that he had saved many lives.

The Finucane killing was part of 'Operation Snowball', an onslaught against suspected members of republican paramilitary groups. Stevens concluded that 'the murders of Patrick Finucane and Brian Lambert could have been prevented', declaring: 'Collusion is evidenced in many ways. This ranges from the wilful failure to keep records, the absence of accountability, through to the extreme of agents being involved in murder' (Stevens Report 2003: 16, paras. 4. 6–4. 7: 16). These were far from the only suspected cases at the time, but they were perhaps the most high-profile allegations. Others included the murders of Loughlin Maginn, which led to the first Stevens Inquiry after the UFF claimed that it had seen RUC intelligence documents stating that Maginn was a member of the IRA; Terence McDaid, mistaken for his brother, and Gerard McSlane. All these killings were undertaken by the UFF, apparently acting on information from the FRU (see British-Irish Rights Watch 1999; <www. cain.ulst. ac.uk/issues/violence/birw0299.htm>).

Prior to the Finucane killing, senior RUC officers compromised a Home Office minister, Douglas Hogg, in providing briefings that led to his claim in standing committee in the House of Commons that 'there are in Northern Ireland a number of solicitors who are unduly sympathetic to the cause of the IRA' (*Hansard*, 17 January 1989, col. 508; Stevens Report 2003: 11, para. 2. 17). Hogg had been briefed on the matter by the RUC Chief Constable and other senior officers, including members of RUC Special Branch, in November 1988. In January 1989, Hogg was sent, as 'proof', documents outlining the activities of Pat Finucane (Cory Collusion Inquiry Report 2004a: 92). His words were immediately criticized by the SDLP MP, Seamus Mallon, who presciently remarked that 'following the Minister's statement, people's lives are in great danger' (*Hansard*, 17 January 1989, col. 511).

The FRU and the RUC Special Branch obstructed all three of Stevens's investigations. Intelligence on republican suspects passed to Brian Nelson by the FRU was taken back by that unit in September 1989 and concealed from Stevens. The British Army's General Officer Commanding, Northern Ireland, met with the Chief Constable of the RUC before Stevens's investigators arrived in 1989 and agreed, in what the Cory Report labelled 'the wilful concealment of pertinent evidence and the failure to cooperate with the Stevens Inquiry', that 'the Stevens Inquiry would have no access to intelligence documents or information, nor the units supplying them' (Cory Collusion Inquiry Report 2004a: 96, para 1. 269). Under considerable pressure, the Army and the RUC later relented, and documents were released to the Stevens team. There were other cases of the Stevens Inquiry being undermined. Brian Nelson was tipped off regarding his impending arrest in 1989, and, on the eve of the revived plan for his arrest, the room used by the Stevens Inquiry team was incinerated. The government Security Minister, Adam Ingram, later claimed that 'all evidence that had been gathered was stored in duplicate on computer in Great Britain' and that 'the cause of the fire could not be categorically established' (*Hansard*, 2 April 1998, col. 75). Stevens (2003: 13, para 3. 4) was more forthright, blaming a 'deliberate act of arson'. Although he did not elaborate further, the FRU headed a fairly short list of suspects.

Brian Nelson was not the only agent involved in the killing of Pat Finucane, as the British Army and the RUC ran their own agents involved with the assassination and did not necessarily share information. William Stobie, a former member of the British Army and the UDA's West Belfast 'quartermaster', was recruited as an agent by RUC Special Branch in 1988. Stobie, an accomplice to the murder of Brian Lambert, passed information on the planning of what appeared to be Finucane's murder. He was asked to collect a firearm, almost certainly used in the murder, from a UDA member a few days after the assassination of Finucane. None of these details were passed by RUC Special Branch to the murder inquiry team, and the RUC failed to monitor the weapons electronically.

The RUC was also implicated as an accessory to the murder in the claim, as yet unproved, of a member of the UDA, that he received advice on the location of road blocks in the area of Finucane's home on the day of the killing (BBC *Panorama*, *Licence to Kill*: Part I, 11 July 2002). Members of the UDA, including its leader, claimed that they were encouraged by RUC officers to shoot Finucane (Lawyers Committee for Human Rights 2002).

The investigation of the Finucane murder was a protracted affair. A retired police officer, Johnston Brown, was later to claim that he was threatened by RUC Special Branch officers when he tried to pursue the case, after revealing that a loyalist confessed the Finucane murder to him in October 1991 (Lawyers Committee for Human Rights 2002: 58–9). In 2001 William Stobie was tried on the charges of aiding and abetting the murder of Pat Finucane, nearly ten years after the Director of Public Prosecutions had initially decided not to prosecute. However, the judge returned a verdict of not guilty after the key prosecution witness was ruled to be no longer credible. His work as an agent exposed, Stobie was executed two weeks after the collapse of the trial by the Red Hand Defenders, a pseudonym used by the UFF for killings after its cease-fire. In the words of the Cory Report on the Finucane case, Stobie 'controlled, stored, maintained and supplied weapons for attacks on targets and collected them after they were used'; yet the RUC Special Branch did not inform two murder inquiry teams of this role (Cory Collusion Inquiry Report 2004a: 69). The key allegations of misconduct in respect of military intelligence and RUC Special Branch can be summarized thus: that they sanctioned and financed agents involved in illegal activity, that they failed to pass information to front line police and army units which might have prevented murders, and that they failed to co-operate with, or deliberately hampered, subsequent investigations into their actions. The image provided by Stevens was of sections of the security and intelligence services operating private fiefdoms, beyond the rule of law and devoid of accountability. A conviction for the Finucane murder was finally secured in 2004, the loyalist paramilitary Ken Barrett sentenced to life imprisonment (but one which would possibly be covered by the early release terms of the Good Friday Agreement) after confessing to the killing following an elaborate police operation.

The Impact of the Use of Agents

The Stevens Inquiries and the Cory Reports highlighted the lack of co-operation between the FRU and the RUC Special Branch. Both valued the work of agents and held the same approach that their protection was paramount, even if this involved lawbreaking by their sources. Of the FRU, in particular, it was declared that it 'considered 'the normal rules – including the rule of law – to be suspended and the gathering of intelligence to be an end that was capable of justifying questionable means' (Cory Collusion Inquiry Report 2004a: 93). Agents were passed information on republicans, sometimes upon request but often on an unsolicited basis. The ends were indeed important, and lives may have been saved, but the claims made in this respect could be risible. The FRU claimed in testimony that Nelson had helped to save 217 lives, a hugely exaggerated claim, dismissed in the Cory Collusion Inquiry Report on the Finucane case as 'based on a highly dubious numerical analysis that cannot be supported on any basis' (2004a: 103). The claim was based upon the number of individuals mentioned by Nelson, however tenuously, as possible UDA targets, irrespective of whether an attack had ever been set up and regardless of whether Nelson had intervened. The combined Cory investigations discovered only one clear instance where Nelson's work and the co-operation of the FRU and the RUC Special Branch saved a life. The FRU conceded in its own documents in respect of Nelson that 'it is often unclear when the targeting has been completed and an attack is to take place', making life-saving intervention difficult (Cory Collusion Inquiry Report 2004a: 43).

Reflecting a broader strategy of the British government of police primacy, the RUC was supposed to occupy a superior position in the intelligence network, collecting intelligence from the FRU, recording it in 'Intelligence' or 'Threats' books, depending upon its seriousness, and determining what action should be taken. The activities of the FRU and the RUC Special Branch were overseen by the Security Service, which rarely interfered in operational matters. Yet separatism rather than integration was the norm in respect of the FRU and the Special Branch. The Special Branch regarded the intelligence from the FRU's agents as inferior to its own, even describing Army sources as 'rubbish and of a poor standard' (Cory Collusion Inquiry Report 2004a: 56). The contrast with the FRU's assessment could hardly be starker. The FRU regarded Nelson very highly, even though he had proved unreliable, passing information to the UVF as well as the UDA, and acting as an accessory to murder in his first spell as an agent in 1985–6. Following this stint, the Security Service disapproved of his re-engagement as an agent, but the FRU rated his performance much more highly, encouraging him to arm the UDA via South Africa. The FRU appeared to prioritize Nelson's protection and promotion within the UDA above all else, even as Nelson continued to commit crimes. According to a soldier in the FRU, an agent 'is bound to get himself involved in some degree of criminality' in order to preserve credibility within a paramilitary organization (Cory Collusion Inquiry Report 2004a: 52). As such, Home Office guidelines to the contrary were unrealistic. The FRU believed that, thanks to Nelson, the UFF had moved from random sectarian assassinations to a more sophisticated form of targeting, although the notion of a 'better class of murder' was unlikely to prove a strong defence against charges of collusion.

The FRU updated Nelson's intelligence through provision of vehicle registration details of republicans and facilitating photographic surveillance. Even with his work exposed, the FRU remained loyal, defending the value of Nelson's work during his trial. Given that, in 1992, Nelson pleaded guilty to twenty terrorist-related offences, including five charges of conspiracy to murder, a much lengthier sentence than ten years might have been expected had the FRU's testimonial not been lodged with the court. In contrast, the RUC appeared less keen to protect Stobie, although the force did warn of the threat to his life, and it was the Northern Ireland Office which declined to provide protection. They were keen to prevent revelations of the Finucane case emerging, and the disclosure of Stobie's previous convictions at his trial in 1990 on weapons offences, collapsing the trial, attracted suspicion as a non-accidental 'blunder' (Lawyers Committee for Human Rights 2002: 33). Despite the rivalry between the FRU and the RUC Special Branch, information was transmitted as a matter of course between the two organizations, but it was not always acted upon by the 'rival' force. As was noted by the inquiry into the Finucane case, Nelson was 'a prolific agent whose information was often proven to be correct by subsequent events. It was therefore difficult to understand why Special Branch paid virtually no attention to his intelligence reports' (Cory Collusion Inquiry Report 2004a: 88–9). A former member of the FRU claimed that extensive information concerning the targeting of Finucane was passed to the RUC (Lawyers Committee for Human Rights 2002: 40). In defence of the RUC, it has been claimed that the intelligence passed to them by the FRU was often watered down, either to protect the identity of FRU agents or to prevent the RUC from intercepting an operation (Ware 1998: 16).

Structural and attitudinal explanations can be offered for the seeming inertia of the RUC Special Branch. The force appeared to construct a hierarchy of offences, demonstrating much less interest in recording threats made by the UDA against suspected republicans and concentrating instead upon information received regarding republican threats to their opponents. Republican threats were officially logged in the Special Branch's Threats book at a rate of 8.5 to 1 relative to loyalist threats, an imbalance only partially mitigated by the greater level of republican paramilitary activity (Cory Collusion Inquiry Report 2004a: 89). On those occasions when threats to republicans were recorded, the RUC often failed to take preventative measures, such as warning targets to increase their personal security or ensuring an enhanced police presence in vulnerable areas. This one-sided approach was most startling in the Finucane case. Via the Security Service, the RUC Special Branch received information in 1981, 1985 and 1989 that solicitors perceived to have republican leanings were possible targets. The 1989 intelligence, emerging from a meeting of UDA commanders in 1988, provided the most specific evidence. Moreover, the RUC was given the opportunity, through advance warning from William Stobie of his delivery of weaponry to UDA members, to track the guns used in the Finucane murder through bugging devices.

Having IRA family members, involvement in civil rights campaigns, and association with the families of hunger strikers, links detailed in RUC and FRU files, all made Finucane a potential victim, guilty by association, and he was indeed named as a potential target. Finucane had also played an instrumental role in launching compensation claims against the RUC for false imprisonment. The lack of willingness of the RUC Special Branch to act to protect Finucane, interpreted by Cory as a form of collusion, was partly to protect sources. It also reflected a disinterest in republican victims, relative to those threatened by republicans. With Finucane having often antagonized members of the RUC through his work, he was the subject of fairly open hostility from members of the force. The FRU did record threats to republicans and their associates, although at times it appeared to endorse or tacitly approve such targeting. Brian Nelson claimed to have warned his handlers over the possible shooting of Pat Finucane only days before the murder took place.

Goodbye to All That? Implementing Change and Ending Collusion

Appointed Commissioner of the Metropolitan Police during the course of his investigations, Sir John Stevens conducted thorough investigations into collusion and kept his position, unlike one of his predecessor investigators of the RUC, John Stalker, in the mid-1980s. Collusion dwindled as Stevens's rigour took root. As one UVF member asserted, 'the files just stopped coming through then' (Cusack and McDonald 2000: 263). Stevens was anxious that no individual or organization be spared, even preparing a case for prosecution of the former head of the FRU, Brigadier Gordon Kerr. Three problems emerged, however, First, it was claimed that the removal of sections of the UDA involved in handling leaks led to the replacement of the 'old guard' by even more militant loyalist paramilitaries (McDonald and Cusack 2004). Secondly, the problem of collusion had been so embedded as to make it difficult to hold to account all those responsible. The third Stevens Inquiry found that eighty-one people had handled confidential documents to which they had no right of access, indicative of how a casual culture of rule breaking had permeated a section of the security forces (Stevens Report 2003: 10). Thirdly, the recommendations of worthy reports required proper implementation, an aspect which might not be forthcoming. Stevens claimed that 'from day one my Enquiry team has been obstructed in its work'. It was evident that putting in place his recommendations might also be problematic (speech at Europa Hotel, Belfast, 17 April 2003). The FRU was the main culprit in obstructing Stevens, holding on to materials in respect of the handling of Brian Nelson, tampering with the evidence, and, most dramatically, attempting to wreck the investigation through arson.

In response to a parliamentary question from Kevin McNamara, MP, the Security Minister, Adam Ingram, declared in 1998 that, in respect of the first Stevens Inquiry, all recommendations *accepted by the RUC* had been implemented by May 1995 (*Hansard*, C37736, 28 April 1998; italics added). The organization that had been the subject of sharp criticism was thus given the opportunity to determine which aspects of change it fancied implementing. Given that the RUC had dismissed an Amnesty International claim of 'mounting evidence' of collusion as 'utter nonsense' in 1994, the RUC's motivation for change might not have been operating at maximum capacity (<www.cain.ac.uk/issue/violence>).

The RUC did act swiftly after the second Stevens' Inquiry, arresting thirty members of the UDR as requested, of whom nine were charged (reply to Kevin McNamara by Adam Ingram, *Hansard*, C37739, 28 April 1998, col. 75). Six of those arrested later won undisclosed damages from the RUC. The recommendations of the third Stevens Report came at a time when the intelligence agencies had reformed in terms of co-operation. Military Intelligence and Special Branch were required to consult prior to the recruitment of agents, ending the dangerous unilateralism of earlier decades, and the use of *agents provocateurs* was forbidden.

Astonishingly, the Patten Report into policing in 1999, which effectively replaced the RUC with the Police Service of Northern Ireland (PSNI), said virtually nothing about collusion between the RUC and loyalist paramilitaries, even though this was, for many nationalists, the most damning evidence of all concerning the partisan and illegitimate nature of policing in Northern Ireland. The Patten Report (1999: 26) declared that the 'RUC has had several officers within its ranks over the years who have abused their position', but made no reference to systematic collusion. Whilst acknowledging the 'crucial role' of the Special Branch in countering terrorism, there was criticism of the manner in which the RUC Special Branch acted as a 'force within a force', although the report did not indicate why and how this was a problem (1999: 72–3). RUC Special Branch controlled all intelligence operations within the RUC and ordinary officers were unaware of its operations. Patten (1999: 73) recommended 'linking Special Branch and Crime Branch' under the command of a single Assistant Chief Constable. This would end what was seen as the unhealthy insulation and isolation of the Special Branch, although linkage was not the same as abolition, and it appeared that the Special Branch would remain. Noting that legislation was already in preparation to ensure that covert policing complied with the European Convention on Human Rights, Patten (1999: 38) recommended that a commissioner for covert law enforcement be established in Northern Ireland. Human rights-based approaches to policing were encouraged, to be closely monitored.

Patten's recommendation in respect of the Special Branch's merger with the Crime Branch under a single authority was 'accepted in principle' by the government and Chief Constable, with a promise to 'review the scope' for such change in 2001 (Northern Ireland Office 2000: 54). The non-committal language raised nationalist fears that this key structural reform would not take place, concerns heightened by the dilution of other proposals of Patten (see Tonge 2005: 232–3). Most of the Patten proposals were duly implemented by 2003, after initial prevarication under the Secretary of State Peter Mandelson (O'Leary 2001).

Collusion and Partisanship in the late 1990s

The failure of Patten to discuss the impact of allegations of collusion upon nationalist perceptions of the RUC was an oversight, even allowing for the fact that such matters were under investigation by Stevens and through the Cory Reports. Following multi-party negotiations between the political parties and the British and Irish governments, six cases of collusion (not all involving British security forces) were selected to be reviewed to determine whether a public inquiry should be held into each of them. The cases of Robert Hamill, Rosemary Nelson and, from an earlier period, Patrick Finucane, were chosen in respect of allegations of collusion involving the RUC and the British Army. All six cases were investigated by the Canadian judge Peter Cory, with the Cory Reports published in 2004. Cory's recommendation that a full public inquiry be held into the most controversial cases, such as the Finucane murder, was downgraded by the Secretary of State to that of an independent inquiry, leading to the withdrawal of co-operation by the Finucane family.

The case of Robert Hamill in April 1997 was an example of partisan policing and connivance, rather than direct collusion with external agents. Hamill, a Catholic, was attacked by loyalists and kicked to death when returning from a Catholic social club in Portadown, at the time an area of particularly high sectarian tension. The attack was witnessed by a number of RUC personnel. Despite this, the officers did not intervene to prevent the incident, nor did they arrest the offenders, even though they had the opportunity. The eventual arrest of suspects led to six men being charged with murder, but these charges were eventually dropped. Cory indicated that there was 'sufficient evidence of police collusion to warrant the holding of a public inquiry' (Cory Collusion Inquiry Report: 2004b:

76). In particular, Cory suggested that the actions of a Reserve Constable, alleged to have helped dispose of the clothing of one of the perpetrators of the murder, whom he had known for a number of years, would, if proved, 'constitute a flagrant and deliberate act of collusion' (Cory Collusion Inquiry Report 2004b: 71). Cory also demanded further investigation of the apparent failure of the RUC to anticipate disturbances, despite their frequency in the locality (police records indicated seventeen incidents at the junction where the murder occurred in the previous six months), and the inadequate, deliberate or otherwise, positioning of officers. There was also an apparent failure to seal the scene of the attack for forensic purposes and the possible premature release of suspects.

In 1999 allegations of collusion resurfaced when the Catholic solicitor Rosemary Nelson was killed by a car bomb. Like Finucane, Nelson was seen as a solicitor with republican leanings. She had attracted the opprobrium of the RUC through stout defences of IRA suspects and through high-profile criticism of policing during the Drumcree dispute over the route of an Orange parade. Shortly after her murder, the United Nations Special Rapporteur, Param Cumaraswamy, criticized the RUC for harassing defence solicitors (<www.cain.ulst.ac.uk/collusion>). The Cory Report (2004c: 70) into the Nelson case agreed that there was a need for a public inquiry, suggesting that the

> failure to take any action to protect Rosemary Nelson could be found to be troubling when it is considered against the background of the earlier murder of Patrick Finucane. By disregarding a significant body of evidence of threats against Rosemary Nelson, it could be found that the NIO [Northern Ireland Office] engaged in conduct that was collusive in nature.

The NIO failed to pass on some of the threats against Nelson to the RUC, whilst several RUC officers were alleged to have made demeaning comments to Nelson. Cory rejected evidence offered by some witnesses close to the case; for example, he found the level of security force activity in the murder area to be normal and not indicative of collusive activity. His main concerns rested, first, upon the inadequate protection offered to Nelson, despite warnings of the risk she was under from 'reputable organizations' and documented threats (Cory Collusion Report 2004c: 74). Secondly, Cory believed that the 'alleged threats and demeaning remarks made by the RUC officers while interrogating clients of Rosemary Nelson about her', which might be seen as 'encouraging threats by others', warranted proper investigation (p. 73).

For republicans in particular, the conclusions of Stevens, whilst acknowledged as far from a whitewash, laid too much emphasis upon out-of-control handlers, rather than on collusion being a systemic failing within the security apparatus. The first Stevens Inquiry concluded that collusion was 'restricted to a small number of members of the security forces', and was 'neither widespread nor institutionalised' (Stevens Report 1990: 1, para. 41). As a percentage of the thousands of security force members, the extent of collusion was indeed low, but there was evidence of it being a considerable problem within two wings of those forces: the FRU and the RUC Special Branch. Moreover, the initial Stevens Inquiry failed to root out the culprits, with prosecutions confined to the receivers of information within the loyalist paramilitary groups. There appeared to be a reluctance to prosecute in the most sensitive cases; for example, Brian Nelson was not charged in respect of the Finucane case, being prosecuted on other matters.

The third Stevens Report contained twenty-one recommendations. Stevens pointed out that the recommendation to establish a dedicated unit to investigate terrorist offences had been made in his first report (Stevens Report 2003: 17). Other proposals included adoption of the National Intelligence Model used by police forces elsewhere; Patten-type proposals for the harnessing of anti-terrorist activity under the responsibility of an Assistant Chief Constable; a full review of training for all agent handlers, to cover issues of integrity and record keeping; and the establishment of an internal investigation department by the PSNI. Given previous experience, Stevens (2003: 19) was anxious that these recommendations not be diluted, recommending 'an independent audit and review . . . within an agreed time frame'.

Moving On: New Policing, New Methods

The more peaceful modern climate in Northern Ireland has allowed changes in structures and forms of policing. The Stevens and Cory reports exposed substantial wrongdoing by elements within the security forces, sections of which at times appeared to be far too closely aligned with loyalist paramilitaries, even whilst other branches were prepared to imprison members of the UVF and the UDA. The early release of paramilitary prisoners under the terms of the Good Friday Agreement was tacit recognition of paramilitaries as prisoners of war, rather than common criminals. This 'official' recognition of the war provided justification for those who had engaged in 'special methods' of fighting the war.

The Patten Report promised radical overhaul of policing in several aspects. Although the title-deeds of RUC were kept, in effect a new police service was born, the PSNI. Most notable in respect of the new proposals were those to achieve 50/50 recruitment from the Protestant and Catholic communities to lessen the religious imbalance; enhanced accountability through a strengthened Policing Board and District Policing Partnerships; an oath of human rights to be sworn by all officers and the non-association with the British state, with a new, specially designed emblem reflecting the neutrality of the force. The Policing Board ought to be capable of holding the police to account rather more than the old Police Authority, of which McGarry and O'Leary (1999: 100) were succinctly dismissive in declaring: 'Rather than representing the community to the police, it has appeared more interested in representing the police to the community.' Meanwhile, a more peaceful Northern Ireland would lead to a substantially reduced police force.

All of these changes will make policing more consensual in Northern Ireland, although the absence of war will be the single most important factor. The initial changes were insufficient for Sinn Fein, which, in contrast to the SDLP, declined to join the Policing Board overseeing the PSNI. However, a shift in Sinn Fein policy on the issue was set to accompany the restoration of devolved government. There remain questions over the role of the security and intelligence services, most notably in respect of the PSNI raid upon Sinn Fein's office at Stormont in 2002, which precipitated the collapse of a tottering Northern Ireland Assembly. Despite various claims at the time of the existence of an IRA spy ring, successful prosecutions are still awaited, and the raid's purpose has yet to be fully justified. The RUC Chief Constable, Sir Hugh Orde, subsequently apologized for the manner of the raid, but has not elaborated subsequently upon its value. Added to an unattributed break-in at Castlereagh police station, blamed upon the IRA but for which evidence is awaited, there remains controversy over the neutrality and techniques associated with the policing of Northern Ireland. The silence of the Policing Board on these issues has not encouraged the belief that full accountability has been reached. Collusion between the legal forces of the state and its ultras, loyalist paramilitary groups, may have ended, but the overall problem of political policing has not entirely vanished. The teething problems of a transition to normal policing will none the less diminish sharply when Sinn Fein signs up to the new arrangements, a remarkable shift in policy which may be accompanied by the devolution of policing and justice responsibilities to a devolved administration. Such developments will enhance scrutiny of an area enveloped in mystery and controversy for several decades.

The Politics of Sinn Fein

The most remarkable feature of Northern Ireland politics in recent decades has been the emergence of Sinn Fein as a strong political force. Since contesting elections in 1982, Sinn Fein has grown to be a formidable party, its role as IRA cheerleader replaced by a dominant position within the republican movement. This process has involved abandoning an 'ourselves' approach, based upon purist principles and political isolation, in favour of a more pragmatic approach which has shifted republican tactics and, more contentiously, principles.

The representative of most nationalists in Northern Ireland, Sinn Fein has also become a significant party in the Irish Republic, capable of helping form a coalition government. Yet, although the party had briefly represented the will of the majority of the Irish people from 1918 to 1920, most of the subsequent period, a brief revival in the 1950s notwithstanding, had been marked by isolation and irrelevance. Accordingly, the formation of Provisional Sinn Fein in January 1970, pledging allegiance to the Irish Republic proclaimed in the rebellion of 1916, was not seen as a landmark at the time. The focus of attention had been the street disturbances of summer 1969, not internecine feuding within largely dormant Irish republican circles. The emergence of Provisional Sinn Fein followed the split in the IRA and, for the first decade of the Troubles, Sinn Fein's primary role was to act as a support network and political cheer-leader for the PIRA. Sinn Fein's role was unsurprising, given that the party, all but extinct by the 1940s, had come under direct IRA orders since 1948, a move that had rescued a party in desperate straits and at least given it a role as a 'political ancillary' to armed republicans (Feeney 2002: 189). As Sinn Fein was re-launched at the start of the 1970s, amid a deteriorating political situation, it remained subordinate, and was 'looked down upon as the "poor relations" of the republican movement, containing those unable or unwilling to join PIRA' (Danny Morrison, quoted in Feeney 2002: 260). Sinn Fein also had to operate underground, being banned as a political party by the British government, although this ban was lifted in 1974 in an attempt to steer republicanism in a more political direction.

Like the armed wing it supported, Sinn Fein demanded unconditional British withdrawal from Northern Ireland, although the time-scale varied for this. In recent times, Sinn Fein has become much vaguer about when and how Britain can withdraw, referring to the need to establish a united Ireland 'within our lifetimes', although exactly whose lifetimes is unclear (<www.sinnfein.ie>). As the only significant all-Ireland party, Sinn Fein has developed electoral strength in both parts of the island, but this flowering has been achieved mainly through the party's replacement of the IRA armed struggle, rather than as an adjunct to the campaign, as originally envisaged. The metamorphosis of Sinn Fein from military support group to the fastest-growing political force in Ireland, and the implications for party ideology, are explored below.

The Vision of Irish Unity

Whilst it was the IRA's role to force British withdrawal from Northern Ireland, it was Sinn Fein's task to sketch the shape of a sovereign, independent, thirty-two-county Ireland. The problem of what to do about the loyalists ought to have loomed larger in Sinn Fein's thinking than was the case. Republicans were anxious to insist that the rights of unionists and Protestants would be guaranteed, being critical of the fusion of church and state in the twenty-six counties. Yet it was self-evident that one right claimed by unionists – to be

British – could not be maintained in a non-partitioned Ireland. The answer for the Provisionals to this conundrum was to offer a federal Ireland via their Eire Nua policy, in which each of the four ancient provinces of Ireland would have its own parliament and considerable autonomy, the central authority in Dublin confining itself mainly to the 'high' politics of foreign policy. The advantage for unionists was that they would be likely to command a narrow majority in an Ulster parliament, and thus exercise a considerable amount of political, social, cultural and possibly economic freedom. The Provisionals insisted that their plan was not to coerce unionists into a united Ireland; indeed the term 'united Ireland' was rarely used until the 1980s. Instead, Sinn Fein offered unionists a role in one of the four federal Irish parliaments, with the British connection severed.

In 1982 Sinn Fein abandoned the romantic federalism of Eire Nua in favour of a unitary state, as part of a more uncompromising stance towards loyalism. This stance included a hardening of the demand for British withdrawal, which, following a 1980 *ard fheis* decision, was required immediately, rather than within the lifetime of a Westminster parliament. Prior to the formal abandonment of Eire Nua, Sinn Fein had been 'informed' by the IRA that it no longer supported the programme, a fairly clear hint as to which way Sinn Fein was to move (Moloney 2002). Like militarism and abstentionism, federalism became elevated to a principle by some within the republican movement. Yet the tangible gains offered by federalism were uncertain. The provinces of Ulster, Munster, Connacht and Leinster were of historical importance, but of scant contemporary economic or political salience to justify their award of a parliament. The northern element of the IRA, based where the war was being fought, had little time for the endless articulation of the finer points of Eire Nua, given that it was 'a document written by Southerners from a Southern perspective and the symmetry of its proposals betrayed its origins' (Bishop and Mallie 1988: 329).

The republican leadership claimed that its anti-loyalist approach and withdrawal of support for Dail Uladh, the Ulster Parliament in which loyalists would have enjoyed institutional recognition of their autonomy, did not alter their position in respect of Protestants in the north. Republicans were anxious to stress that their insistence on a unitary Irish state was not linked to Catholicism, insisting that the republican movement 'is no defender of Catholic theological interests', and that the location of the republican base was due to 'historical circumstances' and 'Britain's use of religious differences' (*An Phoblacht/Republican News*, 8 July 1982: 1, 'Tyranny of Sectarianism'). Loyalists would be guaranteed their religious rights, but as Irish citizens they would no longer be 'slaves to British imperialism' and 'corrupted by colonialism'. The constitutional form of the new Ireland demanded by republicans had changed, but the perceptions of loyalists had not altered.

The end of federalism had been preceded by a leftward shift within Sinn Fein, as the party began to place extra emphasis upon the imperialist nature of British rule and the exploitation of Irish resources. Aspects of these claims were unconvincing, given that Northern Ireland was a drain upon the British Exchequer, particularly given the need to deploy large Army numbers. The harsh fiscal approach of monetarism, evident elsewhere in the United Kingdom, was never applied to Northern Ireland after Margaret Thatcher became Conservative Prime Minister in 1979. Instead of Thatcherism, welfarism was applied to Northern Ireland, creating a dependency culture amid the near-absence of viable indigenous industry (Gafikin and Morrisey 1990). Although the presence of large numbers of security personnel was indicative of British colonialism, there appeared to be no economic logic underpinning the British government's continuing claim to sovereignty. Sinn Fein's critique of imperialism convinced few, eventually disappearing from the party's politics during the 1990s. The left turn had worried conservatives within the movement, and was played down to Sinn Fein's support base in the United States.

Political Isolation and Moral Condemnation

Sinn Fein's problem lay in converting residual sympathy for the cause of Irish unity into support for the only party which did not pay mere lip-service to its promotion. The violence of the IRA led to political ostracism for Sinn Fein and moral condemnation from the Roman Catholic Church, still a hugely influential organization in Ireland until the 1990s. Such condemnation highlighted the erroneous nature of claims from religious loyalists that there was a basic unity between the Roman Catholic Church and the IRA. The appeals for an end to IRA violence came from the top downwards, the Pope having pleaded for PIRA to end its campaign on his visit to Ireland in 1979, whilst recognizing that nationalists sought justice. The Pope's message was clear, but was rejected, albeit in courteous tones, by republicans, who were infuriated by condemnation of the IRA from leaders of the Catholic Church in Ireland. Perhaps the most vocal critic, Bishop Cahal Daly, was dismissed as 'not opposed to the British maintaining partition at the point of a gun, just republicans trying to remove it by the same means' (*An Phoblacht/Republican News*, 7 July 1983: 1, 'Bishop defends Unionism'). Cardinal Tomas O'Fiaich, leader of Ireland's Catholics throughout Ireland and perhaps more sympathetic to republican ideals than others in the Church hierarchy, condemned participation in IRA activity as a 'mortal sin', insisting that 'justice can be achieved through political means' (*An Phoblacht/Republican News*, 26 November 1981: 12, 'Hierarchy expose fear of republican progress'). Dr Edward Daly, the bishop of Derry, denounced the IRA and threatened to excommunicate Catholics within the organization in a pastoral letter in autumn 1981.

Whilst Sinn Fein was anxious not to alienate its own support base by becoming embroiled in a dispute with the Church, the repeated criticisms of the IRA were sometimes met with equal denunciation of the Catholic Church, as relations between the two organizations, often hostile, worsened after the IRA hunger strike. There were three elements to the mutual hostility: history, theology and radicalism. In terms of history, Sinn Fein pointed out that the Catholic Church had condemned the 1916 Easter Rising, opposed the war against the British Army's Black and Tans in the early 1920s and had supported the Anglo-Irish Treaty in 1922, yet, as part of its 'consistently expedient attitude', condemned partition and itself operated on an all-Ireland basis, ignoring the border (*An Phoblacht/Republican News*, 19 May 1983: 2, 'Guns and God'). The dispute had a theological component, Sinn Fein insisting that the IRA's campaign was in accordance with the Catholic concept of a just war, given the lack of alternatives, whereas the Catholic hierarchy argued that there were political avenues for republicans to pursue.

The Sinn Fein president, Gerry Adams, defended armed struggle as a 'necessary and morally correct form of resistance in the six counties against a government whose presence is rejected by the vast majority of Irish people' (*An Phoblacht/Republican News*, 17 November 1983: 9, 'Armed Struggle'). The Church also disliked the leftward drift of the IRA, whilst republicans broadened their attack beyond the normal confines of criticism of individual members of the Church hierarchy:

> The Catholic hierarchy are correctly fearful that IRA-led progress towards a united independent Ireland prefaces their own rejection, together with that of the SDLP leadership, from the backs of the nationalist people, as the people throw off their conservative ideological chains in favour of radical working class republican socialist politics. Both the Catholic hierarchy and the SDLP leadership represent Catholic middle class opinion bent upon collaboration with, and servility to, the British and the preservation of the political status quo and of capitalist stability.
>
> (*An Phoblacht/Republican News*, 26 November 1981: 12)

Irish citizens rejected partition, but could not bring themselves to support Sinn Fein. The view espoused by Cardinal O'Fiaich, that partition was 'almost the worst possible solution', and that it was 'wrong to prevent half a million Catholics from being united with the rest of the country', found favour among his flock, but equally they accepted the words of his predecessor, Cardinal Conway, reinforced by O'Fiaich, that 'you can't bomb a million Protestants into a united Ireland' (quoted in Mallie and McKittrick 1996: 69).

Aside from its difficulties with the Catholic Church hierarchy, Sinn Fein could find little support from other mainstream sources. There remained sympathy for the 'cause' among many Irish-Americans, although financial support from Irish Northern Aid (NORAID) declined during the 1980s. Part of the reason was the establishment of the Congressional 'Friends of Ireland' organization in 1981 by the 'Four Horsemen': the House of Representatives Speaker Tip O'Neill, Senators Edward Kennedy and Daniel Moynihan, and the Governor of New York, Hugh Carey. Its aims were to undercut Irish-American support for the IRA campaign via NORAID; to tone down the activities of the Irish National Caucus, which was severely critical of some aspects of British rule in Northern Ireland; and to bolster the constitutional nationalism of the SDLP (*An Phoblacht/Republican News*, 21 March 1981: 6, 'No Friends of Ireland'). The group was largely successful in its aims. The earlier radical statements of, in particular, Kennedy were replaced by more circumspect pronouncements that appeared to accept the constitutional *status quo*, whilst the IRA encountered greater difficulty in fundraising and having its members escape the authorities.

Sinn Fein was also isolated by most political groups, despite attempting to cultivate links for much of the 1980s. The party attempted to develop broad alliances during the hunger strike campaigns of 1980–1, no longer requiring unconditional support for the IRA's campaign. Outside the Troops Out Movement, the republican cause attracted little support in Britain. The Sinn Fein leadership, particularly Adams, attempted to engage in a dialogue with sections of the Labour left, encouraged by the prescient comments of the leader of the Greater London Council, Ken Livingstone, that the British government would be obliged eventually to engage in talks with militant republicans. In 1981 the Labour Party adopted a policy of support for Irish unity by consent, rejected by republicans as a perpetuation of the unionist veto, whatever the sympathy with Labour's preferred eventual constitutional outcome. In 1987, a senior Labour Party delegation met Sinn Fein, but the party leader, Neil Kinnock, refused to participate. The dialogue on social and economic aspects of policy in Northern Ireland was prefaced by Sinn Fein's insistent upon the 'right to self-determination of the Irish people as the basis of any settlement', although Sinn Fein was encouraged by the description of Northern Ireland as a 'colonial situation' by the visiting party (*An Phoblacht/Republican News*, 22 January 1987: 3, 'Sinn Fein Meets British Labour Party'). The appointment of Kevin McNamara as Labour Party spokesman on Northern Ireland also signalled a somewhat more nationalist approach from 1988 to 1994. Generally, however, the Labour left appeared more concerned with other 'anti-colonial struggles' than the one on their own doorstep, and debates at party conferences, although passionate, attracted only the committed.

In the Irish Republic, Fianna Fail's rejection of Britain's sovereign claim to Northern Ireland allowed its continued self-labelling as the 'republican party'. Given that support for Irish unity among the wider population was characterized by extensiveness rather than intensity, this type of republican rhetoric did Fianna Fail no harm. The lack of support for violence to achieve the unity vaguely desired by the Irish people meant, however, that Sinn Fein's electoral space was constrained and that republicans (of the actual, rather than aspirational variety) generally enjoyed electoral success only when emotion ran high, as in the immediate aftermath of the hunger strikes of the early 1980s. This ought not to have surprised Sinn Fein; had republicans awaited a mandate from an Irish people often acquiescent to British rule, a shot might never have been fired in anger in Ireland. Sinn Fein's electoral success of 1918 owed much to British executions of prisoners; the substantial vote for Sinn Fein, especially in the North, in the mid-1950s was a cry of frustration against a one-party unionist regime and the 1981–2 hunger strike votes for anti-H Block prison candidates were largely a protest against what was seen as unnecessary stridency by the British Prime Minister, Margaret Thatcher. At such times, Sinn Fein could harness latent support for the cause of strong Irish republicanism and a certain ambiguity towards the role of armed struggle. The willingness of nationalists to elect the IRA prisoner, Bobby Sands, in the Fermanagh and South Tyrone by-election of 1981 showed that the cause of republicanism, when it appeared to be the underdog pitted against oppressive British forces, could still rely upon sympathy among swathes of the population. At less heated times, however, the national question prompted either apathy or hostility to armed republicanism amongst the majority of the Irish Republic's electorate. To some extent Sinn Fein 'partitionized' the struggle, placing greater emphasis on social issues in the Irish Republic, but it was still a party seen as dominated by its emphasis upon the national question.

Electoral Politics

The conversion of Sinn Fein into a formidable electoral force in Northern Ireland came in 1982, on the back of the election of hunger strikers to the Westminster and Dublin parliaments. In 1981, the party decided that it would contest future council elections in Northern Ireland, and that successful candidates would take their seats. That year's *ard fheis* heard the party's Director of Publicity, Danny Morrison, asking the (rhetorical) question: 'Who here really believes that we can win the war through the ballot-box? But will anyone here object if, with a ballot-paper in this hand and an Armalite in this hand, we take power in Ireland?'

Privately, Morrison had doubts about the durability of the new strategy, later remarking that 'deep down I knew there were contradictions. I knew there was a ceiling to how far you could go' (quoted in English 2003: 225). At the time, the leadership was concerned more with the reception which the new approach would receive than with its long-term viability. Morrison's rhetoric alarmed some members of the leadership, who regarded his revelation of the new strategy as premature and over-excited, but the speech defined republican strategy for a decade. Rather than concern itself with the impact of violence upon electoral support, the leadership saw its task as reassuring the base that contesting elections did not mean a watering down of principle or fire-power. The primacy of the armed campaign was made clear during and after the *ard fheis*, the leadership asserting that 'republicans do not fool themselves that the ballot-box is a new and powerful weapon against the might of imperialism, neo-colonialism and the physical military occupation of our country' (*An Phoblacht/Republican News*, 5

November 1981: 1, 'By Ballot and Bullet'). Electoral support was useful, but it was designed to complement the armed struggle, as further commentary made apparent.

> The relationship between IRA activity and political change is clear. It is armed struggle which by its relentless application, by its bleeding white the British presence in Ireland, will force a London government, or an opposition party, to the inescapable conclusion that they cannot rule and will have to let us go . . . it is republican dogma that the armed struggle will continue and must continue until the guerrilla war achieves its end . . . However the war can undoubtedly be shortened – not ended – by victories on the political front delivered by the republican machine behind Sinn Fein.
>
> *(An Phoblacht/Republican News*, 12 May 1983: 1,
> 'The IRA and the Election')

The message was reinforced by the Sinn Fein leadership, with the president of the party insisting: 'armed struggle becomes unnecessary only when the British presence has been removed . . . if at any time Sinn Fein decide to disown the armed struggle they won't have me as a member' (Gerry Adams, quoted in McIntyre 1995: 101).

Prior to the hunger strike electoral campaigns, Sinn Fein's disdain for elections had allowed the SDLP to offer itself as the only significant electoral force. It was obvious, however, that there was a sizeable nationalist constituency wishing to express itself in a more radical direction, not only through armed struggle but also through the ballot-box. This was evident not merely in the scale of the anti-H Block vote, but also through the showing of the Irish Independence Party (IIP), a party formed in 1977, declaring 'our first basic principle is to secure a British withdrawal' (Irish Independence Party 1977: 1). As a green nationalist, non-socialist party with no commitment to any political structure in the event of withdrawal, the IIP had pockets of support in nationalist areas, attracting more than 12,000 votes in mid-Ulster in the 1979 Westminster election and approximately 10 per cent of the nationalist vote in the 1981 council election. When Sinn Fein joined the electoral fray, however, the IIP vote collapsed, not helped by its principled decision that it would not contest the 1982 Northern Ireland Assembly elections, leaving the way clear for the SDLP and Sinn Fein to fight the contest, on abstentionist tickets.

The 1982 elections revealed that approximately one-third of Catholics in the North supported Sinn Fein and, by logical conclusion, sympathized with the IRA's armed struggle. This pattern was repeated in the 1983 Westminster election, in which Gerry Adams captured West Belfast; but the signing of the Anglo-Irish Agreement bolstered support for the SDLP, and Sinn Fein's plan to become the larger nationalist party subsided. Although Sinn Fein continued to poll substantial Catholic working-class votes, its failure to make large inroads into the nationalist middle class meant that the room for electoral growth was limited. To represent only a minority of a minority was of limited utility in the promotion of republican ideals. For a time, Sinn Fein dismissed the relevance of its electoral performances, insisting that the 'cutting edge' of the IRA was the decisive factor in the republican struggle. Yet the party was wounded by the loss of Adams's West Belfast seat to the SDLP in 1992. The IRA's campaign had become increasingly marginalized by the security forces and declining support from overseas; now Sinn Fein also faced political confinement to a static core.

The electoral problems of Sinn Fein highlighted the limitations of the armalite and ballot-box strategy. Council election successes drew the party into ever closer contact with the northern state, through the (diligent) work of these councillors. The election appeal of Sinn Fein candidates was not based merely upon the national struggle, although the 'military' credentials of such contestants tended to be emphasized, particularly in the early years. Sinn Fein was also highlighting the need for better jobs and services. Although the extent to which Northern Ireland's councils could alter the problem of high unemployment was minimal, there was an obvious paradox: Sinn Fein candidates appealed for economic growth and investment, whilst their counterparts in the IRA continued to attack economic targets and discourage investment in the North. The first to break ranks publicly on the contradictory strategy was the Belfast councillor Martin O'Muilleor, who suggested that Sinn Fein's calls for job creation looked hollow set against the destruction wreaked by the IRA (Patterson 1997: 216).

Sinn Fein hoped to improve election performances in the Irish Republic after the ending of the party's abstentionist stance in 1986, but the converse was true. The party received an abject 2 per cent of the vote in the 1987 national contest in the South. How could a party that articulated the aspiration of Irish unity held by nearly three-quarters of the Republic's population do so badly? The IRA's ideals and motives, but not its methods, were supported by around two in five of the Republic's population during the 1980s (Patterson 1997: 207). Given their status as 'politicos' rather than members of the paramilitary organization, Sinn Fein candidates ought to have harnessed greater support. However, few drew the distinction, whilst many believed that the IRA's struggle was not the most pressing political issue for them. Indeed, there was a paradox, in that partition shaped politics in the Irish Republic for generations, yet few regarded Northern Ireland as a particularly salient issue. Even during the 1997 Irish general election, for example, amid a rapidly developing peace process, only 14 per cent of voters regarded the North as a key issue, a figure which fell to a mere 4 per cent by 2002 (Garry et al. 2003: 127).

Sinn Fein's poor performances in the Irish Republic perplexed those who had invested heavily in the end of abstentionism. The policy change was a fundamental, if long overdue, shift from what was seen as a republican article of faith, that Sinn Fein would never take seats in partitionist parliaments in Ireland, or at Westminster. The party clung to the view that the only legitimate parliament was Dail Eireann of 1918–19, which attempted to govern all of Ireland following Sinn Fein's overwhelming 1918 election victory. For traditionalists within Sinn Fein, the usurping of the will of the majority by the colonial power rendered all subsequent parliaments illegitimate pending the restoration of national sovereignty. This republican orthodoxy was articulated by Ruairi O'Bradaigh, who argued that once seats were taken in a partitionist parliament in the twenty-six counties, there was no ideological barrier to taking seats in a similar institution in the North. O'Bradaigh was backed in his interpretation by the sole remaining survivor of the 1918–19 Dail Eireann, Tom Maguire, who had backed the Provisionals in 1970 due to their fidelity to republican principles and now refused to back the changes led by Adams and other Northern leaders of Sinn Fein. Maguire insisted: 'I do not recognize the legitimacy of any army council styling itself the council of the Irish Republican Army which lends support to any person or organization styling itself as Sinn Fein prepared to enter the partition parliament of Leinster House' (*An Phoblact/Republican News*, 30 October 1986: 1, 'Forward in Unity'). The republican leadership replied that abstentionism and the IRA's legitimacy were two separate issues, the latter pre-dating the First Dail and being drawn from the continued British 'occupation' of part of Ireland.

The problem for O'Bradaigh was that political principles were outweighed by practical politics. Although there was clearly a continuing case for boycotting Northern institutions, the obvious fact was that the citizens of the Irish Republic accepted their government and parliament as legitimate regardless of their view of British control of the North. In supporting change at the 1986 *ard fheis*, Martin McGuinness criticized the manner in which some republicans wished to 'remain alone and isolated on the high altar of abstentionism, divorced from the people of the twenty-six counties'. He acknowledged that, 'after 65 years of republican struggle, republican agitation, republican sacrifice and republican rhetoric, we have failed to convince a majority in the twenty-six counties that the republican movement has any relevance to them'.

McGuinness sought to reassure those suspicious that the ending of abstentionism would lead to an end to the war by moving to 'reject the notion that entering Leinster House would mean an end to Sinn Fein's unapologetic support for the right of Irish people to oppose in arms the British forces of occupation', insisting that 'the war against British rule continues until freedom is achieved'. The pledge to continue armed struggle answered the other concern of traditionalists, that entry into Dail Eireann would eventually be followed by entry into a parliament of Northern Ireland.

The guarantees of McGuinness would eventually prove to be worthless, but the Sinn Fein leadership won the vote to end abstentionism by 429 votes to 161, narrowly obtaining the two-thirds majority required for constitutional change. There is some evidence that phantom *cumann* (branches) were created to ensure the 'right' result (Moloney 2002). Given that the IRA had approved the change one month earlier, and that Sinn Fein remained, technically at least, under 'Army [IRA]' orders, rejection of change would have been unsustainable. Over a decade later, O'Bradaigh won the argument in terms of future directions as Sinn Fein entered a Northern Ireland assembly and executive, but continued abstention from Dail Eireann would not have benefited the republican cause irrespective of events in the north. The walk-out from the 1986 conference hall to form Republican Sinn Fein by some O'Bradaigh supporters did not lead to the maintenance of a vibrant, ultra-traditionalist republicanism, but instead amounted to a 'small, forlorn group' determined to maintain an unchanging set of principles without adaptation to modern demands (Feeney 2002: 333). The ending of abstention recognized the 'need to blend the national struggle with contemporary reality as perceived by the majority of people in the 26 Counties' (*An Phoblacht/Republican News*, 6 November 1986: 1, 'Going Forward'). Aside from the merits of the debate, O'Bradaigh's walk-out allowed the settling of old scores concerning his former stewardship of the movement, the new leadership insisting that 'there was more chance of the Irish republican revolution being thwarted by the disastrous and confusing 1975 cease-fire which led to a degeneration in the armed struggle, or by the federal policy had it been maintained as a serious basis for a settlement' (ibid.).

Sinn Fein's support remained low, at 10 per cent in Northern Ireland, and 2 per cent in the Irish Republic in the decade after the 1986 abstention decision. The loss of West Belfast in 1992, a contest in which some unionist voters were prepared to support the SDLP's Joe Hendron to defeat Gerry Adams, was indicative of how difficult it was to build substantial electoral support for a party linked to violence. Sinn Fein's main allies outside Northern Ireland, Herri Batasuna, found a similar ceiling to its support due to its links to the violent Basque separatists ETA. It would be wrong, however, to portray a picture of a demoralized republican movement by 1992. Within hours of Adams's defeat, the IRA hit back with the Baltic Exchange bomb which created more damage, in financial terms, than the IRA's entire campaign thus far in Northern Ireland. Electoral reverses and military successes were evident. The difficulty for Sinn Fein was when accidental killings of civilians prompted public outcries.

The impact of the PIRA's cease-fires upon Sinn Fein's election performances was dramatic. Prior to the IRA cessation in 1994, Sinn Fein averaged 11.2 per cent of first-preference votes in the nine elections in Northern Ireland since it entered the electoral fray in 1982. In the first nine elections after the 1994 cease-fire, from 1996 to 2004 inclusive, the party recorded an average vote of 19.5 per cent. Buoyed by its contribution to the Good Friday Agreement, the SDLP retained its lead in the first elections to the post-Agreement assembly in June 1998. However, Sinn Fein overtook the SDLP in the 2001 Westminster and council elections, polling 1 per cent higher and obtaining four Westminster seats, compared to the SDLP's three. In the council elections, the SDLP obtained more seats, but it appeared that this would be the last time such an outcome occurred. In the 2003 elections to the Northern Ireland Assembly, Sinn Fein easily outpolled the SDLP, and became the second largest party, scoring 23.5 per cent, 6.5 per cent higher than the SDLP and netting twenty-four seats, six more than its nationalist rival. Sinn Fein's hegemony within the nationalist community was further confirmed in the 2004 European elections, the party obtaining 26.3 per cent of the vote and gaining its first Northern Ireland seat in the European Parliament, at the expense of the SDLP. In the Irish Republic, Sinn Fein took its first seat in Dail Eireann in 1997 (its previous victors in the 1950s declined to take seats) and won four more seats in 2002, whilst also capturing a seat in the European Parliament. The party aspired to become a government coalition partner in the South, the leadership ensuring at *ard fheisanna* that the membership did not rule out such an option, whilst the party's strength in the North had given it a place in government in the Northern Ireland executive in 1999. Moreover, for the 1999–2002 executive, Sinn Fein chose arguably the two most important ministries, education and health, for the two places in the ten-member executive to which the party was entitled via its assembly representation.

Pan-nationalism and Republican Change

When Sinn Fein emerged as a political force in the 1980s, its primary role was to help the IRA wreck political agreements that threatened to stabilize Northern Ireland. The demise of the 1973 Sunningdale Agreement as a result of the loyalist workers' strike of 1974 was a relief to the republican movement, which feared that the deal could embed power sharing, even against a backdrop of IRA and loyalist violence. Indeed, the collapse of Sunningdale yielded cordial noises of approval from republicans, admiring of how loyalists had defeated their 'imperial masters'. As a significant electoral entity by 1982, Sinn Fein helped block the attempted revival of a Northern Ireland assembly, by boycotting, along with the SDLP, the 'rolling devolution' plan of the Secretary of State, James Prior, in 1982. The plan was a non-starter, comprising a consultative assembly, rather than genuine power sharing, and offering only vague references to an Anglo-Irish Council rather than having a defined Irish dimension. It was dismissed by republicans as merely a 'skilful scaling down of the ill-fated Sunningdale Agreement', itself utterly rejected by republicans (*Iris*, July–August 1982: 1, 'A Riotous Assembly?'). Like the other parties, Sinn Fein was powerless in respect of the implementation of the 1985 Anglo-Irish Agreement, a deal favoured by the SDLP for the consultative rights it gave the Irish government in Northern Ireland. Sinn Fein argued two main points: first, any concessions to nationalists were obtained by virtue of the IRA's role; secondly, the agreement was based mainly upon counter-insurgency, the Westminster government having been influenced by a 1984 report by the Independent Study Group entitled *Britain's Undefended Frontier*, which highlighted how the IRA had been defeated in its 1956–62 campaign because of the unity of security approaches of the London and Dublin governments (and, the report might have added, the Belfast government) (*An Phoblacht/Republican News*, 21 November 1985: 8, 'Defending Britain's Frontier').

Although Sinn Fein's ending of abstention from Dail Eireann made scant difference to the Irish electorate, the move alerted other nationalist parties on the island to the emergent pragmatism within hitherto fundamentalist republicanism. The outcome of this shift was that Sinn Fein moved from leper status to political discussant in 1988, first through secret dialogue with Fianna Fail in the first half of the year, and then through official discussions with the SDLP leadership in autumn, often labelled simply Hume–Adams. A pan-nationalist consensus was forged, which would lead to an IRA cease-fire in 1994, as that consensus appeared to dilute republican articles of faith. Shortly before Adams began to construct a pan-nationalist alliance, the republican leadership had denounced the concept as 'disastrous, because from Fianna Fail and Fine Gael can only come a dilution of the nationalist aspiration, which could be further diluted under the pressure of loyalist and British demands' (*An Phoblacht/ Republican News*, 7 April 1983: 3, 'Fighters against the British Presence'). Adams argued that the demand for Irish self-determination was 'vigorously diluted and undermined by "constitutional" nationalists' (*An Phoblacht/Republican News*, 12 December 1985: 5, 'London–Dublin Accord – What Next?').

In the dialogue with the SDLP, Sinn Fein did not move far from the positions which the party had laid out in its 1987 discussion document, *A Scenario for Peace*. For Sinn Fein, the scenario was one of British withdrawal within the lifetime of a Westminster parliament, disbandment of the RUC and the UDR, withdrawal of the British Army, and, for recalcitrant unionists unable to accept a united Ireland, the prospect of resettlement grants. With the exception of the offer to unionists, these demands were not greatly revised when the document was re-launched in 1989, Sinn Fein arguing that the British Establishment (an ill-defined term) could be engaged in a strategic rethink on Britain's role (Patterson 1997: 220). Indeed

Hume–Adams, in 1988, agreed merely the agreeable: namely that Irish national self-determination was vital for the future of the island. Hume argued that the clear stumbling-block was the division over the means of exercising national self-determination, whereas Sinn Fein's view was that the territorial integrity of the island of Ireland was paramount and should be the basis for the means of self-determination. The other key source of difference between the SDLP and Sinn Fein concerned the attitude of the British government to Northern Ireland. For Hume, the willingness of the British government to face down loyalist protests against the Anglo-Irish Agreement was indicative of British neutrality. For Sinn Fein, the deployment of 14,000 British Army soldiers, 10,000 armed RUC officers and 8,000 UDR personnel to contain insurgency and ensure that Northern Ireland remained in the United Kingdom was a curious form of neutrality.

The symbolism of Hume–Adams c.1988 was replaced by more practical input into the emerging political process in 1992. The Hume–Adams draft document of June that year indicated that the pan-nationalist approach to the question of Irish self-determination had diluted republican ideals concerning the indivisibility of the island of Ireland. The issue of the need for unionist consent for change was now live. The Hume–Adams draft insisted that the 'democratic right of self-determination by the people of Ireland as a whole must be achieved and exercised with the agreement and consent of the people of Northern Ireland'. There remained ambiguity in this draft: notably whether republicans regarded 'agreement and consent' of unionists as a prerequisite for any exercise in national self-determination, or whether agreement and consent could be assumed to follow. None the less, the document's formulation for self-determination was more Hume than Adams, a characteristic that was to be common during the peace process.

The influence of Hume upon republican thinking on self-determination was evident in Sinn Fein's *Towards a Lasting Peace in Ireland* document, published in 1992. This heralded a shift away from the territorial nationalism of previous republican thought in favour of a people-based approach to Irish unity. The separate identity of unionists was acknowledged, and it was now the British government's role to persuade them to change the political perceptions which flowed from this identity. The document spoke of a 'British government joining the ranks of the persuaders in seeking to obtain the consent of a majority of people in the North to the constitutional, political and financial arrangements needed for a united Ireland' (Sinn Fein 1992: 3). What was not stated was what would happen when, as would always be the case, such consent was not forthcoming. The document spoke of persuasion taking place 'within the context of accepting the national right of the majority of the Irish people', which hinted that a consent 'override' existed in the event of resistance. None the less, the more positive role envisaged for the British government in disengagement moved Sinn Fein away from the idea that the only problem was the British. The new approach to unionism embraced 'pluralist language' of accommodation (Bean 2001: 135). An Adams strategist, Jim Gibney, acknowledged this explicitly:

> the traditional position that a resolution to the problems with the Unionists would have to await the removal of the British government's involvement in Ireland was wrong. We must now accept that there are divided political allegiances within the nation and that Unionists have a dual identity that must be accommodated.
>
> (*An Phoblacht/Republican News*, 2 March 1995)

The changes in *Towards a Lasting Peace in Ireland* were accompanied by recognition that the IRA Army Council was no longer the legitimate government of Ireland. Instead, Sinn Fein was merely one political actor competing in the marketplace, whose contemporary mandate had to be respected, but could no longer be enlarged by the legacy of the republican dead. This was made clear by Gibney at the 1992 Wolfe Tone commemoration at Bodenstown, when he dismissed the idea that the republican leadership was a 'government in waiting' and urged republicans no longer to be 'deafened by the deadly sound of their own gunfire'.

Four years later, Gerry Adams abandoned any traditional republican demands in advance of negotiations, when he told the 1996 *ard fheis* that Sinn Fein 'remains willing to enter into dialogue without pre-conditions. We do not want a veto over the agenda for negotiations or the outcome of those negotiations' (*An Phoblacht/Republican News*, 'Sinn Fein Ard Fheis 1996', 30 March 1996: 11). It was difficult to imagine unionist leaders entering negotiations similarly, without a baseline position that the Union remained intact. Moreover, Adams insisted that 'proper all-party talks have a definite potential to create a democracy within which the struggle for the republic can be pursued' (*An Phoblacht/Republican News*, 'Sinn Fein Ard Fheis 1996', 30 March 1996: 10). Previously, the Republic and the democracy were the same entities.

From Oghlaigh n-haEireann to Office: Sinn Fein enters Government

The peace and political processes of the 1990s had a long gestation, during which the British government had full knowledge of the long-term project of Gerry Adams to shift republicanism decisively away from armed struggle. The British government could hardly fail to be aware, given that Adams had undertaken initiatives in the 1980s which involved indirect contacts with that government, bypassing the IRA Army Council and the Sinn Fein leadership (Moloney 2002). Such unilateralism was necessary, in that few republicans would have considered dialogue with the Thatcher government a worthwhile enterprise. Adams offered the prospect of a pan-nationalist consensus built upon agreement on the need for national self-determination. This demand was in line with republican principles; where Adams deviated was in indicating that British withdrawal might not be an inevitable consequence of the exercise of such self-determination, at least in the short term. The search for an agreed formula for self-determination became public through dialogue with the SDLP in 1988. At this time, however, the British government was publicly offering a mantra of 'not talking to terrorists', and indeed introduced a broadcasting ban against Sinn Fein. Despite this, the British government had always kept open lines of communication with the IRA. In the early 1990s, representatives of MI5 and MI6 each had indirect contact with Martin McGuinness, a member of the IRA's Army Council (P. Taylor 1997). Whilst clandestine, due to the political fall-out had such meetings become public knowledge, the indirect dialogue did not amount to much more than a restatement of British constitutional policy on Northern Ireland, although it did provide an indication of the type of imaginative steps, on prisoners, policing and conflict resolution, that the British government might engage in if an IRA cease-fire were called.

Contact between British government intermediaries and the IRA was placed on a sounder footing, but still on the basis of deniability through the establishment of the Back Channel in 1990 (Mallie and McKittrick 1996). The 'military' aspect of the Back Channel explored possible conditions for an IRA cease-fire. The political aspect allowed input to the debate on an agreed formula for Irish self-determination. Documents from the British government underwent detailed, often tortuous scrutiny within the republican leadership, the IRA Army Council passing its commentary to the Sinn Fein leadership (there was considerable overlap, but the formal distinctions were maintained). The climax of the preparatory stage of the peace process was the 1993 Downing Street Declaration offered by the British and Irish governments, which provided a unionist interpretation of national self-determination in terms of substance, even if the language of Irish self-determination offered some succour to nationalists. The Declaration insisted that 'it is for the people of the island alone, by the agreement between the two parts respectively, to exercise their right of self-determination on the bases of consent, freely and concurrently given, North and South, to bring about a united Ireland, if that is their wish'.

An undergraduate scholar could work out that the Downing Street Declaration represented *plus ça change*. The language was of Irish national self-determination, but it was qualified by an obvious opt-out for Northern Ireland, hitherto known by Sinn Fein as the unionist veto. Despite this, Sinn Fein had engaged in too much dialogue over the meaning and exercise of national self-determination to row back at this point. Instead, therefore, the party 'had to ransack its full vocabulary of opaque political language to find an appropriate response to the Downing Street Declaration' (Boyce 1991: 421). Sinn Fein sought clarification of the Declaration, yet, upon receipt, neither rejected nor accepted its contents, although the IRA's 1994 cease-fire statement pointedly declared that it was not a solution. Ultimately, whatever the language of the Declaration, the people of the island were not afforded the opportunity to exercise the right of self-determination to bring about a united Ireland. Such an option was never laid before the electorate, and even if it had been the exercise would have been futile given the continuing Northern veto.

Following the statements of principles that underpinned the Downing Street Declaration, there was still the task of producing detailed political agreement. Sinn Fein played little part in negotiating many of these details, and meekly accepted a very limited cross-border aspect to the bi-governmental, multi-party deal finally agreed on Good Friday in April 1998 (Hennessey 2000; Tonge 2005). Gerry Adams was later to claim that he knew from 1997 onwards that Sinn Fein would be entering a government of Northern Ireland. Not many members had been told, however, as they mobilized on a 'No return to Stormont' platform. The initial denial that Sinn Fein would enter a Northern Ireland executive and assembly meant that the party did not greatly shape any of the three institutional strands of the deal. Sinn Fein's securing of a good deal on IRA prisoners, allowing them all to be released within two years, allowed the leadership to sell the deal to most party members as recognition of the validity of the IRA's war. Cross-border bodies, although limited, were sold as a withering of the border. The amendments to Section 75 of the 1920 Government of Ireland Act, which formed the basis of Britain's sovereign claim to Northern Ireland, allowed the leadership to create the impression, however illusory, of a reshaping of Northern Ireland's constitutional position within the United Kingdom. Moreover, Sinn Fein's leadership could point to the prospect of genuine internal changes within

Northern Ireland, an appealing prospect to the many Provisional republicans motivated politically by the unacceptability of aspects of the northern state rather than affiliation with the twenty-six counties. The agreement's offer of commissions on policing, human rights and equality were attractive to those republicans who wished to see the last vestiges of the 'Orange state' removed.

The combination of these selling points allowed the Sinn Fein leadership to sell the deal to party members more easily than might have been expected given the U-turns they represented. Critics at the dual 1998 *ard fheis* (an April event was held for discussion, a May event for voting) were disarmed (metaphorically, initially) by the leadership's acknowledgement that the GFA was not a republican document. By not overselling the deal, but instead promoting it as a transitional document (although notions of transition were, at best, vague), and by emphasizing practical benefits, highlighted by the parading of soon-to-be-released prisoners, the Sinn Fein leadership did a skilful job in managing change. This leadership could then anticipate the tangible benefits of holding office in a state they had once pledged to end, and within 18 months of the 1998 *ard fheis*, the party helped form the new governing executive of Northern Ireland.

Sinn Fein's willingness to negotiate within the framework of an agreement that meant tacit acceptance of Northern Ireland and entry into a partitionist assembly was smoothed by the international kudos afforded to the party leadership. The US President Bill Clinton's involvement in the Northern Ireland peace process stemmed not merely from 'personal and emotional reasons', but also from his belief that all of the conflicts in Europe were solvable, with Northern Ireland 'the most ripe' (interview, *The Politics Show*, BBC Northern Ireland, 18 July 2004). The IRA's armed struggle had become routinized, whilst sectarianism and societal abnormality were the norm in a state dysfunctional since birth. Clinton encouraged Adams in his struggle to move republicans from violence.

Adams succeeded in restoring the cease-fire in 1997 through two key events. First, he managed to keep hard-liners in the movement at the level of the IRA executive, rather than in the upper echelon of the IRA Army Council (Moloney 2002). Secondly, the arrival of a Labour government in the UK in 1997, with a huge parliamentary majority, ensured that IRA decommissioning was relegated to a successor to a political deal, rather than a prerequisite or accompaniment. This allowed Adams to continue to offer the line that any IRA or Sinn Fein moves were only tactical, with all options retained.

Sinn Fein's arrival in government in 1999 was the climax of the party's movement from abstention to participation, and emphasized how equality rather than unity was its new *raison d'être*. The party's choice of the education and health ministries under the D'Hondt allocation formula, based upon assembly seats, provided an opportunity to defend the interests of its increasingly broad nationalist constituency. Opposition to the 11+ transfer test in schools was popular among most nationalists. Other education policies, most notably the introduction of Private Finance Initiatives (PFI) by Martin McGuinness as Education Minister, were also radical, but not in the manner in which Sinn Fein supporters might once have envisaged. Sinn Fein merely blamed the British government for the need for PFIs. The Sinn Fein Health Minister, Bairbre de Bruin, was accused of partisan decision-making on behalf of the nationalist community on such matters as hospital location decisions, yet objective analysis suggests that the Sinn Fein ministers settled quickly into roles they could scarcely have envisaged a few years earlier.

Understanding the Changes within Sinn Fein

Although there was a determined effort by the British and Irish governments to ensure that Sinn Fein could conclude a deal without a trace of humiliation, the GFA amounted to a seismic shift in republican thinking. Assessing the extent and rationale of changes in Sinn Fein is not easy, given the obfuscation sometimes provided by its leadership and the lingering conspiratorialism which pervades a once militaristic movement. The leadership has endorsed considerable change, adopting a New Labour-type rationale of offering traditional values in a modern setting. Despite the difficulty in analysing the degree of movement, three clear conclusions may be drawn. First, republican 'theology' has been replaced with pragmatism, according to which all that was once held as principle has become tactical. This is a less dramatic change than it sounds, given that the republican ideological compass had few fixed points and numbered among its adherents people with very different experiences and motivations. Beyond the republican desire that the British government end its sovereign claim to Ireland and that national self-determination be exercised by the Irish people (assumed to be all the citizens of the island), there is no clear definition of what republicanism comprises. The problem with this inter-pretation of republicanism is that it leaves it as all or nothing, ranging from the aspirational form offered by Fianna Fail, or even Fine Gael or the SDLP, to the militancy of the Real and Continuity IRAs and their political associates.

For many within the new nationalist consensus, including Sinn Fein, transition towards the exercise of national self-determination is the new republican politics, allied to a new political pluralism designed to create an 'Ireland of equals'. For traditionalist critics of the new approach, outcomes must be defined, as supposedly transitional routes have historically always been political cul-de-sacs, although this outcome could equally be said to be the end-product of militaristic republi-canism. The harder, traditional form of republicanism, which post-1998 has again found itself marginalized, lays much greater stress upon definitive outcomes: British withdrawal within a specified time frame, establishment of an indivisible thirty-two-county independent Ireland, and the defence of Irish national sovereignty. There is impatience with the new stress upon identity politics. As one critic of Sinn Fein's dilution of republicanism put it: 'The accommodation of diversity and national reconciliation have in fact been British policy for the last 70 years. It's called partition' (E. Anderson 1993: 15). The 'hard republican' ideological framework is clear enough, but the means to attain its goal are far less obvious, not merely because of partition, but also because of the new, reduced forms of national sovereignty accruing to all nation-states in an era of transnationalism and a supposedly post-sovereign global order. For Ryan, Irish republicanism has died due to this new order, which diminishes parochial local contests amid a hegemonic (capitalist) framework (Ryan 1994, 1997).

The second conclusion is that ideological change has been hastened by structural alterations in Northern Ireland. The rise of the nationalist middle class, hitherto 'impervious to republicanism and hostile to the armed struggle', posed considerable challenges for an increasingly electorally oriented Sinn Fein (Bean 1995). Republicanism in its pure form was a scarce enough commodity in its urban working-class base, most of Sinn Fein's grass roots being '1969ers', motivated by the street riots of that year. Outside this base, with the exception of poor rural and border areas, republicanism held little appeal. For the creed to survive, it necessarily had to be diluted to maintain relevance to new generations. Whilst republicanism could convert itself to community politics in urban areas, this was more difficult elsewhere. Republicanism failed to connect to the nationalist middle class, and the conditions of its working-class base improved due to a combination of equality laws and welfarism, removing some of the republican ghetto mentality.

Thirdly, electoral politics offered a continuing outlet for republicanism as the politics of protest, and appeared a more viable route than militarism. Electoral politics carried fewer personal risks and could be seen to be successful, not in the attainment of the Holy Grail of the Irish Republic, but in shaping the daily lives of nationalist citizens. Ultimately, republicans could achieve greater gratification from Sinn Fein electoral gains than from the killing of enemies; the latter proved of limited utility over three decades, whereas the potential of electoralism has not yet been exhausted. The emergence of those who 'fought the fight' at the negotiating table with the British created the impression that the war had been concluded with an honourable draw, and that the continued elevation of Sinn Fein as a political force would secure a nationalist-oriented peace. Moreover, Sinn Fein, as an all-Ireland party,

had room to expand beyond the confines of narrow, sectio
northern nationalism. The dilution of republicanism amid tne
pluralistic tones of pan-nationalism could be tolerated by
many if it meant electoral gain.

Conclusion

The Provisional republican movement had begun life as a
group of irreconcilables who could not be defeated. For the
first time since partition, an IRA was established which 'might
not be able to win but after a generation could not be
defeated', even if, in broader political terms, republicans lost
(Bowyer Bell 2000: 269). A return to armed struggle for the
Provisionals became unthinkable, given the hegemonic position of Sinn Fein within the movement and the arrival of the
party as a significant all-Ireland entity for the first time since
partition. It is conceivable that Sinn Fein will become the
largest party in Northern Ireland. It has ended the structural
exclusion of nationalists from Northern Ireland and helped
convert them into a substantial voting bloc no longer dominated by unionists.

What is perhaps most striking is how little the IRA's violence yielded Sinn Fein in terms of Northern Ireland's constitutional position. Instead, the durability of the armed struggle,
combined with Sinn Fein's sizeable mandate, produced a
republican veto, in that no viable settlement could be imposed
without the consent of Sinn Fein (Bean 1995). Equally,
however, republicans proved incapable of ending the unionist
veto, and did not shift the balance of constitutional forces
decisively towards Irish reunification. Thirty years of conflict
produced six weak cross-border bodies that fell woefully short
of a decisive shift towards joint British–Irish sovereignty over
Northern Ireland. The only significant constitutional shift
went in the opposite direction, the Irish government renounc-
ing its territorial claim to sovereignty over the six counties in
favour of an assertion that all citizens on the island had the
right to belong to an (ill-defined) Irish nation. Given the
failure of the IRA to shift British and unionist constitutional

entrenchments, it is far from clear that the political approach of Sinn Fein will be more successful. A likelier conclusion is that Sinn Fein will continue to develop what the IRA perhaps achieved: substantial internal reforms in Northern Ireland.

6 Republican Ultras ──────

The IRA has long been an organization vulnerable to fragmentation. Since the partition of Ireland and the Anglo-Irish Treaty in 1920–1, the IRA has seen divisions between pragmatists, willing to accept deals as the best available and as a basis for improvement via constitutional politics, and fundamentalists, for whom any compromise short of a thirty-two-county independent Irish Republic is unacceptable. During the 1980s and 1990s, the rapid changes in the Provisional republican movement yielded the latest splits between those prepared to accept the lure of constitutionalism (or semi-constitutionalism) and those for whom fidelity to the supposed principles of republicanism outweighed the benefit of 'respectability' conferred by entry into conventional politics.

The peace process of the 1980s and 1990s saw the emergence of two small splinter IRAs, the Continuity IRA (CIRA) and the Real IRA (RIRA), both rejecting the view of the Provisional IRA (PIRA) that armed struggle had run its course. Although labelled 'dissidents', the ultra IRAs were continuing advocates of a violent republicanism which has always existed within the Irish version. Irish republicanism has always fused violence with peaceful methods, but the balance has fluctuated, and the physical force wing was in retreat within Provisional republicanism from the 1980s. The 'dissidents' of the CIRA and RIRA are merely the residual ultra wing that has always existed within Irish republicanism.

A historically determinist view of Irish republicanism notes its tendency towards compromise and marginalization of erstwhile 'comrades'. The heterogeneity of the republican movement provides a partial explanation, as the IRA has comprised, among others, variously nationalists, republicans, socialists, Marxists, Catholics and Protestants, often holding different perspectives. The other key explanation of the regular shifts towards constitutionalism is the overwhelming odds against IRA success. In the most recent major phase of armed struggle, the PIRA was opposed by 30,000 British troops and local security personnel, loyalist paramilitaries, animosity from a million unionists and, frequently, antipathy, or at best, indifference, from the bulk of nationalists throughout Ireland. Given this range of counter-forces, the temptation for diversion into mainstream politics is considerable. None the less, there remained small groups determined to maintain some form of armed campaign against British rule in Northern Ireland.

The Emergence of the Continuity and Real IRAs and their Political Associates

The CIRA and the RIRA and their political affiliates emerged from the PIRA and Sinn Fein. Both ultra IRAs have struggled to maintain campaigns amid penetration from the security services and lack of support. The CIRA and its political associate, Republican Sinn Fein (RSF), are 'purist' republicans, opposing the 'partitionist' institutions of the twenty-six-county Irish state and those in Northern Ireland. Republican Sinn Fein was born in 1986, rejecting Sinn Fein's lifting of the ban on elected party candidates taking seats in the Irish parliament. For Republican Sinn Fein, the only true Dail Eireann was that established after Sinn Fein won the 1918 all-Ireland elections, which claimed jurisdiction over the entire island. The election result and the First Dail were replaced by 'partitionist' political institutions: a twenty-six-county parliament in the South and a six-county parliament in the North. Provisional Sinn Fein (PSF) formed in 1970 pledged allegiance to the First Dail, having split from what became known as the Official IRA and

Official Sinn Fein, because it had voted to enter a 'partitionist' parliament. However, in 1986, PSF and the PIRA abandoned this principle, recognizing that the twenty-six-county parliament was accepted by the vast majority of citizens under its jurisdiction. Whilst pledging to continue armed actions in Northern Ireland and insisting that the change was not a precursor to entry to Stormont, Sinn Fein's Martin McGuinness justified the U-turn as acceptance of reality:

> We are not at war with the government of the 26 Counties . . . we have failed to convince a majority in the 26 Counties that the republican movement has any relevance to them. By ignoring reality we remain alone and isolated on the high altar of abstentionism, divorced from the people of the 26 Counties and easily dealt with by those who wish to defeat us.
>
> (Quoted in Feeney 2002: 232)

Republican Sinn Fein argued correctly that accepting the legitimacy of a twenty-six-county Irish parliament would lead eventually to PSF taking seats in a parliament of Northern Ireland. The party demands British withdrawal from Northern Ireland within the lifetime of a Westminster parliament and offers a federal Ireland (Eire Nua) as the replacement, with parliaments for each of the historic four Irish provinces (Republican Sinn Fein 2001). Unionists are viewed as Irish citizens who would accept Irish unity in the event of British withdrawal. These ideas and policies are identical to those offered by Provisional Sinn Fein policy until the early 1980s. Few PSF members joined RSF, however, and the republican purists remain isolated with a tiny, elderly membership.

According to the president of RSF, Ruairi O'Bradaigh, the 'overwhelming' Irish historical lesson is 'that there has always been resistance', and the CIRA's actions are 'indications that militant republicanism is not dead', even if, 'instead of a flame they are only a spark' (*The Times*, 13 February 2003: 8, 'Republican Die-hard Awaits New Militancy'). In its view, the twenty-six counties constitutes a neo-colonial state, and the North is a directly controlled British colony, and hence armed resistance to foreign colonial rule is justifiable and necessary.

The 'necessity' argument is based upon the belief that the British have never left colonies on an entirely voluntary basis. RSF places itself within the Wolfe Tone tradition of unity of Catholic, Protestant and Dissenter within an independent Ireland, the 'source of all evils', the British, having been removed.

The CIRA did not emerge until ten years after the RSF–PSF split, bombing a Fermanagh hotel in 1996. Although RSF denies that it is the political wing of the CIRA, the RSF publication, *Saoirse*, publicizes the activities of the CIRA, and a link is evident. The CIRA's 'military credentials' have been scorned, not merely by the PIRA, but even by other ultras in the RIRA (Mooney and O'Toole 2003). Nevertheless, the CIRA has maintained a campaign of low-level violence since 1996, attacking a variety of targets, including police stations, commercial premises and the residence of the British Secretary of State for Northern Ireland.

The RIRA and its political outlet, the 32 County Sovereignty Movement (32 CSM) emerged as the PIRA declared cease-fires in 1994 and 1997, and Sinn Fein moved towards a power-sharing agreement. Those who formed the RIRA and 32 CSM had stayed with the PIRA and Sinn Fein after the 1986 split, reassured that the military campaign to remove British sovereignty from Northern Ireland remained intact. When the PIRA restored its cease-fire in 1997, without advancing the republican position, the PIRA quartermaster Michael McKevitt resigned and formed the RIRA, joined shortly afterwards by nearly forty serving or former PIRA members (O'Brien 2000).

The RIRA launched its campaign in early 1998, first appearing through the staging of road blocks in South Armagh, when it awarded itself the title 'Real IRA' (Harnden 1999). In 1998, RIRA bombs destroyed the town centres of Moira and Banbridge, after which the RIRA undertook its disastrous bombing of Omagh, killing twenty-nine civilians and draining the organization of what little sympathy it may have had. The public outcry was such that the RIRA was forced to call a cease-fire. The Omagh bombing appeared to highlight the danger and futility of continued armed struggle, and the dissidents, dismissed as 'militarily useless' by Sinn Fein's Martin

McGuinness, have struggled to maintain an armed campaign (BBC Northern Ireland, *Newsline*, 25 September 2003). None the less, the RIRA mounted eighty operations from January 1999 to July 2002, and claimed its first post-Omagh victim in August 2002, when a bomb at a Territorial Army base in Londonderry killed a civilian contractor.

The RIRA's 'military' commitment and the record of its adherents in the PIRA in earlier years made it potentially a bigger threat than the CIRA, although for both groups desire exceeded ability to disrupt, with the clear exception of the Omagh bombing. The Irish Taoiseach Bertie Ahern sent his special adviser, Martin Mansergh, to meet the RIRA's leader, Michael McKevitt, twice, in July and December 1998, to 'underline the Irish government's belief that there was no future in armed struggle' and to insist upon RIRA disbandment (quoted in *Sunday Times*, 19 October 2003). Given the sensitivity attached to talking to the RIRA, Ahern informed Dail Eireann in 2002 that 'no member of the government' had met the group, technically true given Mansergh's status as an *ad hoc* special adviser (Tonge 2004). Mansergh had played an important role in steering the PIRA towards peace, but found the RIRA unreceptive.

In 2000 a bombing campaign began in London, which included a highly publicized attack outside the BBC, an attack on the headquarters of MI6, and a car bombing in Ealing, which injured eleven people. The campaign spread to Birmingham in autumn 2001, but the RIRA cell was then arrested and imprisoned. A RIRA attempt to import weapons from Iraq was thwarted after its team was arrested in Slovakia and convicted in May 2002. In 2003 the RIRA began a campaign of intimidation of members of District Policing Partnerships, and at the end of 2004 undertook a fire-bombing campaign in stores. As the RIRA maintained its campaign, the Northern Ireland Office began to segregate republican and loyalist prisoners in Maghaberry Prison, reviving a limited form of special status for paramilitary prisoners and claimed by the RIRA/32 CSM as 'de -facto' recognition of the existence of 'prisoners of war' (*Sovereign Nation*, June–July 2004: 1, 'Hunger Strike Imminent'). Segregation followed a short 'dirty protest' by republicans, as they hoped to elicit sympathy on the issue of the holding of Irish prisoners in British jails.

The 32 CSM began as a pressure group within Sinn Fein, anxious to prevent a leadership sell-out. Such concern was unappreciated by the Sinn Fein leadership, which expelled the group and prevented its members entering the 1998 *ard fheis* at which support for the GFA was confirmed by Sinn Fein members. The 32 CSM rejected entry to any parliament of Northern Ireland, or any political deal maintaining the 'unionist veto'. Its concern was with ending partition, and it was not interested in the opposition to Dail Eireann perpetuated by the republican purists of RSF. For the 32 CSM and the RIRA, there was a need to concentrate upon ending British rule in Northern Ireland, rather than engaging in concerns about the validity of the 'Irish Free State' to the South. The 32 CSM declared its objective to be to 'successfully pressure the British into relinquishing its [*sic*] claim to sovereignty over part of our country and withdrawing from Ireland' (*Sovereign Nation*, 2.6, 2000: 5). Optimistically, the 32 CSM challenged partition through the United Nations Human Rights Commission in 2001, claiming that the division of Ireland was a violation of 'human rights' of sovereignty, and demanding 'an end to Britain's illegal occupation in Northern Ireland and the restoration of Ireland's national sovereignty' (*Sovereign Nation*, 4.2, June/July 2001: 'Mackey Slams Naïve Andrews').

The Ultras' Critique of Sinn Fein and the PIRA

The emergence of 'dissident' IRAs accompanied the seismic shift in the political direction of Sinn Fein and the PIRA, which culminated in Sinn Fein's support of the 1998 Good Friday Agreement (GFA). The deal fell substantially short of the republican goal of a united, independent Ireland, and Sinn Fein did what it had hitherto always stated it would never do: enter a government of Northern Ireland. Soon afterwards, the IRA began to decommission part of its weaponry, and pledged to put it all beyond use in the event of a permanent inclusive settlement. In previous decades, republicans had declared that only a British declaration of intent to withdraw from Northern Ireland would suffice, but nothing in the GFA could be construed at tantamount to such an utterance. Given the scale of republican compromise, what was surprising was the lack of dissent from Adams's leadership. Adams acknowledged that IRA decommissioning had 'caused little earthquakes' within the republican constituency (*Irish News*, 28 November 2001: 1, 'IRA Arms Move Caused "Little Earthquakes" in Republicanism'). Republican ultras claimed that the PIRA's removal of its weapons, unprecedented in the IRA's history, amounted to the 'final betrayal' (*Sovereign Nation*, 4. 5, December 2001: 1).

The critics who emerged were not merely advocates of continuing armed struggle, as an eclectic grouping of academics, writers and former prisoners opposed to violence offered their opposition to Sinn Fein's 'new republicanism' in journals such as *Fourthwrite*. However, there remained republican diehards, for whom violence was a necessary and just means of opposing British rule in Northern Ireland. These 'dissidents' argued that they remained true to republican principles. As such, the label 'dissident' is perhaps misleading, Sinn Fein offering a Herbert Morrison-type view of republicanism – it is what (Provisional) Sinn Fein does, leaving ultras to ask republicans to 'seriously consider whether their allegiance is to one particular political party or to the goal of a 32 county, sovereign island' (Rory Dougan, 32 CSM, quoted in *Independent*, 25 October 2001: 6, 'Republican dissident factions hope to recruit those who still believe in violence').

According to critics of Sinn Fein's acceptance of the GFA, there is nothing transitional towards a united Ireland in the contents of the deal. The British Prime Minister insisted that 'a political settlement is not a slippery slope to a united Ireland', and that the British government 'will not be persuaders for unity' (Tonge 2002: 179). Instead, the GFA reformed Northern Ireland under British rule, whilst offering a token all-island dimension through the establishment of cross-border areas in anodyne arenas such as inland waterways and food safety. In the words of Bernadette Sands-McKevitt, member of the

32 CSM and sister of Bobby Sands, the first imprisoned IRA hunger striker to die in the 1981 prison strike: 'Bobby did not die for cross-border bodies with executive powers. He did not die for nationalists to be equal citizens within the Northern Ireland state' (Hennessey 2000: 112). Echoing such criticisms, the former PIRA prisoner Marian Price argued that 'to suggest that a war was fought for what they [SF/PIRA] have today . . . diminishes anybody who partook in that war, anybody who died in it and went out there and sacrificed their lives and liberty' (quoted in English 2003: 317). As Sinn Fein's Francie Molloy admitted, his party was now 'prepared to work an Executive. We are really prepared to administer British rule in Ireland for the foreseeable future. The very principle of partition is accepted and if the Unionists had held that in 1920 they would be laughing' (quoted in *Sunday Times*, 28 March 2003).

For such critics of Sinn Fein, there is no demographic route to Irish unity if the border is recognized. The Catholic population in Northern Ireland, not all nationalist, rose by only 2 per cent between 1991 and 2001, and the percentage of the Northern Ireland population supporting a united Ireland is approximately 30 per cent (Northern Ireland Life and Times Survey 2002). Republican ultras resent the dilution of Sinn Fein's agenda through the demands of pan-nationalism, and oppose the diversion of republican politics into social and cultural campaigns around the equality agenda of the Good Friday Agreement. Such militants criticize the manner in which 'the Provisional leadership are not fighting for "Brits out" – instead they seek parity of esteem . . . We are not a defence committee; what we want is a campaign against the English' (*Saoirse*, 121, May 1997: 1, 'Continuity IRA to Target British Crown Forces').

Republican ultras resent the condemnation of their violence by Sinn Fein, given that party's support for PIRA violence for nearly three decades. Sinn Fein argues that dissidents 'have no strategy to secure a united Ireland and no support within the community', both valid criticisms, if also applicable to the IRAs of 1916 and 1970 (*Irish News*, 1 December 2001: 1, 'Chaos blamed on dissident group'). The RIRA's killing of a civilian worker at a Territorial Army base was condemned by

Sinn Fein's Martin McGuinness as 'not a blow for Irish freedom . . . nothing of the sort', even though the PIRA to which McGuinness had once belonged carried out hundreds of similar operations (*The Times*, 2 October 2002: 4, 'Three held as Real IRA is blamed for killing of TA man'). The CIRA dismissed condemnation from Provisional republicans as the words of 'nauseating hypocrites' (*Saoirse*, 154, February 2000: 7, 'CIRA warns against RUC meetings'). With nearly 200 republican ultra prisoners incarcerated by 2002, the claim by Sinn Fein's Martin Ferris that there were 'no political prisoners' appeared a case of selective amnesia given Provisional republican experiences over three decades (quoted in *Saoirse*, 167, March 2001: 1, 'Prisoner to stand in W. Belfast?'). The ultras expect Sinn Fein to join the Policing Board in Northern Ireland and assist in the arrest of militant republicans, following historical precedents set by Eamon de Valera, after his Fianna Fail party, formed from the IRA in the 1920s, adopted entirely constitutional methods.

Insurmountable Odds?

Republicans wishing to maintain an armed campaign were confronted by the most difficult set of circumstances faced by any IRA. Whilst militant republicans had long been isolated, the problems faced by the CIRA and the RIRA exceeded those confronting previous IRAs. Republican ultras have been ostracized by erstwhile comrades, former sympathizers and all governments.

Following the attacks upon the United States in 2001, any residual sympathy for some forms of terrorism evaporated. Even prior to 9/11, the ultras found the United States infertile territory. The majority of Irish-Americans sympathetic to the PIRA and Sinn Fein backed Adams's peace strategy, the Friends of Sinn Fein organization, which emerged during the 1990s, proving a major fundraiser. Republican ultras complained that 'the Irish National Caucus, Ancient Order of Hibernians, Political Education Committee, Irish American Unity conference, Friends of Sinn Fein etc have all been bought by the

British peace process, which is not about Irish unity' (*Saoirse*, 132, April 1998: 'A Final Wake-up Call to the Irish American Community'). A National Irish Freedom Committee and fundraising bodies in the United States, *Cummann na Saoirse*, with branches in seven cities in north-east America, have been established in support of RSF and the CIRA, but their memberships and fundraising are low.

As Provisional republicans moved towards peace, the US government adopted a more relaxed attitude towards them. By contrast, the US government proscribed the RIRA and the CIRA and their political wings as terrorist organizations in May 2002, prohibited fundraising for the dependants of prisoners, and closed sympathetic websites. An FBI agent was the main provider of evidence leading to the imprisonment of the RIRA leader Michael McKevitt in 2003. In the United Kingdom and Ireland, counter-terrorist measures were further strengthened after the Omagh bombing and extended after 9/11. Dissident republicans in the Irish Republic have been liable to have financial assets seized.

The Irish government abandoned its territorial claim to Northern Ireland, the voters of the Irish Republic approving its downgrading to an aspiration for Irish unity in the May 1998 GFA referendum. The aspiration for unity remained extensive, but lacked intensity (Hayes and McAllister 1996). Only 6 per cent (85,748 voters) opposed the change, with a further 1 per cent (17,064) spoiling their ballot-paper. Turnout was modest, at 56 per cent, meaning that an overall majority of electors had yet to formally endorse partition. None the less, the substantial vote for change meant that the symbolic position of the IRA as the 'cutting edge' of the national will was removed. Although republican ultras were contemptuous of the lack of interest of 'Free State' governments in pursuing Articles 2 and 3, the existence of the constitutional claim had meant that the difference between the twenty-six-county government and the IRA was essentially one of methods, not substance. The change to the articles indicated that Irish reunification was no longer a constitutional imperative, heralding the death of traditional republicanism in Ireland (Ryan 1994).

Republican ultras are also devoid of a significant support base in nationalist areas, a crucial element in the maintenance of a sustained campaign. The IRA's 1956–62 border campaign withered due to the lack of support, the IRA claiming that the population had been 'deliberately distracted from the supreme issue facing the Irish people – the unity and freedom of Ireland' (Coogan 1989: 418). Following the PIRA's cease-fire in 1994, Sinn Fein's electoral support soared, the party becoming the dominant nationalist party by 2001. Sinn Fein hegemony, rather than defections to the ultras, has developed. The Omagh bombing and the international 'war on terror' are major explanatory factors. According to Sinn Fein/PIRA, 'any struggle which adopts the tactic of armed force is in danger of succumbing to militarism . . . The continuation of the armed campaign itself becomes the objective', rather than a realistic political agreement (*An Phoblacht/Republican News*, 20 August 1998).

Sinn Fein declared its opposition to an armed campaign, and the PIRA indicated its evolution into a 'comrades club'. However, the slow pace of movement towards this kept some members active and prevented defections. In 1995, prior to the collapse of the first IRA cease-fire, the Sinn Fein president, Gerry Adams, told republican doubters that 'They [the IRA] haven't gone away you know' (Moloney 2002: 437). Two years later, the republican base was told that if negotiations did not work, the IRA could 'simply go back to what we know best' (Francie Molloy, Sinn Fein, quoted in *Daily Telegraph*, 17 November 1997: 'Talks under threat as IRA is primed'). Sinn Fein's office at Stormont was raided in 2002 amid (unsubstantiated) allegations of an IRA spy ring, and the IRA was also blamed for the theft of intelligence files from police headquarters at Castlereagh. In 2004, three IRA members were convicted in a Colombian court of assisting FARC rebels, whilst in Belfast the IRA was accused by the Chief Constable of the Police Service of Northern Ireland of mounting a £26.5 million bank robbery, the largest mounted in the United Kingdom. These events undermined confidence in the political process, but reassured doubters that any IRA 'retirement' was from a position of strength. For former PIRA members, new roles were created within Sinn Fein, many becoming elected councillors as the party continued to expand.

The republican leadership indicated its long-term ambitions, even prior to PIRA's formal declaration of an end to violence in 2005. In 2004 Gerry Adams called for the IRA to be 'removed' as an excuse for Unionists to block 'progress' (*The Times*, 6 August 2004: 4, 'Time to get rid of the IRA, says Gerry Adams'). In 2005, Adams called for the IRA to stand down. The PIRA's war was over, indicated by the willingness of some senior members to assist the British Army as a riot developed in Ardoyne in North Belfast after the Orange 12 July parades in 2004, a move that attracted the scorn of ultras (*Saoirse*, 208, August 2004: 1, 'Provos protect British soldiers'). Moreover, the PIRA was prepared to move on occasion against dissidents, exemplified by its killing of a member of the RIRA in west Belfast in 2000. The mainstream republican movement's occasional ambiguities with respect to violence and semi-constitutional approach ensured continuing loyalty from adherents. There were few incentives to join rival IRAs, given that the PIRA, despite its expertise and weaponry, had failed to end British sovereignty in Northern Ireland.

Sinn Fein electoral buoyancy masked the political reverses of the GFA, whilst divisions within unionism in the early post-GFA years helped create the illusion of republican success. Support for 'armed struggle' had always been a minority taste among northern nationalists, the majority not believing that a united Ireland was worth the sacrifices of an armed campaign, whilst support for violent republicanism was confined to the emotional, post-hunger strike period in the Irish Republic. Nationalists were willing to back the GFA, and a Sinn Fein, no longer supportive of violence, indicated its willingness to prioritize internal political change over longer-term constitutional ambitions. Of course, the option of a united Ireland was not placed before the nationalist electorate, but, had it been, a much smaller majority, 58 per cent, indicated that they would support a united Ireland in a referendum (although only 20 per cent would oppose), compared to a 99 per cent vote in favour of the GFA (MacGinty 2003).

Republican Sinn Fein and the 32 CSM lack political support,

although, according to their republican 'theology', the vanguard role of the IRA, the position of its Army Council as a government in-waiting, and the illegitimacy of partition and British 'occupation', given the 1918 all-Ireland election result, dispense with the need for majority support in elections. The 32 CSM does not contest elections, and none of the seven council candidates fielded by RSF in the Irish Republic in the 2004 local elections were elected. RSF wished to field an imprisoned CIRA member in the 2001 Westminster election, but was barred from doing so under electoral rules created by the British government after the election of the IRA's Bobby Sands in 1981. Instead, RSF urged voters in West Belfast to spoil their ballot-papers, and more than 1,500 did so; but the size of any protest was hidden amid the vast majority enjoyed by Gerry Adams. Whilst RSF claimed that its 2004 *ard fheis* took place in a 'packed hall', the reality was somewhat different, a mere sixty delegates being confined to a modest Dublin hotel room (*Saoirse*, 212, December 2004: 7, '100th *Ard-Fheis* of Republican Sinn Fein held in Dublin'). In March 2004 RSF undertook an internal review, which acknowledged as weaknesses the 'failure to attract new members', 'small cumainn' (branches) and the inability to be 'outward looking' (Ruairi O'Bradaigh, presidential address to 100th *Ard-Fheis* of Republican Sinn Fein, 14 November 2004).

One piece of evidence does offer an indication of a modicum of support for ultras. In October 2002 RSF and 32 CSM were listed as a voting option in a BBC Northern Ireland *Hearts and Minds* survey (<www.news.bbc.co.uk/1/hi/northern_ireland>, 12 November 2002) amid disenchantment with the GFA as its institutions collapsed. The combined support for republican ultras amounted to 7.1 per cent of nationalist preferences, surprisingly high given the tendency to understate support for 'extremes' (Sinn Fein's support, 49.8 per cent in this survey, is consistently understated in polls, despite the party's new respectability) and taking into account that the Omagh atrocity occurred only four years earlier. Of these supporters, 3.8 per cent claimed to back RSF, with a further 3.3 per cent supporting the 32 CSM. There was also a wider perception that republican ultras might become more significant. In 2003,

68 per cent of UUP supporters and 53 per cent of Sinn Fein supporters believed it 'probable' or 'very probable' that dissident republican paramilitary groups would become more active (Irwin 2003).

The pressures faced by republican ultras led to internal divisions, reviving the old adage of Brendan Behan that the first item on an IRA agenda is the split. Beset by arrests, and isolated following revulsion over the Omagh bombing, some republican ultras decided that continued armed struggle was futile, whilst maintaining opposition to the GFA. In October 2002 the RIRA split, a section acknowledging 'that there is no support for armed struggle in Ireland at this time' and urging the RIRA leadership to 'stand down with ignomiiny', claiming it had neglected prisoners, fraternized with 'criminals', and lacked strategy (*Forum*, 1, February 2003: 1, 'Interview with Republican Prisoners'). As the RIRA fractured, the CIRA declared that it had 'no animosity towards the "Real" IRA, but we are two entirely separate organizations and that is the way we will stay. There is no question of even co-operating with the "Real" IRA' (*Irish Times*, 21 February 2003; *Saoirse*, 191, March 2003). None the less, it was clear from evidence in respect of the Omagh bombing that there was co-operation between dissident republicans purportedly belonging to different groups. Their political wings kept their distance from each other; the 32 CSM derided by RSF for having stayed with the Provisionals until 1997, and RIRA was criticized for wanting to assume control of continuing violence. There was also tension between the CIRA and the RIRA over the representation of prisoners, the Irish Republican Prisoners Welfare Association being seen as a RIRA entity, with RSF preferring alternative campaigns on behalf of CIRA prisoners.

It was the impact of the security services, however, that did most to deter the ultras, who found their attempts to mount a campaign frequently thwarted. Of the 101 'political' killings between 1998, the year of the Good Friday Agreement, and July 2002, 70 per cent were committed by other groups, mainly loyalists. The two dissident groups were responsible for only 20 per cent of the 1,833 shootings (excluding punishment shootings) and bombings during this period (Police

Service of Northern Ireland 2003). The scale of dissident IRA attacks is limited, compared to the previous limited IRA campaigns of 1939–40 and 1956–62 when the IRA averaged over 100 operations annually (Tonge 2004).

Conclusion

Republican ultras are confronted by a very unfavourable international environment, domestic hostility, especially since the Omagh bombing, penetration from the security services, and an inability, through lack of weaponry and volunteers, to sustain a campaign of violence. Sinn Fein's hegemonic position among nationalists in Northern Ireland has been at the expense of that party's commitment to armed struggle, whilst the previous mantras of the illegitimacy of partition emanating from the Irish government have disappeared. As such, militant republicanism has rarely been as isolated in political and 'military' terms. Republican ultras have endured previous difficult eras, and the collapse of the GFA in 2002 offered some succour to the 'end-of-history' approach of militants that Northern Ireland remained an unworkable entity and that only a thirty-two-county Irish Republic would endure.

It was evident, even perhaps to ultras, given the experience of thirty years of PIRA involvement in conflict, that armed struggle could not remove the British government from Ireland. The level of PIRA bombings of British cities assisted Sinn Fein's entry into multi-party negotiations, but the outcome of these negotiations was not a marked shift towards a united Ireland. Republican ultras could offer a persuasive critique that the GFA would not achieve Irish unity and could point to the number of ideological somersaults of Sinn Fein, whose entry into political institutions allowed the 'illegitimate' state of Northern Ireland to become embedded. The difficulty lay in advancing an alternative, beyond mantras concerning Eire Nua. The main role of ultra IRAs was to emphasize the 'colonial' nature of British rule, by re-creating the need for repressive security measures in Northern Ireland, lending the impression that the British Army and the police service were 'forces of occupation'. Meanwhile, continued violence stressed the abnormality of Northern Ireland, a fragile polity which lacked consensus.

Loyalist Violence

Arguably the most important feature of the Irish conflict in the twentieth century was the threat, and sometimes actuality, of loyalist violence. Had the British government not been obliged to factor the risk of such violence into its calculations, an undivided Ireland would have been awarded self-government prior to the First World War. Instead, the presence of the heavily armed Ulster Volunteer Force (UVF) deterred the British government from introducing self-government for Ireland, even though parliament had passed the measure in 1912. Far from accepting the will of their sovereign parliament, unionists raised an army in defiance. The continuing threat from this quarter made redundant the 1918 all-Ireland election result, even though the aggregate verdict (the normal means of assessing such contests) was a victory for Sinn Fein, campaigning for an independent (and of course non-partitioned) Ireland. Put simply, the threat of loyalist violence overrode the expressed will of the British parliament and the Irish people. This achievement means that fashionable talk of 'taking the gun out of Irish politics' and the need to 'get rid of private armies' needs to be set against historical realities; Northern Ireland's existence was partly a consequence of the formation of a 'private army'. Without guns, the UVF would have been a stage army. Instead, it was heavily armed and enjoyed support from some British Army officers, even if their supposed mutiny at the Curragh after the third Home Rule bill of 1912 was utilized for political ends by a British government anxious to evade its responsibilities.

Loyalists drew up historical lessons for much of the post-1969 conflict. Their threat of civil war in the event of British withdrawal remained a bigger barrier to a united Ireland than British commitment to retain Northern Ireland. As the combined loyalist paramilitaries asked rhetorically: 'Do you, the Irish, seriously believe we will sit back and allow ourselves to be coerced and persuaded into an all-Ireland [sic]?' (Rowan 1995: 60). Loyalists remained the only group with a selfish and strategic interest in keeping Northern Ireland as part of the United Kingdom. Although only 28 per cent of deaths from 1969 to 1998 were caused by loyalist paramilitaries, compared to 60 per cent caused by republican activity, the threat of civil war acted as a significant barrier to withdrawal by British governments which held no emotional commitment to the preservation of the Union (Fay, Morrisey and Smyth 1999).

Who are the Loyalists? Loyalist Narratives and Counter-arguments

To reassert the basic truth of how Northern Ireland's position in the United Kingdom was created and maintained through the threat of violence has become unfashionable. The willingness of the descendants of settler colonials to threaten force divided Ireland. In this respect, theories of neo-colonialism are valid in explaining the loyalist ultra position, with an indigenous local force willing to uphold the colonial power. Thus Clayton (1996: 22) argues that 'it was no accident that three of the world's main trouble spots in the 1970s, Northern Ireland, Israel and Rhodesia, could be directly attributed to the British empire's original interference with smaller and weaker communities than itself and the incursion of settlers'. As a new Northern Irish politics has emerged, arguments grounded in colonial theory have diminished, although, as Miller (1998) argues, it is never made clear when Britain's hold on Ireland ceased to be colonial. The basic lesson is that 'gun politics' ('Ulster will fight and Ulster will be right') were as influential as 'electoral politics' in creating Northern Ireland. The main caveats to this fundamental republican version of Irish history can be summarized thus. First, loyalists are not settler colonials, because their ancestors landed in 'Northern Ireland' long before Ireland ever fell under British colonial rule. Loyalist narratives stress the presence of 'their' Ulster-Scots leader, Cruithin, in the north-east corner of the country in the seventh and eighth centuries, prior to the arrival of Celts in the province (Adamson 1982; Graham 1997). Secondly, a loyalist opt-out from an all-Ireland election result was justified, given that the British government, in altering the *status quo*, was attempting to expel loyal citizens from the United Kingdom, forcing them into an increasingly independent Ireland. Thirdly, such forced 'repatriation' would render the Protestant-British population subject to political and religious subordination, claims that loyalists argue were vindicated by subsequent events, as Ireland became a Catholic state for a Catholic people. The formation of Northern Ireland was defended as mature recognition of the coexistence of two nationalities within the same land mass.

Whatever the political merits of the unionist case, the importance of loyalist threats of 'armed struggle' have been played down in unionist-leaning accounts of the formation of Northern Ireland, in favour of more contentious notions of rights of self-determination. Ironically, republicans, whilst correct in emphasizing the electoral illegitimacy of the formation of the northern state, ignored the lesson of 1913–20, that a loyalist military threat exists independently of their British 'masters' and is the ultimate barrier to Irish unity. As such, the republican perception that their struggle was purely against British colonialism was misguided. The group that drew perhaps the most apposite lessons from history were the post-1969 loyalist paramilitaries. Distrustful of the Westminster government, their violence brutally but effectively emphasized to it that Northern Ireland could not be abandoned. The links between the UVF of 1913–20 and the Troubles version were tenuous, in terms of size, support and status. None the less, the UVF and its counterpart, the Ulster Defence Association (UDA) were rational actors, even if some individual members were psychopaths. They realized that a shift within the UK government towards withdrawal could be derailed if it was evident that civil war would be a consequence. Indeed, whatever the criminality of their actions, the UVF and the UDA were, in some respects, less defiant than their predecessors. They did not openly defy the will of parliament on the future of Ireland, unlike loyalists from 1886 to 1918; nor did they reject the results of a fair and democratic election, as had loyalists in 1918.

Loyalist paramilitarism represented the cutting edge of the unionist veto enshrined by partition in 1920. Orthodox republican thinking, evidenced by the output of Sinn Fein from the 1970s until the 1990s, suggested that loyalists were misguided Irish people, deluded by their British imperial masters, who remained the enemy. Loyalists would accept a united Ireland when the British no longer supported their veto. Whilst this was useful for republicans in providing justification for avoidance of a civil war with loyalists, it appeared an exceptionally optimistic scenario. Republicans could point to French withdrawal from Algeria, despite the existence of a pro-French minority. Furthermore, republicans offered a secular, federal Ireland, rather than a Catholic united Ireland, in their Eire Nua strategy from 1970 to 1981. Yet Eire Nua, with its promise of a federal Ulster parliament, failed to register in the nationalist Falls, let alone the loyalist Shankill area. By the 1980s, the emergent northern leadership of Sinn Fein instead offered a 'no concessions to loyalists' policy. Although this owed more to recognition by the leadership of the popularity of the slogan than any belief that loyalists could somehow be defeated, it represented the hostility of Northern republicans to a loyalist 'enemy' often situated only hundreds of metres away, on the other side of a sectarian interface. The draft version of *A Scenario for Peace*, Sinn Fein's 1987 policy document, offered repatriation grants to those loyalists unwilling to live in a united Ireland. Without the ability or willingness to impose a defeat upon loyalist paramilitaries, who also enjoyed some unofficial backing within elements of the security forces, republican paramilitarism was doomed to struggle. An outright civil war was neither desirable nor likely to be winnable.

The Growth of Loyalist Paramilitaries

Following the heady days of rebellion of 1913–20, many units of the UVF were absorbed into policing structures in the newly formed Northern Ireland. This meant that, for many nationalists, policing was undertaken by a sectarian militia, the exclusively Protestant Ulster Special Constabulary (B Specials) being regarded with particular opprobrium. With policing structures proving more than capable of dealing with episodic IRA activity, the re-emergence of the UVF in 1966 came as a surprise and an insult to many. First, there was little threat from a moribund IRA at the time. Secondly, the actions of a handful of murdering drunks from the Shankill, awarding the title of UVF to their group, antagonized ordinary Protestants, acutely aware of the mass basis of the UVF in days of yore. The UVF's indiscriminate killing of two Catholics, unconnected to the tiny IRA, and one other person in 1966 attracted widespread condemnation, particularly from a unionist government with little to fear from the IRA. Armed republicanism had appeared to have ended four years earlier with the dismal end of the IRA's largely unsupported border campaign. Later, the self-styled leader of the UVF, Gusty Spence, claimed that senior unionist politicians suggested that he form such a group, a grandiose claim without foundation. Important unionist politicians, notably William Craig and Ian Paisley, did dabble episodically with paramilitary groups, but never turned such flirtations into marriage, the politicians ensuring that any links with extra-constitutionalism could not be construed as aiding paramilitary activity. Paisley insisted that the Protestant community 'will not bow to intimidation, either from the IRA or any so-called Protestant group' (*Irish Times*, 20 March 1973; Bruce 1989: 26). During the 1980s, Paisley joined the anti-Anglo-Irish Agreement movement, Ulster Resistance, on an Antrim hillside to wave firearms certificates. Paisley promised to give Ulster Resistance 'all the political cover' it needed, but claimed that he withdrew support when it was clear that a section of that group was arming.

The Prime Minister of Northern Ireland, Terence O'Neill, acted immediately to ban the reconstituted UVF, describing it as 'this evil thing in our midst' (Elliott and Flackes 1999: 494). Apart from a brief period in 1974–5, when the UVF was being encouraged to 'go political', it remained a proscribed organization. For the UVF of the late 1960s, there was no IRA to fight, and the organization turned its attention to removing the relatively liberal O'Neill from office. This required the invention of an IRA as part of a supposed threat to Ulster, which O'Neill was apparently ignoring. Accordingly, the UVF and the semi-constitutional Ulster Protestant Volunteers (UPV) blew up water supplies in Northern Ireland in 1969, explosions for which the almost non-existent IRA was blamed. With the Northern Ireland Civil Rights Association already perceived as republican by many unionists, this apparent revival of the IRA put more pressure on the concessionary approach of O'Neill, who rapidly became outflanked by hardliners. As the situation deteriorated to the point where it was felt necessary to commit British troops to prevent intercommunal violence, the reviving loyalist paramilitary groups found a niche as supposed community defenders.

As nationalist demands for civil rights grew from the mid-1960s onwards, unionist politics fractured, and paramilitarism revived. A range of forces emerged as challengers to the orthodox voice of unionism as represented by the Unionist Party. The UPV evolved into the Protestant Unionist Party in 1969 and the Democratic Unionist Party two years later, led by Paisley. The Vanguard movement, led by William Craig, emerged in the early 1970s as the authentic voice of working-class mobilization for many Protestants. Craig regarded himself as a politician, and in the mid-1970s signalled the end of his own career by calling for an emergency power-sharing coalition with the SDLP. In earlier, less compromising guise, he suggested that 'it will be our job to liquidate the enemy' (Bruce 1989: 24). Added to these groups was Tara, a short-lived extreme associate of the non-violent Orange Order. Tara attracted fundamentalists who believed that the Protestants of Ulster were the lost tribe of Israel. These Israelites needed to keep their purity, threatened by groups such as Catholics. Such groups were regarded as bizarre by the majority of Protestants. Of much greater significance, however, were the far less religious emergent paramilitaries of the UVF and the UDA, the latter remaining legal until 1992, despite a persistent history of sectarian assassination under its cover name of the Ulster Freedom Fighters (UFF). Although pledged to defend Protestants, these groups had no religious basis. None the less, the loyalists sometimes drew parallels with the struggle of the Israelis, the UFF arguing: 'We have more in common with the state of Israel . . . like the Jewish people, each time an act of aggression is committed against our people, we shall retaliate' (cited in Brewer 1998: 154). Whilst loyalist paramilitaries do not subscribe to theological notions of a chosen people, an element of 'we are the people' pervades and conditions their outlook. The main components of this are a sense of being the underdog and, it is even claimed, a vague sense that loyalists are supported by God (Morrisey and Smyth 2002: 55–7). An early edition of *Loyalist News* (August 1971) argued that 'the enemies of the Faith and Freedom are determined to destroy the state of Northern Ireland and thereby enslave the people of God'. Although the religious dimension of loyalism is far less explicit than that found in Paisleyism, there is hostility to what is seen as expansionist Roman Catholicism and a lingering belief in the superiority of the United Kingdom to the Irish Republic.

The UVF and the UDA were both formed supposedly to 'defend Ulster' from its 'enemies', the IRA. The desire to keep Northern Ireland in the United Kingdom was expressed through a willingness to kill known republicans or, more commonly, members of the Catholic community from where the IRA drew support from 1970 onwards. Loyalist paramilitarism was a peculiar form of ultraism, condemned by the British government, which, whilst not averse to subjugating due processes of law to expediency, paled at the activities of those whose place in the United Kingdom was under threat. The UVF and the UDA attempted to establish themselves as legitimate armies complementing the work of the British Army. They even aped the Army's rankings, if tending to over-promote through the readiness to award the title of 'Brigadier' even to humble volunteers. Bruce (1992: 113) punctures the grandiose claims of loyalist paramilitaries thus: 'a "company" was any self-identifying group of men who joined the UVF. In Belfast this usually meant a group which drank in a particular pub . . .. Assembling on parade meant turning up at the bar.'

None the less, Bruce understands the supposed rationale to the brutality of loyalist violence, and is far from dismissive of the capabilities of the paramilitaries. For Bowyer Bell (2000: 107), the loyalists are to be unfavourably compared to their republican counterparts in terms of organization and conduct. Whilst the Provisional IRA resembles a genuine secret army, 'the Protestant loyalists resplendent with titles – Ulster Volunteer Force or Red Hand Commandos – are neither secret armies nor really even defenders but rather vigilantes waiting for an opportunity to commit sectarian murder – a posse of hard men drinking in the upstairs room of a pub as comfortable in their structure as is the IRA on parade'. Accusing loyalist paramilitaries of naked sectarianism, Bowyer Bell (2000: 113) claimed that 'these "working class bigots" . . . sometimes can kill Irish republicans but mostly they make do with Irish Catholics and rationalizations legitimized by self-awarded titles and forms"'.

For such critics, the UVF and their loyalist paramilitary associates have never been an army. In terms of political support, the UVF and the UFF were never 'people's armies', unlike the IRA, which enjoyed demonstrable support within the nationalist community, if measured in terms of votes for Sinn Fein, a party which unambiguously supported the IRA in the 1980s. The UVF and the UFF did not seek such support, nor would it have been forthcoming; but their targeting of republicans did not bring howls of protest from the loyalist community. During the late 1980s and early 1990s, as the loyalist 'death-squads', to use the vernacular of republicans, targeted their supposed rival army, loyalist paramilitary activity appeared to adopt a profile more compatible with that of an army 'at war'. What is not considered in Bowyer Bell's work is whether the loyalists' willingness to commit violence to keep Northern Ireland within the United Kingdom affected British policy. Acknowledging that the British government abandoned its plans to concede semi-independence to the entire island of Ireland at the beginning of the twentieth century partly due to the threat of loyalist violence, it is plausible to contend that British policy was similarly affected by its actuality towards the close of that century. This is, of course, a necessary but insufficient explanation of British policy. Arguably, IRA violence was far worse than anything the loyalists could have managed; yet it failed to reshape British policy towards the constitutional position of Northern Ireland in the United Kingdom. Furthermore, the number of loyalists prepared to engage in loyalist paramilitarism, beyond the early street patrols of the UDA, was low. Yet IRA violence could, eventually, be contained by the British. The number of combatants and the extent of violence within a civil war, in the event of a British declaration to withdraw, could not be gauged. Just as the IRA enjoyed a sizeable number of 'sneaking regarders', so loyalist paramilitaries believed that they had a wider constituency upon which to draw should the British government ever signal its intention to leave Northern Ireland. For loyalist paramilitaries, the threat or use of violence was required to maintain the *status quo*. Politics were less important, to be developed after Northern Ireland's constitutional position had been secured.

Both the main loyalist paramilitary organizations gathered support from the *ad hoc* community defence groups which arose from inter-communal rioting in 1969. The UDA prospered in harnessing the combined strength of these local defence committees. Allied to trade union support, fostered by the Loyalist Association of Workers, the UDA became a large organization, capable of mobilizing thousands of Protestants on the streets of Belfast in the early 1970s. Its federal structure reflected its formation, an amalgamation of a loose network of community organizations. Local autonomy for UDA groups meant that the organization had significant community roots. The UDA's original role sometimes complemented that of the British Army, in patrolling the streets, supposedly to deter republicans. As such, the UDA enjoyed a greater level of respectability than the UVF, reflected in its legality and level of backing. Against this, the UDA's lack of central command meant that its units were often out of control, and the organization was prone to splits, local racketeering and alcohol-fuelled violence.

The UVF was (re-)created as a secretive, tightly knit organization. Its origins lay less with local community defence and more with a self-ascribed defence of the Protestant population against republicans. In common with the IRA's purported defensive role, this claim of deterrence was largely delusion. Insistent that its war was with 'Crown forces', the IRA rarely chose to attack Protestants just because they were Protestants. As such, the 'defence' was not under direct attack most of the time. When notable exceptions occurred, such as during the latter half of 1971 and the IRA's nakedly sectarian phase of the mid-1970s, including the sectarian bombing of the Bayardo Bar on the Shankill Road in 1975 and the Kingsmill massacre of Protestants in 1976, the UVF was powerless to defend Protestants. The Bayardo bombing was partly retaliation for the UVF's killing of three members of the Miami Showband, when the group was returning to the Irish Republic after playing a concert in Northern Ireland. In January 1976 the UVF murdered six Catholic civilians in one day, a move followed by the IRA's sectarian massacre of ten Protestants (only the Catholic bus driver was spared) at Kingsmill, under the cover name of the Republican Action Force, a South Armagh unit of the IRA. For the IRA, this was a 'success' in temporarily halting sectarian killings in the area; yet neither loyalist nor republican paramilitary groups could defend communities. Instead, each action generated a backlash against innocent members of the community from which the paramilitaries came.

The majority of IRA killings, albeit only a narrow one, were of security force personnel. The majority of UVF and UFF killings were of ordinary Catholic civilians. In the peak loyalist killing years of 1972 and 1976, over 100 people were killed by the UFF and the UVF, the vast majority having no connection with the IRA. These facts do not necessarily confirm the IRA as containing a 'better class of terrorist'; nor do they exonerate the IRA from the charge of sectarianism. The IRA had uniforms to shoot at or blow up, readily identifiable targets in the RUC, the British Army and the UDR. They do, however, indict the loyalist paramilitaries, most of whom were too lazy, incompetent and ill-informed to seek IRA targets for much of the 1970s and 1980s, until the targeting strategy of the late 1980s. There were exceptions; for example, the UVF shot Gerry Adams in 1984. Generally, however, the UVF and the UFF chose the easiest possible targets: innocent Catholics picked up inside, or travelling to or from, Catholic areas. Until the late 1980s, when collusion with the security forces became more organized, the UVF and the UFF lacked proper information on members of the IRA. Instead, they chose to kill members of the community from which the IRA drew support, irrespective of whether the individual slain supported the IRA. The *perception* of loyalists was that they were a community under siege, victims of ethnic cleansing, suffering large enforced population movements in urban areas and witnessing the growth of an encroaching Catholic population.

The UVF committed some of the worst atrocities of the Troubles, with no IRA members killed in some of these incidents. Under the pseudonym of 'Empire Loyalists', its bombing of McGurk's Bar in Belfast in 1971 slaughtered fifteen civilians. In a rare attack upon the Irish Republic, the Dublin and Monaghan bombings in 1974 cost thirty lives. In the chaos that engulfed Northern Ireland during the worst years of the Troubles, combatants stood a reasonable chance of not being captured. In 1972, there were more than 10,000 shootings and 467 deaths, yet only 531 people were charged with terrorist offences, and only three Protestants were charged with murder (Cusack and McDonald 2000: 116). The UVF had an *alter ego*, the Red Hand Commando, often with overlapping membership, and sometimes used the label Protestant Action Force as a flag of convenience for its actions. Membership of loyalist paramilitaries was fluid, although generally there was a clear division between the UDA and the UVF.

It was perhaps surprising that so few operations were carried out against a state laying claim to Northern Ireland. Part of the reason lay in the consistent condemnation of the IRA by the government of the Irish Republic, although other factors were more important. Members of the PIRA, certainly the ones inflicting damage upon the Protestant community, operated mainly in the North, often only a few streets away from loyalist heartlands. Nearby Catholic communities also provided the support base for the IRA. As such, in the loyalist mind-set, it was members of that local community who needed to be deterred from providing such succour. Not all UVF 'commanders' believe that the civil war strategy was entirely appropriate, one commenting, in respect of any post-cease-fire move towards joint British–Irish authority, that 'if there is to be a resumption in the future caused by Dublin moving things too far, then the organization will be looking across the border' (Cusack and McDonald 2000: 402).

Although many loyalist paramilitaries accepted that the Union was secured by the Good Friday Agreement, they remain suspicious of the British government. This scepticism is shared by unionists of various hues; only 5 per cent of the membership of the Ulster Unionist Party, for example, believes that the Westminster government can be trusted on Northern Ireland (Author's membership survey, 2001. For discussions, see Tonge and Evans 2001; Tonge 2003).

The notion that loyalists are 'Queen's rebels' has long been evident in analyses of loyalism (Miller 1978). Loyalists adopt the maxim that their duty to obey is conditional upon protection from their sovereign government. As such, their only 'crime' is conditional loyalty. For some, British policy in respect of Northern Ireland is predicated upon the idea of eventual withdrawal. This view is maintained despite the contradictory evidence of successive political deals during the conflict, all of which have been based upon the principle of majority consent in Northern Ireland for constitutional change, a device clearly preserving the Union. In the early years of the conflict, the suspicions of loyalist paramilitaries were exacerbated by the willingness of the British government to meet the PIRA. To describe the July 1972 talks as negotiations would be to grossly exaggerate the exchange of ideas. None the less, that the dialogue occurred fuelled the fears of loyalists that the British government could not be trusted. The subsequent PIRA onslaught merely confirmed the belief of 'Ulster's uncertain defenders' that a government that negotiated with republicans could not be trusted.

Community Control, Racketeering and 'Policing'

Despite the protestations of loyalist paramilitaries that they existed to defend Ulster, for much of the 1980s it appeared that the UDA leadership functioned to line its own pockets. Racketeering reached its height whilst the UDA's chief fundraiser was Jim Craig. Through extortion, blackmail and secret contacts with republican 'enemies', Craig and, to a lesser extent, John McMichael, the leader of the UDA in south Belfast, enjoyed a lucrative existence from their cut of funds supposedly destined for the UDA. With the organization's commitment to politics failing to fully embed within the movement and the control of areas complete, there was considerable scope for the diversion of monies towards leadership, rather than movement, benefit. Craig's execution in 1989 was undertaken by a UFF tired of his racketeering; John McMichael's demise two years earlier was at the hands of the IRA, but there were unproved suggestions of loyalist complicity (McDonald and Cusack 2004; P. Taylor 2000).

The loose structure of the UDA allowed its 'brigadiers' to run particular areas as 'personal fiefdoms' (P. Taylor 2000: 199). The organization failed to develop a strategic coherence during the 1980s under the long-standing leadership of Andy Tyrie. His departure (a bomb was placed under his car as 'encouragement' to quit) saw the rebirth of the UDA as an effective fighting force. Loyalist paramilitaries had begun to be seen as pariahs within their own community, although the extent of such views is difficult to quantify. The community tolerated attacks on republicans and, as with republican tolerance of IRA 'punishment attacks' in nationalist areas, even accepted loyalist 'policing' of the local area, whatever the condemnation of such activities outside those communities. As the UDA south Belfast leader Jackie McDonald put it: 'A UFF commander or a UVF commander doesn't just wake up some morning and say, "I think I'll go and beat wee Billy . . ." It's because the community has asked for it, or some members of the community have asked for it' (quoted in P. Taylor 2000: 260).

Members of the community appeared to be 'asking for it' in greater numbers. The number of 'paramilitary-style attacks',

mainly punishment attacks, committed by loyalist paramilitaries rose sharply after their 1994 cease-fire. Shootings doubled
from fifty-five in 1994–5 to 110 by 2002–3, whilst assaults,
consisting of beatings of varying severity, rose from forty-six in
1994–5 to ninety-four in 2002–3 (Police Service of Northern
Ireland 2003: 21). These increases reflect several aspects of life
in a contemporary loyalist community. First, there is a heightened determination among paramilitaries to maintain control
of their community (the figures for republican shootings and
assaults also rose during this period, albeit by much less).
Secondly, ordinary crime has increased in Northern Ireland, as
a conflict which engaged a substantial section of the working
class has subsided. Thirdly, allowing punishment attacks to
continue has been a means of keeping members of paramilitary
'armies' occupied and those groups intact. Fourthly, although
never publicly admitted, 'internal housekeeping' by paramilitaries, whilst a symbol of a dysfunctional society, is not a major
concern of the British government and has rarely been a major
issue in the peace or political processes, even though punishment attacks have been cited as breaches of cease-fires. Despite
their self-ascribed roles, loyalist paramilitaries have lacked a
mandate from their own people. Electoral support from the
Protestant community for their representatives was minimal
and increased only slightly during the peace process. Moreover,
the Protestant population wanted loyalist paramilitaries to disappear. Post-GFA, a higher percentage of Protestants (80 per
cent) felt it very important that the UVF begin to decommission
its weaponry than did Catholics (57 per cent) (Irwin 2002: 52).

The loyalist paramilitaries also lacked international support,
but they profited sometimes from ambiguous attitudes among
some Protestants and secret backing from elements of the security forces. Generally, the front line security forces treated loyalist paramilitaries with the same disdain they felt towards the
IRA. The argument of the UVF and the UFF that 'their only
crime was loyalty' received little sympathy, and convicted loyalist paramilitaries received similar sentences to their republican counterparts. Loyalist no-go areas were removed under
Operation Motorman in July 1972, in similar fashion to those
in republican areas, and the majority of the British Army and

the RUC were contemptuous of 'armies' which murdered innocent Catholics. Belatedly, internment was extended to cover
Protestants from 1973 onwards, although the intelligence used
for such detention was only marginally superior to that which
wrongly detained many Catholics in 1971. Protestants desirous
of an active role in defending their state were hardly short
of outlets. They could join the RUC, either full-time or as
reservists, or join the even more overwhelmingly Protestant
Ulster Defence Regiment (again on a full- or part-time basis),
effectively the replacement of the old B Specials abolished
in 1969.

Cease-fire: Victory and Feuding

In October 1994, six weeks after the PIRA's cessation of violence, the Combined Loyalist Military Command (CLMC)
announced its own cease-fire. With no IRA to fight, the rationale for loyalist paramilitarism had disappeared. However,
the uncertainty over the durability of the initial IRA cessation
fuelled the arguments of loyalist cease-fire sceptics, found particularly, but not exclusively, within the ranks of the UDA.
Loyalists were soon reassured regarding the other aspect of
the IRA cessation that attracted their suspicion. The assur-
ances from the British government that a secret deal had not
been done with the IRA proved true. In the run-up to the
cease-fire, loyalists denounced the establishment of a 'pan-
nationalist' front of the SDLP, the Irish government and Sinn
Fein as a threat to Northern Ireland. SDLP members were targeted in 1993, although the intention was to frighten rather
than execute constitutional nationalists. Loyalists misread
pan-nationalism as a threat; its main contribution was the
dilution of republicanism into a more ambiguous, pluralist
form, less concerned with the assertion of territorial Irish
unity. Indeed, the position offered by the CLMC differed little
from that of the SDLP in its acceptance of 'unthreatening' –
i.e. non-political – all-Ireland co-operation.

The loyalist cease-fire followed several years of sustained
activity by the UFF and the UDA, which had seen the increased

targeting of Sinn Fein party members. In 1992 and 1993, the loyalist paramilitaries killed more than republicans. Loyalist killings rose from single figures in 1983–4 to more than forty by 1990 (Morrisey and Smyth 2002: 52). The loyalists believed they were winning the war, as republicans found the costs of their continued campaign prohibitive. The PIRA was forced to divert some of its energies into dealing with the loyalist onslaught. Its response went disastrously wrong, with the attempt to blow up the loyalist paramilitary command in October 1993 resulting in the deaths of nine civilians and the bomber. The loyalist response promised that 'John Hume, Gerry Adams and the nationalist electorate would . . . pay a heavy, heavy price'. Predictably, even in an era of refined loyalist targeting, it was the nationalist electorate rather than the IRA, that paid the price, with thirteen deaths occurring in the following seven days (Rowan 1995: 53). The IRA and the INLA did succeed in targeting loyalists in 1994, emphasizing strength and settling scores, whilst engaging in precisely the kind of sectarian war they had often pledged to avoid.

Once the IRA had announced its cease-fire at the end of August 1994, loyalist reciprocation was inevitable, arriving six weeks later, but not before several further killings. Imprisoned loyalists proved influential in fostering the cease-fire, offering three reasons. They suggested that prolonging violence would be detrimental to the loyalist cause, acknowledged the difficulty of 'targeting known republicans' as the security focus switched to loyalist areas, and appreciated the 'unacceptability of targeting non-combative nationalists' (message from UDA/UFF prisoners to UDA leadership, cited in Rowan 1995: 120–1).

Despite the loyalist constitutional victory, those who believed themselves to be the architects of that success did not feel that they had netted the spoils. The cease-fire had a destabilizing effect upon the order established over the previous 30 years. Those who had profited from the police concentration upon republican violence found their illegal activities targeted by a force with more investigative time. There was also a sense of redundancy, as 'cease-fire soldiers' found themselves inactive. Loyalist paramilitaries had long believed that they had been exploited, first, through a unionist leadership which had taken the loyalist working class for granted, and, second, through politicians who flirted with them when it suited their needs. In 2001 the Secretary of State for Northern Ireland, John Reid, warned against Northern Ireland becoming 'a cold house for Protestants'. For some loyalist paramilitaries, Northern Ireland had always been a 'cold house'. They had been excluded from the economic spoils of partition, and now saw republicans achieve post-Agreement gains through an 'equality agenda' which the Protestant class had never enjoyed. The result was internal loyalist conflict over whether to sustain support for the GFA. In 2000 this erupted in conflict between the UVF in the Upper Shankill and 'C' Company of the UFF, led by Johnny Adair, in the Lower Shankill. Although McDonald and Cusack (2004: 399) argue that the loyalist feud in 2000 'had everything to do with the peace process and the Good Friday Agreement', this assessment is not shared by those who saw the internecine loyalist disagreements as connected to control of drugs rackets. The truth is a combination of the two arguments. Undoubtedly, personal fiefdoms were of importance to 'leading' loyalists, but there were also interconnected organizational and political rivalries. The UVF remained committed to the GFA through its political intermediary, the PUP, which won representation in the Northern Ireland assembly. The UDA/UFF cease-fire was ruled invalid by the Secretary of State for Northern Ireland from 2001 until 2004. Most visibly perhaps, the UFF was involved in disturbances arising from the Holy Cross School dispute in 2001, when loyalists demonstrated against Catholic parents taking their children to school in a Protestant area. Under a cover name, the Red Hand Defenders, the UFF was also involved in killings, perhaps the most prominent of which was that of a Catholic postman, Daniel McColgan, in a brief return to the random sectarian assassinations that characterized the 1970s and 1980s.

The UDA's political representatives at the time of the GFA, the Ulster Democratic Party (UDP), did not achieve political representation in the assembly, confirming the suspicions of its unreconstructed members that there was no political way.

From this point, a turf war developed over control for the loyalist heartlands between the UDA, elements of which developed links with the Loyalist Volunteer Force (LVF). The LVF was an anti-Agreement offshoot of the UVF, based mainly in mid-Ulster, particularly the Portadown area, where it had taken a hard-line stance in defence of the Orange Order's right to march down the nationalist Garvaghy Road during the Drumcree dispute in the mid-1990s. The LVF's leader, Billy Wright, was killed in prison by the INLA in December 1997. Those associated with the politics of the UDA tended to drift from politics during the loyalist feud, although some stayed despite the slide of the UDA into violence. The latter element included the deputy lord mayor of Belfast, who sat on a platform from which shots were fired during a loyalist 'day of culture' in 2000, which ended in feuding between the UVF and UDA/UFF. Throughout the Troubles, the two main wings of loyalist paramilitarism had retained rigid divisions in terms of structure, command, finance and support networks. Even when in prison, loyalists relied upon different support networks, those in the UDA looking to Loyalist Prisoners' Aid, whilst UVF prisoners depended upon the Loyalist Prisoners' Welfare Association. Long-standing rivalries between the two organizations came to the fore, with hundreds of families having to be rehoused. However, one of the main catalysts of the confrontation was the desire of Adair to command loyalist paramilitarism. As a consequence, when the feud with the UVF subsided, the UDA/UFF turned on itself in a battle which was predominantly about empire building rather than politics, most of the UFF having turned against the GFA by 2000. The killing of an Adair rival, John Gregg, proved too much even for many erstwhile Adair supporters, and the power struggle resulted in defeat for the imprisoned Adair and internal exile in the United Kingdom for his supporters.

The CLMC only papered over divisions during the run-up to the cease-fire. Intra-loyalist divisions had earlier been overshadowed by the need to fight a common republican enemy. Post-cease-fire, the rationale for loyalist paramilitarism vanished, and the need for a plethora of self-styled groups appeared incomprehensible. The peace process brought problems for those loyalists who had enjoyed a 'good war' in terms of personal empires, now subject to greater police scrutiny against a less violent backdrop. The GFA brought difficulties for loyalist paramilitaries, as it did for unionism more generally, over whether to accept the constitutional victory and move on, or continue with a form of politics based upon an increasingly imagined enemy. Given that the history of Northern Ireland unionism and loyalism was based partly upon threat perception, it was unsurprising that the new politics emergent after the Agreement destabilized adherents to the traditional 'No Surrender' form.

Conclusion

For some loyalists, the conflict will not end until republicans drop their plans to create a united Ireland. This exaggerates the strength and coherence of modern Irish republicanism, as represented by Sinn Fein, which no longer directly challenges British rule in Northern Ireland. Even for those loyalists prepared to immerse themselves in politics, there is sometimes a lack of recognition that they have won, or that the war is over. Thus one former UVF member claimed that the 'conflict is merely going through a political stage' (Interview with Eddie Kinner, Progressive Unionist Party, 30 November 2002). The former UDA leader, Andy Tyrie, argued that although Gerry Adams had 'lost the war', he was trying to 'win the peace' by gaining concessions for republicans (quoted in Rowan 1995: 160). Loyalist paramilitaries thus justified 'continued vigilance', and were more reluctant than the PIRA to decommission their armoury.

If one adopts an approach grounded in historical determinism, the current phase might be seen merely as a fairly peaceful interval in a conflict that has adopted different forms through the decades. As loyalists point out, few anticipated the revival of the IRA in 1970, only six years after the organization appeared to have been given a quiet burial. Moreover, the aspiration for Irish unity within the Irish government and people and, most obviously, among republicans remains extensive. Yet the threats from the IRAs, Provisional, Continuity or Real, in modern Northern Ireland appear exaggerated by loyalists. Loyalist paramilitarism revived in the 1960s partly due to an exaggerated sense of threat. It continues to exist today for a variety of reasons, including those that place profiteering before politics. At its heart, loyalist paramilitarism retains a political dimension, although one that has diminished in a post-cease-fire era, where a clear paramilitary enemy has removed itself from the stage, to be replaced by racketeering (again) and feuding. The political components remain the same: the sense of siege, suspicion of the British government's intentions, and fear of republicanism, all over-emphasized in the current context, which fuelled loyalism in previous decades.

8 War by Other Means or the Triumph of Moderation? The Party System

Politics in Northern Ireland has always been characterized by rigid ethnic bloc voting. The link between Protestant-British identity and voting for unionist parties is matched in the rival ethnic bloc by votes for nationalist parties by those holding a Catholic-Irish identity. Although there are important exceptions and nuances to these traits, this political fault line dominates the politics of the region. The single transferable vote system, normally used in all non-Westminster elections in Northern Ireland, allows voters to grade preferences for all candidates on their ballot-papers, but few avail themselves of the opportunity to transfer across the divide and register a lower-preference vote for a candidate from the rival ethnic bloc. Any electoral thawing has been slight, although it is detectable. In the 1982 Assembly election, only 368 voters in Northern Ireland transferred votes from the Ulster Unionist Party (UUP) to nationalist parties, whilst in the brief euphoria following the completion of the Good Friday Agreement, the June 1998 Assembly elections recorded 4,303 transfers from the UUP across the divide (Kelly and Doyle 2000: 10). These transfers represent a paltry 0.2 and 2.5 per cent respectively of (first-preference) votes cast for the UUP.

The term 'sectarian politics' is used glibly to describe politics in Northern Ireland, on the grounds of the connection between religious affiliation and voting patterns. There is nothing intrinsically sectarian, however, in supporting a united independent Ireland or preferring Northern Ireland to remain in the United Kingdom, the two competing aspirations that have dominated the politics of the region. A better term than 'sectarian' would be 'ethno-national-religious', as national identity and religious affiliation (often intertwined) are the most important variables in terms of party choice. This is likely to remain the case for some time, even if the constitutional question of Northern Ireland's status diminishes in importance. A strong link between national and religious identities is obvious, one that shows scant sign of withering in post-conflict Northern Ireland. The level of support for the maintenance of Northern Ireland's position within the United Kingdom has averaged more than 85 per cent among Protestants in Northern Ireland Life and Times surveys since the 1998 Good Friday Agreement. Among Catholics, average support for Northern Ireland remaining part of the United Kingdom has been below 20 per cent.

From the 1920s until the 1970s, the depth of this division and the hegemonic position of a single party within each bloc, the UUP and Nationalist Party respectively, ensured that politics were dull and, to some extent, meaningless. There was some working-class radicalism, reflected by a willingness to support the left-leaning Northern Ireland Labour Party in significant numbers, but it was the UUP, as the supposed embodiment of the wishes of the unionist community, that held unbridled power in a majoritarian, winner-takes-all political system. The ineffectiveness of the Nationalist Party was compounded by its understandable refusal to play a stooge role of official opposition until the mid-1960s.

The Emergence of Intra-bloc Rivalry

After the conflict began in 1969, Northern Ireland politics became more dynamic, as intra-bloc rivalry began to accompany the (still overarching) inter-bloc contest. The one-sided UUP versus Nationalist Party contest was displaced by the birth of three significant parties in 1970–1. First-born was a party which wished to erase traditional bloc voting, the cross-community Alliance Party in April 1970, an organization which adopted unionist constitutional principles, but did not wish to be categorized as a unionist party. It believed that the British state offered better protection of liberal principles, an implicit condemnation of the confessional Irish Republic of the time. Alliance operated as a bi-confessional party within a confessional party system (McAllister and Wilson 1978). The party attracted support from Protestants and Catholics. Alliance succeeded in attracting votes from both communities, although the majority come from Protestants, and the party's membership, although largely Protestant, includes 20 per cent Catholics (Evans and Tonge 2003: 31). Despite Alliance's 'non-sectarianism', its members divide on important questions according to religion, Protestant members being more hostile to conflict resolution measures such as prisoner releases and policing changes. Most Catholic Alliance members see themselves as Irish, whereas most Protestant members see themselves as British (Evans and Tonge 2003: 29).

The nationalist Social Democratic and Labour Party (SDLP) was founded two months after Alliance. The SDLP's founding constitution proclaimed the party 'socialist', and the term 'nationalist' did not appear. According to the party's first leader, Gerry Fitt, the aim of the new organization was to be a 'social democratic and labour party that would engage the sympathies across the sectarian divide in Northern Ireland' (*Irish News*, 17 August 1995).The SDLP was nevertheless more nationalist than the old NILP, which had a partitionist approach, whereas the SDLP made clear that Irish unity, or an 'agreed Ireland', was its preferred solution. Given the SDLP's origins in the civil rights movement and its stance on the constitution, it was always seen as a nationalist party and attracted few unionist votes. It was seen as a party for Catholics, even though it was much less clergy-influenced than the Nationalist Party. Protestants form only 2 per cent of the party membership, and the party became increasingly green and nationalist in outlook (Evans, Tonge and Murray 2000).

The SDLP's virtual monopoly of the nationalist vote came under challenge from Sinn Fein from 1982 onwards, as the IRA's campaign was gradually converted from a military to a political activity. The slowness of that conversion allowed the SDLP to hold its lead position until 2001, when, with Sinn Fein's commitment to the peace process firmly established, the nationalist electorate made the party previously seen as the political wing of the IRA its favoured choice. Previously, the division between the two nationalist parties over the utility and morality of violence worked in the SDLP's favour. A majority of the nationalist electorate declined to support Sinn Fein because of its unconditional support for PIRA violence. Condemnation of the IRA by the Catholic Church added to Sinn Fein's problems in winning votes among Catholics. Sinn Fein's supporters added to the SDLP's lead in terms of council seats by showing a willingness to transfer lower-preference votes to their moderate nationalist rival that outstripped SDLP transfers in Sinn Fein's direction. One-third of SDLP first-preference voters transferred lower-preference votes to Sinn Fein in the mid-1980s, a figure that had risen to over 70 per cent by the 2003 Assembly elections.

On the unionist side, the UUP lost its status as the main unionist party to the Democratic Unionist Party (DUP) at the 2003 Assembly elections, amid disaffection with the Good Friday Agreement. The DUP emerged in 1971 under Ian Paisley, who previously led the Protestant Unionist Party, from which the DUP took two-thirds of its original recruits (Bruce 1986).The DUP adopted an even tougher line than the UUP on constitutional issues, its Protestant Unionist Party ancestor having emerged in opposition to the modest reformism of the UUP Prime Minister, Terence O'Neill, in the 1960s. Paisley effectively ended O'Neill's career by polling only 1,414 votes fewer when, as a Protestant Unionist candidate, he opposed the Prime Minister in O'Neill's Bannside constituency in 1969. The by-election was a landmark event, 'the most devastating electoral blow sustained by the governing Unionist Party in the history of the Northern Ireland state from 1921 to 1971' (Walker 2004b: 69). It confirmed the lack of receptiveness of a section of the unionist community to political change, the mild reformism of O'Neill being derided by Paisley as part of an incremental sell-out of the Union. The theme of 'Lundyism', treachery and betrayal of the Protestant people, had a long history, and was now revived to the advantage of hard-line unionists. The DUP moved unionism away from the patrician politics of the UUP towards a tougher, less deferential loyalism with appeal to the Protestant urban working class and to conservative Protestants in rural areas. Paisley's demagoguery impressed loyalists, although those of a paramilitary bent became less enamoured; rural evangelicals were impressed with Paisley's religious commitment, and DUP activists in the party's early years were drawn from Paisley's Free Presbyterian Church at a rate hugely exceeding what might have been expected from a church to which only 2 per cent of Protestants belonged. The Free Presbyterian Church enjoyed a twelve-fold increase in members to 12,363 from 1961 to 1991, but even this rise left it the seventh largest church in Northern Ireland, way below the 280,000 and 337,000 figures for the Church of Ireland and the Presbyterian Church respectively (Cooke 1996: 120).

Sectarian Politics? Unionism and Orangeism

The link between religious affiliation and voting patterns has been apparent since the formation of Northern Ireland. Within nationalism, the link between the Catholic Church and the Nationalist Party was superseded by the rise of the SDLP and Sinn Fein. Neither of these parties has any links with the Catholic Church, although the two parties draw the overwhelming bulk of their support from Catholics. Within unionism, there was a formal association between religion and politics through the presence of the Protestant Orange Order, the largest civil organization in Northern Ireland, within the UUP. In March 2005, the governing Grand Lodge of the Orange Order voted by eighty-four votes to sixteen to end the century-old link, cognizant that many members no longer gave their support to the UUP, having defected to the DUP.

In helping create the Ulster Unionist Council (UUC) in 1905, the Orange Order acted as midwife to an Ulster Unionist Party which fused Britishness with Protestantism. Historically, the Orange Order opposed those elements within the UUP who encouraged Catholics to join the party (Walker 2004a). Although religious or theological objections to Irish unity have diminished in salience within unionism, particularly given the increasingly secular nature of the Irish Republic, the Orange Order offers a religious component to an essentially territorial political argument.

The Order remains a 'partisan unionist' organization (McGarry 2004: 310). Although in decline in terms of political influence since the collapse of unionist majority rule in 1972, the Orange Order remains a sizeable organization, which claims a membership of 80,000, amounting to one in four Protestant adult males (Elliott and Flackes 1999: 380). Added to the informal, but strong, link between the DUP and the Free Presbyterian Church, it is evident that unionist politics possesses a religious flavour. Conflict over territory may wane, but Northern Ireland politics may continue to have sectarian associations. The irony is that the two main traditions in Northern Ireland share a common conservative culture in a polity in which religious worship (42 per cent attend church weekly) is substantially above the European norm (Fahey, Hayes and Sinnott 2005).

For many Orange Order members, the restrictions, rerouting or outright bans on its parades in recent years form part of a process of retreat for Protestants, in which the dynamics of the political process are diluting expressions of their culture (McAuley 2002). Approximately fifty parades annually are subject to restrictions or rerouting, less than 2 per cent of the total of more than 3,000, but such prohibitions are often disputed. The bitterest dispute, leading to the establishment of the Parades Commission, was at Drumcree in the mid-1990s, when nationalist protests against the Order's desire to process along its traditional route led to the march being prevented, in 1997, from entering a predominantly nationalist area.

The severance of the link between the UUP and the Orange Order became inevitable as the UUP continued to back the GFA against strong opposition from many Protestants. In the 1998 referendum on the GFA, the Order urged a 'No' vote, placing it in opposition to the leadership of the party to which it was linked. Whilst 70 per cent of the UUC and 57 per cent of Protestants voted in favour of the deal, only 34 per cent of members of the Orange Order supported the GFA (Tonge and Evans 2001; Hayes and McAllister 2001). By 2004, only 12 per cent of Orange Order members claimed that they would support a similar deal.

The Orange Order promotes itself as a repository of unionist unity and was critical of inter-party unionist rivalries. Eighty-one per cent of Orange Order members support the idea that the two main unionist parties should unite, a plea common in Orange literature (see, as examples, 'Unionists must unite now', *Orange Standard*, November 1994; 'Unity is strength', *Orange Standard*, June 1998). The Order still clings to the aspiration for a single, 'catch-all' unionist party operating within the Protestant bloc. However, the long-standing desire of Ian Paisley to 'dominate both the ecclesiastical and political arenas' ensured that the search for Protestant and unionist unity was chasing after a rainbow (Cooke 1996: 223). The unity envisaged by the DUP was under its own banner. As relations between the Orange Order and the UUP became strained, the question raised was whether Orangeism had become realigned with the DUP. Eighty per cent of those members of the Orange Order who voted 'No' in the 1998 GFA referendum claimed to support the DUP. Previously, the association of the DUP's leader, Ian Paisley, and many of his party activists with the Free Presbyterian Church led to disdain by the Orange Order.

Explaining the Party Vote

An examination of election results in Northern Ireland since 1982 (when Sinn Fein entered the electoral arena) confirms how unionist and nationalist votes dominate those of other parties. Table 8.1 highlights three key developments: first, the previous leaders of the ethnic blocs, the UUP and SDLP, have been usurped; secondly, there has been a growth in size of the nationalist bloc, reflecting the growth in size of the Catholic population in Northern Ireland, from 38 per cent in the 1991 census to 41 per cent in 2001. Thirdly, the centre ground, as

Table 8.1 Election results in Northern Ireland, 1982–2005 (first preference, %)

Election	UUP	DUP	SDLP	SF	APNI
1982 Assembly	29.7	23.0	18.8	10.1	9.3
1983 General	34.0	20.0	17.9	13.4	8.0
1984 European	21.5	33.6	22.1	13.3	5.0
1985 Local	29.5	24.3	17.8	11.8	7.1
1987 General	37.8	11.7	21.1	11.4	10.0
1989 Local	31.3	17.7	21.0	11.2	6.9
1989 European	22.2	29.9	25.5	9.1	5.2
1992 General	34.5	13.1	23.5	10.0	8.7
1993 Local	29.4	17.3	22.0	12.4	7.6
1994 European	23.8	29.2	28.9	9.9	4.1
1996 Forum	24.2	18.8	21.4	15.5	6.5
1997 General	32.7	13.6	24.1	16.1	8.0
1997 Local	27.8	15.6	20.7	16.9	6.5
1998 Assembly	21.3	18.1	22.0	17.6	6.5
1999 European	17.6	28.4	28.1	17.3	2.1
2001 General	26.8	22.5	21.0	21.7	4.8
2001 Local	22.9	21.4	19.4	20.7	5.2
2003 Assembly	22.7	25.7	17.0	23.5	3.7
2004 European	16.5	31.9	15.9	26.3	Did not stand
2005 General	17.7	33.7	17.5	24.3	3.9
2005 Local	18.0	29.6	17.4	23.2	5.0

represented by the Alliance Party of Northern Ireland (APNI), has shrunk in terms of vote share.

The Single Transferable Vote (STV) system used in all Northern Ireland elections except Westminster contests has not facilitated the growth of centre parties, but it has helped the Alliance Party to survive. The party continues to receive substantial exit (final) transfers from bloc voters unwilling to cross the divide and support a party in the rival bloc. As a result, Alliance was the party most over-represented in the Assembly after the 2003 election, 3.7 per cent of first-preference votes yielding 5.6 per cent of the seats. Overall, however, STV produces a highly proportional result (Mitchell 1999). The distortions of the first-past-the-post system used for Westminster elections favoured the UUP, until the more even division of the unionist vote in 2001 reduced this anomaly. The only seriously disproportional contests held under STV are European elections in which the low district magnitude – only three candidates are elected – is unhelpful in a polity in which four parties have dominated, obtaining over 90 per cent of the vote in these ballots. The consequence is that there is one big loser; in 2004, the SDLP's 15.9 per cent of first-preference votes were wasted, as the party failed to get its candidate elected. Previously, the major loser had been Sinn Fein.

The early optimism that the GFA would wither the sectarian voting divide was not confirmed by the 2003 Assembly election (although this does not eradicate the possibility of electoral thawing), which saw an increase in in-house transfers in the unionist and nationalist blocs. The 1998 contest produced a 5 per cent increase in unionist transfers to the SDLP, an increase matched by SDLP transfers to pro-GFA UUP candidates (Kelly and Doyle 2000). In the rare cases where no Alliance candidate was available, slightly over one-third of final UUP transfers went across the divide to the SDLP. However, the hardening of the UUP position on the GFA in the 2003 contest, following the collapse of political institutions in 2002, meant that cross-community transfers on a deal whose honeymoon period had long expired were more difficult to achieve in the second set of Assembly elections. The lack of cross-community vote transfers was also evident in the 2004 European election, when 87.1 per cent of the DUP's 38,441 surplus votes were transferred to the UUP, with only 1.2 per cent transferred to the SDLP.

Although STV has not proved an incentive to cross-community voting, it may have encouraged moderation by political parties, in order to achieve a higher number of lower-preference vote transfers within their ethnic bloc. The growing moderation of Sinn Fein has meant that SDLP voters are prepared to transfer to their nationalist rival in ever increasing numbers, rather than help Alliance. The dual party system provided incentives for Sinn Fein to moderate its agenda. Whilst much of Sinn Fein's success lies in mobilizing young voters and previous non-voters, the party also attracts an

increasing number of lower-preference votes from SDLP supporters, and now captures many first-preference votes of previous SDLP voters, feats achieved since the party distanced
itself from political violence. Sinn Fein could not remain an
anti-system party forever, condemned to permanent minority-
of-a-minority status.

There are important alternative explanations of why the
PIRA abandoned violence, including lack of ideology
(McIntyre; 1995), the end of the Cold War and subsequent
changes in British policy (M. Cox, 1998; M.Cox et al. 2001),
the squeeze from the British military (Taylor 1997; O'Brien
2000; Moloney 2002), and the reduction in importance of
national sovereignty (McCall 1999). None of these claims is
invalid, but the possibility of electoral reward for Sinn Fein is
perhaps the most convincing, offering a more attractive late
career flourish for its leaders than the permanent isolation and
insecurity of continued militarism. In a STV system in which
votes were unlikely to stray outside the nationalist bloc, there
were extra incentives for moderation. Sinn Fein stole many of
the SDLP's political clothes whilst attempting to maintain
'green' credentials. Political U-turns since the 1990s, usually
initially denied to the grass roots, have included the disavowal
of violence, entry to Stormont, removal of the demand for
British withdrawal from Northern Ireland within a specified
time frame, tacit acceptance of the principle of consent for
constitutional change to Northern Ireland, support for power
sharing, acceptance of the European Union, and indication of
a willingness to eventually support the Police Service of
Northern Ireland. Such spectacular changes have not harmed
the electoral performance of the party.

For the SDLP, the problems appear terminal, despite the
party's more consistent line on the range of issues listed
above. Despite its overall policy consistency, the party has
oscillated between nationalist approaches stressing the need
for a substantial Irish dimension to any deal and policies
designed primarily to attain power sharing for nationalists in
Northern Ireland. The party became greener in terms of
members after the collapse of the Sunningdale Agreement in
1974 (Evans, Tonge and Murray 2000). Under the leadership

of John Hume from 1979 until the end of the century, the party drew the Dublin government into the political process of Northern Ireland, the climax of this strategy being the establishment of the New Ireland Forum in 1983, bringing together constitutional nationalists throughout Ireland and the signing of the Anglo-Irish Agreement in 1985. The SDLP's concerns were not merely altruistic; the party feared eclipse by Sinn Fein. The willingness of Hume to engage in a pannationalist project with Adams from 1988 onwards, beginning with a dialogue to create ground rules for peace and culminating in the 1998 Good Friday Agreement, represented a personal and political triumph. Hume's ideas of an 'agreed Ireland' dominated the GFA.

The impressive victories for the DUP in 2003 and 2004 confirmed a reordering of unionist electoral politics, as the party replaced the UUP as the primary recipient of Protestant votes. Within the unionist bloc, the UUP had held its position as the 'natural' repository of unionist votes throughout the conflict, notwithstanding Paisley's large personal vote in European contests from 1979 until 1999. The 2003 Assembly election success was followed by an overwhelming triumph for the DUP in the 2004 European elections, confirming a strong party vote, aside from the 'Paisley factor', when the party fielded a new candidate. The rise of the DUP has confounded (understandable) pre-GFA orthodoxy that 'the party most threatened by long-term peace is the DUP. In conditions of peace, and if proportional representation applies in all elections, there is no compelling reason why the DUP electoral bloc should hold together' (McGarry and O'Leary 1995: 405–6).

The DUP's electoral advance after the GFA was startling. From the 1997 to 2001 Westminster elections, the DUP gained almost 75,000 votes. By 2001, the number of Protestants opposing the GFA outweighed supporters (Northern Ireland Life and Times Survey 2001). In October 2002, as the institutions were suspended, a BBC Northern Ireland *Hearts and Minds* poll reported that only 33 per cent of Protestants still backed the deal. The UUP's entry into government with Sinn Fein after the GFA proved catastrophic for party fortunes. At the 2005 Westminster election, the UUP was reduced to fourth place in representational terms, holding only one seat, whilst the DUP emerged with nine. David Trimble lost the Upper Bann constituency and resigned the party leadership.

Despite intra-unionist rivalry, contests held under STV are marked by in-house transfers. In overtaking the UUP in the 2003 Assembly election, the DUP was assisted by the willingness of pro-Agreement unionists to keep their votes 'in bloc', even if this meant supporting anti-Agreement unionists. The solidarity of DUP voters was impressive, almost four-fifths transferring to other DUP candidates, but nearly half recorded lower-preference votes for pro-GFA UUP candidates in the 1998 and 2003 Assembly elections. Even members of the UUC, the ruling body of the UUP, are reasonably content to transfer lower-preference votes to the DUP, although the possibility is much stronger among those members who opposed the GFA in 1998, a group who were joined in their opposition to the deal by growing numbers within the UUP (see Table 8.2).

The DUP's critique of the GFA was based on constitutional and moral grounds. The party outlined its principles, designed to underpin any re-negotiated agreement, in *Towards a New*

Table 8.2 Potential lower-preference vote transfers to other unionist parties among Ulster Unionist Council members

Mean (s.d)	How voted in 1998 GFA referendum		
	Yes	No	N
DUP	2.65	1.52	264
	(1.14)	(0.95)	
UKUP	2.72	1.46	251
	(1.09)	(0.82)	
PUP	2.85	3.37	226
	(1.03)	(0.86)	

1 = very likely   4 = no possibility   N = 299
UKUP = anti-GFA United Kingdom Unionist Party
PUP = pro-GFA Progressive Unionist Party.

Source: Author's survey, 2000–1: a postal survey of all 858 UUC members was conducted, eliciting 299 replies. More detailed findings are reported in Tonge and Evans 2001.

Agreement (2003), restating the critique evident in the party's 2001 and 2005 election manifestos, *Leadership to Put Things Right* (DUP 2001–2005). Both criticized the presence of 'terrorists' in government, the dilution of British culture, the all-island dimension to the deal, and the morally unacceptable aspects of prisoner releases and policing changes. The party insisted that IRA decommissioning be time-tabled, verifiable and transparent (DUP 2005: 10). The DUP oscillated between outright rejection of the GFA and 'renegotiation' of the deal, to ward off charges of negativity. Untainted by involvement in production of the Agreement, having quit multi-party negotiations in July 1997, the DUP highlighted its unsavoury aspects, describing it as a 'failed agreement', but kept its options open by not rejecting power sharing with Sinn Fein *per se*. The DUP's deputy leader, Peter Robinson, stressed that unionist–republican co-operation on Belfast City Council 'shows that if you have a different structure, it [power-sharing] can work' (BBC Northern Ireland, *Heart and Minds*, 25 September 2003). DUP electoral success was accompanied by 'a more subtle and less hysterical critique' of the GFA (Patterson 2002). With one-third of its supporters claiming to have supported the GFA in the 1998 referendum and half wishing the deal to work, the DUP avoided the charge of outright rejectionism (Irwin 2002). In defence of the Agreement, the UUP correctly highlighted how it constructed a 'Unionist veto' on Assembly decisions and North–South expansion.

The DUP struck a chord in opposing aspects of the GFA, such as prisoner releases and the changes to policing arising from the Patten Commission established by the Agreement. Both these measures were opposed by a majority of pro-GFA UUP members (Tonge and Evans 2002). The moral basis of opposition to the deal was not offset sufficiently by maintenance of the constitutional *status quo* for a large number of unionists. There were fewer incentives to moderation for the DUP than there were for Sinn Fein within the nationalist bloc. Whereas Sinn Fein's electoral conquests were seen as a reward for the development of a new morality, DUP opposition to unsavoury aspects of the GFA was seen as occupation of the moral high ground. The unionist electorate registered majority support (just) for the GFA in 1998, but then opposed unfavourable or supposedly immoral aspects of that deal by supporting the DUP. By 2003, with the DUP having overtaken the UUP, Paisley's party could promise a new deal with the impurities of the GFA removed and confirm its position as the stouter defender of the interests of the unionist bloc. There was of course no prospect of reversing several of the GFA measures, including those on prisoners or policing, but the DUP could blame the UUP for having permitted such developments, The DUP prospered against such expectations by highlighting supposedly damaging effects of the GFA upon the unionist community. The party positioned itself as the stouter defender of the Protestant-British-unionist ethnic bloc, but asserted the desirability of fully inclusive devolved power-sharing government, in a revised agreement that would operate within the framework of the GFA, whatever the party's protestations to the contrary.

The new political dispensation posed questions for both the ethnic blocs in Northern Ireland. As the possibility of a DUP–Sinn Fein deal arose, the old certainties of the previous political order were likely to be dismantled, with former enemies sharing power in a Northern Ireland government. The ethnic bloc system would remain, with its links between nationality, religion and voting, but the old political fault line of support for Irish unity versus defence of the Union could diminish in salience. Given this, normal politics might begin to emerge, based upon rivalries in policy areas such as health and education. The first phase of the Northern Ireland Assembly, from 1999 to 2002, was marked by co-operative committee relationships across the divide, indicative of the form of politics that could develop. However, continuing hostility to the GFA within the DUP and growing disillusionment within the UUP ensured that the governing executive often malfunctioned, even if there were few substantial disagreements on items on which the Assembly actually held legislative power (Wilford 2001; Tonge 2005). The most contentious item was the future of selective education, with unionists (PUP excepted) opposed to the removal of the 11+ transfer test.

In addition to differences across the political divide, there remain differences of emphasis within the unionist and nationalist blocs. The UUP is more integrationist than the DUP. A majority of its members believe that the best solution to the constitutional question is full integration of Northern Ireland into the United Kingdom, a position particularly popular among opponents of the GFA within the party (Tonge and Evans 2002). From 1979 until 1995, integration was the basis of party policy, the UUP leader James Molyneaux having 'recognized the fragility of belief in Stormont as a bulwark against a united Ireland' (Hume 1996: 12). Despite the arrival of a pro-devolution leader in Trimble in 1995, and notwithstanding the restructuring of the United Kingdom by the Labour government since 1997, there is still an integrationist constituency within unionism's largest party. This constituency is less keen, however, upon the logic of integration, by which 'mainland' political parties would contest elections in Northern Ireland. Integrationist UUP members occupy different political terrain from the DUP, which has long been a devolutionist party.

Is There Still Room for Two Nationalist Parties?

The rapid overhaul of the SDLP by Sinn Fein raises the question of whether a dual party bloc system will be maintained, as nationalist voters side increasingly with one party. A similarly valid question has been raised in respect of the unionist bloc, but it is less apparent that the post-GFA problems confronting the UUP could be terminal. Nationalist convergence during the peace process had a long gestation. Although it is often traced to the Hume–Adams dialogue of 1988, it is evident that Gerry Adams, as president of Sinn Fein from 1983 onwards, had formulated a strategy to forge a pan-nationalist alliance, centred upon a concept of Irish self-determination that might not necessarily result in physical British withdrawal from Northern Ireland. This notion of an agreed Ireland has been adopted as Sinn Fein policy, although the language of reunification remains more strident than that offered by the SDLP.

For the SDLP, the problem lies in articulating a nationalist alternative to Sinn Fein, now that the traditional marker between the two parties, Sinn Fein's support for violence, has disappeared. The SDLP needs to develop an appealing nationalism whilst competing against a vibrant, all-island rival, Sinn Fein offering populist republican and left-leaning rhetoric whilst holding genuine prospects of holding office North and South. The SDLP's commitment to nationalism appears tepid by comparison. Among party members, 88 per cent agree that the party is nationalist. Only 7.9 per cent believe that the optimum solution is for Northern Ireland to remain in the United Kingdom in the long term (Tonge 2005: 110), a low figure which renders the SDLP membership greener than the Catholic population in its entirety. However, only 49.5 per cent of SDLP members view a united Ireland as the optimum constitutional solution, and joint British–Irish sovereignty is backed by only 34.5 per cent, whereas the 'GFA/power-sharing' enjoys support from 80.5 per cent of the membership (ibid.). Among members of what was for three decades Northern Ireland's larger nationalist party, there is greater acceptance of a GFA-type settlement, predominantly internal and partitionist, than there is of an end to partition, even though Northern Ireland's long-term presence in the United Kingdom (a likely consequence of the GFA) is not desired by members.

The nationalist electorate can vote for a party which supports the framework of the GFA whilst continuing to pursue Irish unity, but this party is more likely to be Sinn Fein. The SDLP offers a post-nationalist agenda and has long supported the concept of Northern Ireland as part of a Europe of the Regions, but the impetus from the GFA is more bi-national, with embryonic all-island economic structures, rather than post-national. The other difficulty for the SDLP lies in convincing the electorate that it is not merely a party with an important past, in terms of developing the peace process and offering the framework within which a power-sharing deal was constructed. Sinn Fein's dominance of working-class votes and ability to attract younger voters are two assets not available to the SDLP, a party with an ageing membership profile, the average age of members being 57. Even among these members, there is a feeling that their party's work may be complete, 82 per cent concurring that the party has achieved the bulk of its objectives through the GFA, and substantial majorities believing that equality, power sharing and unity are all more likely as a consequence of the deal.

Given the sanguine view of the GFA held by SDLP members (see table 8.3), the obvious question is how the party can build on its success. In comparison to Sinn Fein, the SDLP looks a narrow, sectional northern nationalist party, adding to the party's problems of blurred future agendas, ageing membership and loss of electoral superiority. The early post-GFA aspirations held by some within the party, of sizeable transfers from the pro-GFA wing of the UUP, have not materialized. The

Table 8.3 Attitudes to the Good Friday Agreement among SDLP members

	Strongly agree	Agree	Neither agree/ nor disagree	Disagree	Strongly disagree
The SDLP has achieved the bulk of its objectives through the GFA	25	57	9	6	1
The GFA makes a united Ireland more attainable	14	55	22	7	1
The GFA will give Irish nationalism equal status to unionism	15	53	18	11	2
The GFA will lead to real power sharing in the Belfast Assembly	10	58	20	7	2

N = 528.

Source: Author's survey, 2000. A full questionnaire survey of SDLP members was conducted under Economic and Social Research Council (ESRC) project R000222668, with findings accessible at the ESRC data archive, SN 4406.

11 per cent fall in its European election vote from 1999 to 2004 illuminated how the party has suffered since the retirement of John Hume. Although the party emerged from the 2005 Westminster election with three seats, the swing to Sinn Fein had merely slowed (to 3 per cent), amid controversy over continuing IRA activity, rather than been reversed. The steady growth in the Catholic population has kept the party's vote share high and inflated the overall nationalist bloc vote, but the SDLP's vote relative to Sinn Fein's has declined. One option might be to counter Sinn Fein's structural advantage as an all-Ireland party by entering into a pact with Fianna Fail in the Irish Republic, in which the SDLP operates as a 'Fianna Fail North', but such a plan might have few takers in either party.

Is There Room for a Centre Party amid Movement to a Single Party Bloc System?

Given the party's long-standing advocacy of devolved power sharing, it was natural that Alliance endorsed the GFA. An overwhelming majority (94.7 per cent) of its members voted in favour of the GFA, with 4.4 per cent not voting and only 0.9 per cent opposing. Moreover, 90 per cent still supported the deal in 2001, as confidence began to evaporate among Protestants (Evans and Tonge 2003). None the less, the existing centre party had much to fear from a settlement which moderated extremes whilst consolidating divisions between unionists and nationalists. In the short term, the consociational basis of the GFA institutionalized the unionist–nationalist fault line and rejected implicitly Alliance's view that the Northern Ireland polity should be based upon 'one community'.

For Alliance, politics based upon two communities ignores the sizeable chunk of the population (35 per cent according to the 2002 Northern Ireland Life and Times Survey) which does not view itself as unionist or nationalist. An agreement built upon a fault line was merely a 'band-aid' agreement, which would not address the underlying basis of conflict (Farry and Neeson 1999). Alliance offers a vision of integrative power sharing in Northern Ireland, emphasizing inter-communal reconciliation and attached to accountable North–South structures.

Instead of developing integration on the basis of Northern Irishness, the GFA spoke of the equal legitimacy of both traditions, rather than attempting their fusion into a single entity. In the Assembly terms, this theoretical approach was reflected by a series of measures: allocations of ministerial portfolios to ensure that 'both' communities were represented; the requirement for Assembly members to designate themselves as 'unionist', 'Nationalist', or 'Other', leading to, in 2001, the farce of three Alliance members re-designating themselves as unionist to ensure the re-election of David Trimble as First Minister, as his 'unionist-Unionist' backers diminished; weighted majority voting, or parallel consent, to effect legislation. Beyond the Assembly, the two traditions approach was evident in, for example, policing, with quota (50/50 Catholic/non-Catholic) recruitment introduced, to the chagrin of Alliance.

The party views itself as a Northern Irish party in promoting the replacement of the unionist–nationalist dichotomy with a liberal, pluralist, non-ethnic form of politics. Yet, even within the party, identities and views are linked to religious affiliation. There are clear differences in national identity according to religious affiliation. Only 11 per cent of Protestant members of Alliance view themselves as Irish, compared to 33 per cent of Catholics, whilst only 10 per cent of Catholic members perceive themselves as British, compared to 34 per cent of Protestants (Evans and Tonge 2003). Only half of the party adopts a hybrid British-Irish or Northern Irish label. Protestant members of the party were more hostile to conflict resolution measures of prisoner releases and policing changes.

The difficulty for Alliance was that it opposed the institutionalization of division, yet was insufficiently cognizant of the extent to which *formal* entrenchment of division was accompanied by *actual* reduction of the gap between the two blocs. By offering places in devolved government, Sinn Fein moved from 'no return to Stormont' to defending the Agreement which gave the party places in government. Having claimed to oppose the GFA, the DUP, having emerged as the largest party at the 2003 Assembly elections, found the prospect of a DUP First Minister difficult to resist and attempted to revive devolved power sharing, albeit after transparent decommissioning of IRA weapons. The emergence of Sinn Fein and the DUP may have been viewed as the triumph of the extremists, but was hardly a victory for extremism.

The increase in support for the DUP and Sinn Fein has further marginalized the centre ground, wiping out the other centre grouping, the Northern Ireland Women's Coalition in the 2003 Assembly elections. Alliance's decline in first-preference votes preceded the Agreement, and the party survives, ironically, on the unwillingness of voters to transfer across the sectarian divide with their lower-preference transfers. Cross-community voting increased where an Alliance Party candidate was not present, although such voting occured almost exclusively between the UUP and the SDLP, and it is far from certain that it would become habit-forming in the permanent absence of Alliance. At the 2003 Assembly elections, Alliance retained its six seats, its candidates elected on average at the tenth count, with two of its successes occurring despite the party being seventh after first-preference votes were counted. In four constituencies, successful Alliance candidates were below rivals who were not eventually elected (two SDLP, one Sinn Fein and one UUP).

Conclusion

The triumph of the DUP and Sinn Fein in recent elections has heralded a possible move from Northern Ireland as a dual party bloc system towards a single party per bloc entity. The three moderate pro-GFA parties – the UUP, the SDLP and Alliance – all struggled in the aftermath of the deal, as the electorate shifted to the stouter defenders of their ethnic blocs, or abandoned Alliance by aligning themselves with a bloc. Sinn Fein was rewarded for its moderation and adaptation of some SDLP ideas by ever increasing transfers from its nationalist rival, under a STV system which has worked effectively in encouraging the dilution of bloc militancy, whilst not yet facilitating cross-community voting. Sinn Fein's new constitution-alism, strong campaigning and historic association with a tough defence of nationalist interests has led to mass support from young voters and previous non-voters, particularly among the working class.

The DUP captured the majority of unionist votes by promis-ing to remove the ambiguities of the GFA as negotiated by the UUP. This was a sensible campaigning strategy, given the fragility of Protestant support for the deal, only three in ten claiming to remain consistent 'yes' voters from 1998 to 2003 (Hayes and McAllister 2004: 13). Despite this Protestant hos-tility and DUP rhetoric, it was evident that many aspects of the GFA would remain in a renegotiated deal. Given the extent of policy convergence within blocs, there is no particular reason why two parties need represent each ethnic bloc, and the move towards single party blocs will remove destabilizing intra-bloc rivalries. Increasing pan-nationalism and pan-unionism, each centred upon commitments to devolved power sharing within the context of commitment to long-standing constitutional goals, is the norm, yet the internecine battles within national-ism and unionism have increased. There remain two main ten-sions within unionism. One lies between its civic and cultural forms, the former based upon a commitment to a full acknowl-edgement and embracing of the traditions of the other com-munity (Porter 1996). The other lies in the extent of commitment to devolution among the UUP, which, even when it operated as the largest party in Northern Ireland, contained a sizeable section of members content with direct rule from Westminster. This lack of commitment to devolved power sharing, allied with opposition among many within the party to the terms of the GFA, undermined the party leadership. One reform which might have assisted central control of the party would perhaps have been the introduction of party list STV systems to diminish local autonomy in candidate selection and construct a united representative team. Given the chaotic structure of the UUP, however, such a reform might not have worked.

Within nationalism, the belief of the majority of SDLP members that the party has achieved its objectives highlights its dilemma. Having helped bring Sinn Fein into the political mainstream and secured a political deal supposedly based upon its core idea of an agreed Ireland, the seeming triumph of the SDLP has been followed by a bleak future. The structural advantage of Sinn Fein in being an all-island party, and the political benefits accruing to its role as stout defender of the nationalist 'equality agenda' for constitutional nationalism, are useful assets, set against an ageing rival, confined to a middle-class, six-county base.

The GFA offered inducements to moderation to the so-called extremes, but the political future it envisaged was not based upon a 'one community' approach supported by the Alliance Party. The two communities approach undermines the value of Alliance representation in the Northern Ireland Assembly. The political centre relies upon the keenness of bloc voters to avoid crossing to the rival bloc, instead transferring 'half-way' to Alliance, scarcely the integrative future envisaged by Northern Ireland's only significant 'non-sectarian' party.

9 Auditing the Peace and Political Processes

The 1998 Good Friday Agreement contained elements of conflict management and conflict resolution. The management section was one in which republican constitutional ambitions were put in abeyance pending demographic change, in a bid to neuter violence. Republicans were required not to abandon their objective of dissolving Northern Ireland into a unitary state, but merely to put the project on hold and await demographic and internal change. Conflict resolution elements were those which addressed the main reasons why republicans had resorted to violence. These sections dealt with the remnants of 'second-class citizenry' and inequality with which many Catholics had associated the Northern Ireland polity. Sinn Fein indicated that the Agreement contained the potential to remove the causes of conflict. This was indeed true if one accepted that nationalists had reverted to an entirely civil rights agenda rather than constitutional claims.

Despite the potential of the GFA to bring closure to the conflict, it remained a deal accompanied by a series of wrangles over implementation of the process, arguments set against a backdrop of continuing claims of paramilitary activity. If, as the clichéd response of the two governments suggested, the deal was the 'only show in town', this was perhaps more a comment on the paucity of consensual alternatives than a rousing endorsement of what was on offer. Peace was armed and imperfect, and inched forward against a backdrop of dysfunctional inter-community relations. Moreover, the 'peace process' was seemingly interminable, having lasted longer, even allowing an indeterminate starting date, than the two world wars of the twentieth century by the mid-2000s. It appeared set to reach a conclusion in December 2004, with the DUP prepared to enter government alongside Sinn Fein, the two historic 'enemies' providing the First and Deputy First Ministers. The pact collapsed over Paisley's demands that the IRA wear 'sackcloth and ashes' and allow the decommissioning of its weapons to be photographed. The IRA's formal announcement, in July 2005, of the abandonment of its armed struggle, revived prospects of a deal. The main problems of the process, decommissioning, residual paramilitarism, policing and lack of commitment to inclusive devolved power sharing, all appeared surmountable, but the ambiguities of the GFA ensured that early implementation of solutions was not an option.

Decommissioning

Amid the constructive ambiguities of the Agreement, it was evident from the outset that some items would prove likely stumbling-blocks. The resignation of the then UUP MP Jeffrey Donaldson from his party's negotiating team on the day the GFA was signed, on the issue of the 'fudging' of decommissioning requirements, indicated the most likely potential problem.

Contrary to what has become popular myth, there is no requirement for paramilitary decommissioning within the GFA, an obfuscation which explains Donaldson's disquiet in April 1998. The deal merely required parties to exert maximum possible influence upon paramilitaries to decommission their weapons, as indicated below:

> All participants accordingly reaffirm their commitment to the total disarmament of all paramilitary organisations. They also confirm their intention to continue to work constructively and in good faith with the Independent Commission [on Decommissioning] and to use any influence they may have to achieve the decommissioning of all paramilitary arms within two years following endorsement in referendums North and

South of the agreement and in the context of the implementation of the overall settlement.

(HM Government 1998: 20)

It was left unstated what would happen if the efforts of parties were unpersuasive, notwithstanding the belief of 60 per cent of Northern Ireland's population that Sinn Fein is 'not separate from the IRA' (*Irish Times*, 5 March 2005: 6, 'SF loses credibility, but voters still want deal done'). Moreover, even when decommissioning commenced, the process would be overseen by an International Independent Commission on Decommissioning (IICD), rather than through any stipulations contained in the GFA, a deal which permitted the process of removing arms to be conducted in near-secrecy.

As the head of the IICD stated in respect of decommissioning, 'however symbolic the issue may be in the minds of some, it continues to be the principal source of concern for many in both north and south' (de Chastelain 2004: 178). Decommissioning would provide conclusive evidence that the IRA has 'gone away', and that the war is over. Yet, this key aspect of the peace deal was left uncertain amid the carefully chosen language which yielded the GFA but provided a difficult aftermath. Anxious to persuade the UUP to accept the deal, Tony Blair, hours before its signing, wrote to the UUP leader, David Trimble, to insist that, for the British Prime Minister, paramilitary decommissioning of weapons *was* a requirement. Hitherto, Blair, unencumbered by difficult parliamentary arithmetic, unlike his predecessor, John Major, had been far more concerned with ensuring a permanent end to IRA violence than with dealing with the symbolic issue of decommissioning. Equally anxious to conclude the deal, Trimble placed faith in the idea that letters from a British Prime Minister could supersede the agreed terms of an internationally recognized and painstakingly negotiated agreement. Trimble and Blair recognized that a deal requiring explicit, 'up-front' decommissioning would have created problems for republicans. The IRA had split, albeit with most members remaining loyal to the Provisionals, during the previous year, with the formation of the Real IRA. The GFA still had to be sold by the republican leadership to its base, which, whilst prepared to tolerate entry to Stormont, might not acquiesce in rapidly dismantling the IRA.

Given the lack of compulsion in the GFA, it was hardly surprising that the IRA couched its decommissioning in terms of voluntary acts of goodwill by the organization, rather than as a product of unionist or British demands. From the outset, the IRA had indicated a willingness to disarm as a 'natural development of the peace process' (*Financial Times*, 17 June 1998). Whilst many within the movement hoped that the weaponry would, in the words of one Sinn Fein member of Dail Eireann, Caoimhghin O'Caolain, 'rust in peace', the republican leadership was cognizant of the 'moral', if not written, agenda associated with the GFA, recognizing that much pressure would be placed upon the IRA to disarm. Protracted decommissioning in stages suited Sinn Fein as a means of levering concessions and garnering support from the nationalist electorate as the party that could remove the IRA and deliver a lasting peace. According to the original timetable envisaged by the British and Irish governments, in their *The Way Forward* proposals issued in summer 1999, decommissioning was to be completed by May 2000, in accordance with the deadline envisaged in the GFA. Despite Blair's insistence that decommissioning was an obligation, it was evident that, until devolved power sharing was embedded, major destruction of weaponry was unlikely. Moreover, there was scant movement on decommissioning on the loyalist side, a token gesture from the LVF, although the political associates of the loyalist groups did not, of course, possess the sizeable mandate which permitted Sinn Fein its place in government.

The pressure upon the IRA to begin disarming began in earnest after the UUC voted narrowly (58 per cent to 42 per cent) to 'jump first' and enter government alongside Sinn Fein in November 1999. The UUP's leap was conditional upon a rapid commencement of IRA decommissioning. As the demand was unrealized by February 2000, the UUP effectively collapsed the executive and the assembly, only for the institutions to be restored three months later as the IRA began initiating a process of decommissioning. What followed over the next few years was a tactical game, in which the IRA would engage in decommissioning of weapons at strategic intervals to 'save the peace process', firstly in October 2001, secondly in April 2002 and thirdly, in the run-up to Assembly elections, in October 2003. The third act of decommissioning was acknowledged as substantial by the head of the IICD, but there remained a view among sceptical unionists that decommissioning was a 'smoke and mirrors' act by the IRA. As further indication of movement from conflict, the IRA apologized for the deaths and injuries caused to 'non-combatants'.

Standing Down 'the Army'?

As Aughey (2005: 151) notes, the constructive ambiguity of the GFA allowed republicans to be 'bound into an institutional framework that bore no relationship to their historical demands'. The impact of the apparent compromise of compromises within republicanism was muted by several factors: war-weariness, recognition of the non-imminence of victory, steady movement of Catholics into the middle class, and faith in the signals from the leadership. These signals initially included the possibility that republicans could revert to violence if the British government, or unionists, failed to deliver the GFA. The republican leadership promoted the idea of the 'Tactical Use of Armed Struggle' at the time of the IRA cease-fire in 1994, indicating that the option of a return to 'armed struggle' remained. The temporary renewal of the IRA's campaign in 1996, with large bombings in London and Manchester, reassured the republican base, did not harm Sinn Fein's electoral support, and reminded the British government that the IRA remained a potent force. In terms of its limited ambitions, the 1996–7 IRA campaign was successful in emphasizing the need for the inclusion of Sinn Fein in negotiations. Given Labour's election success in 1997, it was evident that Sinn Fein/IRA was kicking at an open door in this respect.

Sinn Fein's support for the GFA, allied to the unacceptability of support for terrorism post 9/11 (of greater importance among the republican support base in America than domestically), required different things of the IRA than in the run-up to the 1998 deal. With Sinn Fein readily incorporated into the negotiations, the IRA's role, given its unwillingness to fight against British rule in Northern Ireland, became less obvious. A carefully managed process of decommissioning of weapons could be used to extract further concessions from the British government. The IRA could act as a guarantor that the power-sharing deal remained intact, amid suspicion over the extent of unionist commitment to dividing political spoils with nationalists. Equally, however, continued activity remained likely to undermine the GFA.

Ultimately, the PIRA was obliged to disappear, existing only as a 'veterans' association'. At the beginning of the 2005 election campaign, the Sinn Fein President, Gerry Adams, urged the PIRA to embrace fully peaceful and 'democratic' methods, as political alternatives were now available. The timing of the Adams missive was designed to maximize electoral benefit, but it nonetheless represented the logical conclusion of his project of turning republicanism into an unarmed movement in which pragmatism rather than fixed ideology was paramount. Unsurprisingly, the PIRA responded to Adams's request in the affirmative. Whilst protesting the legitimacy of its armed struggle, the PIRA and Sinn Fein had found it impossible to simultaneously ride revolutionary and constitutional horses, opting for the latter. Despite the PIRA climbdown, there remained widespread scepticism over the likelihood of disarming the IRA, two-thirds of Protestants believing that it would never happen and nearly half (45 per cent) of Catholics doubting the likelihood of such a development under the GFA (*Belfast Telegraph*, 11 March 2005).

Prior to its standing down, the PIRA had come under increased pressure following the allegation of the Chief Constable of the Police Service of Northern Ireland (PSNI), Hugh Order, backed by the British and Irish governments, that the Provisionals carried out the Northern Bank robbery in Belfast in December 2004, netting over £26 million. Moreover, the Minister for Justice in the Irish Republic, Michael McDowell, relying upon intelligence gleaned mainly through bugging operations, claimed that the raid had been authorized by Sinn Fein's leadership, whose membership over-lapped with that of the IRA's Army Council, at a time when negotiations with the British government over the supposed 'deal of deals' of entering government with the DUP was taking place. The Independent Monitoring Commission, dismissed by Sinn Fein as anything but independent, given the presence of, among others, political opponents and former anti-terrorist police leaders, reiterated the allegations.

Whilst the claims of the PSNI and by members of the anti-republican Progressive Democrats in the coalition government of the Irish Republic could be seen off by the IRA, pressure on the republican movement increased markedly in January 2005, when several of its members murdered Robert McCartney, a Sinn Fein voter from Short Strand in Belfast. The popular outcry against the murder, led by the dead man's sisters, from within an area where the IRA had enjoyed much support, undermined the last vestiges of the IRA's self-appointed role as 'community defender'. Ironically, the Catholic enclave of Short Strand, isolated amid loyalist heartlands, represented one of the few areas where the IRA's claim to this function was perhaps more credible than similar assertions elsewhere. Criticism from the McCartneys that their brother's killers were 'criminal gangs who are still using the cloak of romanticism around the IRA to murder people' could not easily be ignored by a movement which had always elicited sympathy in such locations (*Times*, 16 March 2005: 1, 'McCartney sisters take battle to IRA in America'). In response, the IRA made a supposed 'offer' (mainly for propaganda, knowing that it would be rejected) to shoot McCartney's killers, and expelled them from the organization. Whilst desisting from urging direct co-operation with the PSNI, Gerry Adams urged republicans to come forward with information about the killing.

Yet even this 'crisis' in the peace process appeared more imaginary than real. Recent controversies have moved Gerry Adams closer to the project he conceived way back in the 1980s: namely, the removal of the IRA. Adams had already moved the IRA in remarkable directions: recognizing the Irish state, declaring a cease-fire, and entering a Northern Ireland Assembly that the IRA had itself smashed during the 1970s.

His attempted end-game – Sinn Fein in coalition government north and south of the border – would remove the IRA as surplus to requirements. By March 2005, even a majority of Sinn Fein supporters (56 per cent) believed that Sinn Fein should 'split from the IRA if the party cannot convince the IRA to end all its activities' (*Irish Times*, 5 March 2005: 1, 'Two-thirds of voters believe Sinn Fein must split from IRA').

Sinn Fein moved slowly towards support for the PSNI, the final taboo for those who fought the war against British 'Crown forces'. At the 2005 *ard fheis*, an event dominated by the furore over the McCartney killing and the surprise conference attendance by the sisters, Gerry Kelly prepared the ground for policing change by warning republicans of the responsibilities that would come with their new role. Motions adhering to traditional republican arguments, in which Sinn Fein *cumann* in Tyrone insisted that the party should never back a six-county police force, were heavily defeated, paving the way for another major shift in party policy.

By 2005, the PSNI comprised 13 per cent Catholics, an improvement on the 8 per cent at the time of the replacement of the RUC, but still a long way from a religious balance reflecting Northern Ireland's population. The government none the less insisted that the PSNI was on target for 30 per cent Catholic representation by 2011, acknowledging that 440 Protestants of acceptable quality had been denied entry to the force in 2004 due to the quota system (Ian Pearson, *Hansard*, HoC, 26 March 2005 (6130)). The extent of change in policing was still seen as insufficient by a sizeable number of Catholics, 42 per cent of whom declared that policing reform had 'not gone far enough', whereas 58 per cent of Protestants thought it had 'gone too far' (Kennedy and Farrington 2005: 105). Twenty-two per cent of Catholics declared that they had 'no confidence' in the police (*Belfast Telegraph*, 11 March 2005: 6, 'What Ulster Thinks'). Sinn Fein's gradualism on the development of support for the new policing arrangements thus reflected continuing reservations within its base.

The display of anger within the hitherto pro-IRA area of Short Strand in Belfast at the killing of McCartney thus assisted Adams's project, whilst the bank robbery reminded the British and Irish governments of the IRA's capability. Removal of the IRA at the behest of Paisley would have prompted disquiet among republicans. The IRA's leaving the stage through community protest was far more acceptable to the ever increasing numbers of Sinn Fein voters. Adams had to endure a bout of ostracism from George Bush, calls from the US envoy to Northern Ireland, Mitchell Reiss, for the IRA to 'go out of business', and comparisons with Yasser Arafat as a leader unable to deliver hard-liners (*The Times*, 10 March 2005: 25, 'Bush's Envoy Calls on the IRA to "Go out of Business"'). These demands and labels were of little account in electoral terms. Moreover, the similar call for IRA disbandment by long-term sympathizer Congressman Peter King was probably of value to Adams within his American base of supporters. United States funding for Sinn Fein, which fell sharply to a record low, albeit temporarily, in the immediate aftermath of 9/11, was secure, although of less value to the party in Northern Ireland, given a tightening of legislation for political parties, concerning money raised overseas. The real concern for Adams was Sinn Fein's electoral support, which surprisingly rose in a by-election in the Irish Republic even amid the McCartney furore. Significantly, although the DUP leadership made ritualistic calls for the Sinn Fein leadership to be arrested, it did not rule out a deal with Sinn Fein in the longer term.

The bigger concern for Adams was not a people protest which moved his party closer to where he wanted it to be. Instead, it remained that very small coterie of republicans opposed to the IRA's disappearance whilst Northern Ireland continues to exist. After all, an IRA accepting of Northern Ireland and a British claim to sovereignty cannot lay claim to the name. An Adams-led decommissioning of the PIRA was not quite tantamount to the removal of all the guns, or other IRAs, from Irish politics. Even after the 1997 split, there remained those within the Provisionals, including its main financier in South Armagh, who were lukewarm towards the inevitable outworking of the peace and political processes.

The main contribution of the protests by the McCartney

sisters may have been to nudge republicans towards co-operation with the police. The sisters also exposed the criminality of those who use the IRA label to bully communities, despite not having fired a shot in anger against British rule in Northern Ireland since 1997. The residual paramilitarism, used as a form of community control rather than the action of an army at war, had provoked increasing disquiet, although the McCartney case was the first to arouse widespread protest. Other killings, such as that of Andrew Kearney in 1998 after a row in a pub with an IRA leader, had led to growing disillusionment with 'cease-fire soldiers'. Long term, however, the lessons for those campaigning against paramilitary violence, most notably from the 1970s, when the Peace People briefly united Catholics and Protestants, were discouraging. Ultimately, the campaign collapsed amid acrimony and recrimination and the 'Whataboutery' which the McCartney family were soon enduring from different sides. Others with relatives killed by the IRA, loyalists or the British Army demanded similar attention, some resenting the media focus on a single case.

Meanwhile, the IRA was also confronted with allegations of criminality, including tax evasion, smuggling and money laundering. Charges were levelled at loyalist groups too, but there were substantial differences in *modus operandi* and sophistry. The differences were acknowledged by the head of Northern Ireland's Assets Recovery Agency, who insisted that loyalists were 'very much at the hard end – drugs, extortion, local armed robberies, prostitution – crimes that are almost all in the community's face and often for personal gain. Republicans have always tended to operate differently. They have moved much more towards excise and revenue-type activities and a few big robberies' (Alan McQuillan, quoted in *The Times*, 25 February 2005: 9, 'IRA PLC Turns from Terror into Biggest Crime Gang in Europe'). Although individual allegations did little to undermine paramilitarism, the collective pressure on the IRA to justify its modern existence was mounting. By the mid-2000s, even a majority (59 per cent) of Sinn Fein supporters believed that the IRA should decommission all of its weapons, a view which could not be attributed merely to socially acceptable answering (*Belfast Telegraph*, 11 March 2005: 1, 'What Ulster thinks now'). Moreover, only 29 per cent of Catholics believed that it was acceptable for parties linked to paramilitary groups involved in violence to form part of a Northern Ireland executive (Kennedy and Farrington 2005: 106).

Institutional Audit

The consociation attempted in the GFA was risky, given the attitudes of the rival political parties who were to form a supposedly coalitional government. The DUP opposed the GFA, although the party's opposition was more to the deal's ambiguities than to its substance; the UUP supported the GFA, but was divided internally; the SDLP offered unambiguous support, whilst claiming that the GFA moved the constitutional scenario closer to Irish unity; and Sinn Fein pledged support for the deal, but the IRA did not leave the stage. Given these positions, it was unsurprising that the institutional apparatus created by the GFA proved fragile. Elections to the Assembly in 1998 placed the UUP and the SDLP as the leaders of their respective ethnic blocs, each with three executive portfolios, but the Assembly strengths of the DUP and Sinn Fein meant that they each had only one seat less.

Against a backdrop of stalemate on decommissioning and DUP hostility to the terms of the GFA, the executive was often dysfunctional. That the GFA had yielded Sinn Fein ministers running Northern Ireland's education and health services was too much for many in the DUP, whilst the supposed interlocking of Northern (Assembly and Executive) and North–South (all-island cross-border) bodies failed to fully develop due to the DUP's boycott of the North–South Ministerial Council (NSMC). The UUP regularly debated the wisdom of being in government with Sinn Fein, and failed to develop an alliance of the moderate centre with the SDLP. The devolution of power to Assembly committees, where relationships were much more consensual, may have been more successful (Tonge 2005).

After the executive was suspended for a fourth, indefinite period in October 2002, it was evident that fresh mandates were required. The triumph of the DUP and Sinn Fein at the November 2003 Assembly elections ostensibly made the restoration of devolution more difficult, yet conversely facilitated a more durable deal in the absence of intra-bloc sniping to end the agreement, as witnessed from 1998 to 2002. For a revived Stormont model to work, a number of changes would be required to move the Assembly from institutional apartheid and party fiefdom in respect of individual ministerial posts. Far from representing genuine power sharing, the 1998–2002 Assembly was an example of power being divided up between rival parties. Moves towards a more collective approach would involve Assembly ratification of ministerial appointments (requiring, for example, the DUP MLAs to endorse Sinn Fein ministers, and vice versa), greater accountability of ministers to the remainder of the executive and the Assembly, and further transfer of legislative drafting and scrutiny powers to Assembly committees. Sanctions, including removal from office, might also be applied to ministers refusing to participate in North–South arrangements, although there is unlikely to be a cross-community consensus for such removals. The NSMC was displaced by intergovernmental action after the collapse of the institutions in 2002. The all-island implementation bodies have operated on a 'care and maintenance' basis since the suspension of devolved government in the North, acquiring no new functions. Other institutions attached to devolution in the North, including the Civic Forum, a pluralist body comprising societal representatives, have been put in cold storage.

Beyond Assembly and North–South institutions, implementation of the GFA has proceeded more successfully, as table 9.1 shows. The Equality Commission absorbed the plethora of earlier statutory bodies designed to eradicate discrimination in employment, housing and public policy. Whilst implementation of equality of opportunity has been largely uncontentious, affirmative action via the use of quotas, most visible in terms of Catholic recruitment to the police, has been more controversial. Such equality measures have been described by critics as the 'clarion call of a Catholic communalism' rather than as about fairness or opportunity (Morgan 2004: 10), although, on this definition, the earlier recruitment imbalances were presumably at least partly a derivative of a Protestant communalism. Although there remain some differentials between the Protestant and Catholic communities,

Table 9.1 Architecture and implementation of the Good Friday Agreement, 1998

Institution	Description	Progress by 2005
Executive	Governing 'cabinet'	Suspended October 2002
Assembly	108-member legislative and scrutiny body	Suspended October 2002
Civic Forum	60-member consultative group	Suspended October 2002
NSMC	All-island Council of Ministers	Suspended October 2002
N–S bodies	All-island implementation/ co-operation	Care and maintenance
British-Irish Council	Federation of devolved institutions	Ongoing advisory forums
British-Irish Intergovernmental Conference	Anglo-Irish body	Ongoing reviews
Decommissioning Commission (IICD)	Paramilitary disarmament	Three acts of IRA decommissioning; ongoing
Equality Commission	Advisory and investigative	Substantial ongoing work
Human Rights Commission	Oversees legislation/ public policy	Substantial, but delays re Bill of Rights; suspension of devolution hampers scrutiny
Policing Commission	Investigated RUC	Reported 1999; led to changes in name, structure, size, recruitment and ethos of police
Victims Commission	Forum for relatives of victims of violence	To be established

most notably in the level of unemployment, the era of economic second-class citizenry for nationalists has disappeared, even if sectarianism as a feature of society has not waned.

Amid the rights-oriented agenda of the GFA, it was inevitable that a Human Rights Commission (NIHRC) would be established. Although the British government was already incorporating the European Convention on Human Rights into UK law, it, along with (in particular) the nationalist parties, believed that a specific Northern Ireland body would be valuable in ensuring local institutional recognition of the human rights protections. However, the Commission soon became a 'prisoner of events', as the frequent collapsing of devolution meant that it had 'little opportunity to exercise its new power to advise the Assembly on compliance of proposed legislation with human rights standards' (Livingstone 2000: 166).

There was also slow progress on formulating a Bill of Rights, although prevarication was perhaps excusable given the broad context of such a bill in Northern Ireland, embracing culture, language, identity, economics, social issues and a legacy of communal disadvantage. The NIHRC was charged with consolidating the concept of parity of esteem between the two communities, whilst articulating the rights of individuals within those communities. Thus the Commission has attempted to balance individual and group rights and to avoid institutionalizing division by merely counterbalancing the rights of two rival communities. In doing so, the NIHRC has utilized a European framework for the protection of national minorities, which refers to members of those minorities rather than simply treating them as lumpen, homogeneous collectives (Flynn 2003). Each individual will supposedly have 'equality of identity' (although, given that Irish republicans will still be living in a British state, the concept is contestable).

Changing Politics or Changing Parties?

The most dramatic development after the GFA was reached was the erosion in support from the Protestant community.

Although far from overwhelming adherents, Protestants offered at least majority (57 per cent) support for the GFA in the 1998 referendum. By October 2002, as political institutions collapsed, support among Protestants had fallen to one-third, and by 2003 only 10 per cent agreed with the proposition that 'the Agreement is basically right and just needs to be implemented in full'; and only 28 per cent vowed to back the GFA in a rerun of the 1998 referendum (Kennedy and Farrington 2005: 103–4).

Post-GFA politics were, superficially at least, a case of *plus, ça change*. The fault line in Northern Ireland politics had not altered, with constitutional preferences virtually unchanged – overwhelming Protestant backing for the Union and few takers for Irish unity; slight majority support among Catholics for Irish unity and only fairly small minority support for the Union (see <www.ark.ac.uk/nilt>). What had changed was the tactics of, in particular, Sinn Fein and the willingness to compromise of the unionist parties. A sympathetic account of Sinn Fein suggests that it has always been a party 'careful not to be too specific about its ideology', a flexibility that has allowed it to move from the rhetoric of revolutionary socialism to a plea for respect for the mandate it enjoys for its mildly leftist (albeit tinged with a radical edge) equality agenda in an 'Ireland of Equals' (Maillot 2005: 4, 184). The adoption of the concept of an agreed Ireland and the diminution of purely territorial aspirations has been accompanied by a rights-based agenda in tune with the GFA.

The SDLP's continuing desire for a united Ireland was outlined in its 2005 document, *The Better Way*, which, like Sinn Fein's demands, urged action from the Irish government on the issue, including the issue of a 'greenprint' for unity and the staging of a referendum on the issue. The party conceded that a majority in the North was required, after which a unitary state would need to be set up irrespective of continuing opposition from a minority. This stance is perhaps now as 'green' as that offered by Sinn Fein, which regularly reaffirms its republican objectives, calls for votes for northerners in presidential elections, and demands representation within the Upper House of the Irish parliament, as first steps towards all-Ireland political harmonization. Despite its supposed republican credentials, yet to extend beyond the twenty-six counties, Fianna Fail is less keen, viewing the presence of northerners in the Irish Republic's legislature and elections as potentially destabilizing and as an example of representation without taxation. The GFA reshaped nationalist demands to make them less threatening to unionists, but the constitutional question has not necessarily been resolved in perpetuity.

Within unionism, the DUP's emergence as the dominant force has seen the arrival of a new party pragmatism, previously displayed by the UUP. Trimble's party was too divided internally, over the rationality of backing the GFA's consent principle versus the concomitant erosion of exclusive Britishness, to fully implement the GFA, a problem compounded by archaic structure (Tonge and Evans 2001). The DUP's new approach has been to reconcile 'a belligerent attitude towards republicans and defence of the Protestant community with full participation in council activities' (Farrington 2004: 9). Combined with greater flexibility, evidenced, for example, by engaging in television debates with Sinn Fein, the DUP has prepared its base for a deal with Sinn Fein, but not before the issues of the status of the IRA and the decommissioning of weapons have been resolved. If the DUP's warning prior to the 2003 Assembly elections that 'we are closer to a united Ireland than we have ever been' appeared outlandish, its seven 'principles' and 'tests' for a new Agreement resonated with a Protestant community which felt nationalists to be the major beneficiaries of the GFA (see <www.dup.org.uk>). Of the DUP's seven 'principles', only the insistence that 'terrorist structures and weaponry must be removed before the bar to the Stormont Executive can be opened' offered a substantive difference to the UUP's agenda between 1998 and 2002. Having obtained its election success in 2003, the DUP prepared to do a deal with Sinn Fein a year later on the basis of the dismantling of the IRA, but with no other fundamental changes to the GFA having taken place. After the collapse of the December 2004 deal, both the DUP and Sinn Fein revisited their twin projects of mandate strengthening.

Conclusion

By the middle of the following decade, the main ambition harboured by the British and Irish governments in shaping the GFA, the dissolution of the PIRA as an armed and active unit, had been realized. Northern Ireland was no longer a state under siege and the visible manifestations of conflict were removed under a process of demilitarization, even though political instability remained. Despite the tribulations in the peace process caused by continued paramilitarism, intra-UUP rivalry and DUP opposition to the initial terms of the GFA, British policy remained fairly consistent. The British government continued to search for a solution based upon inclusive devolved power sharing, regarding a deal without Sinn Fein as a non-runner. Given its sizeable mandate and the reluctance of the SDLP to marginalize its nationalist rival, Sinn Fein now held a veto over political arrangements in the North which matched that yielded by IRA violence in earlier years. Whereas the Conservative opposition at Westminster made ritualistic protests over the 'indulgence' shown towards Sinn Fein and the IRA, attempting, for example, to end permanently all expenses, worth £400,000 annually, for Sinn Fein's abstentionist MPs, the Labour Government operated largely uninhibited. Meanwhile, the presence of a small number of Progressive Democrats in the Irish government did not derail Fianna Fail's approach.

The central requirements of the peace process remained the same: devolution, power sharing, decommissioning, demilitarization and disbandment. The problem was that the precise requirements and modalities for most of these were far from clearly stated in the GFA, ensuring years of subsequent wrangling and re-negotiation, amid institutional collapse. There remained the possibility of an alternative form of devolution built through enhanced powers for local councils, where power sharing was often already a reality, although the model of cross-community co-operation was not always encouraging (O'Muilleoir 2000). The more likely, if unstated, default position of the British and Irish governments was, however, the Anglo-Irish Agreement for slow learners – direct rule with increasing nudges towards joint British–Irish authority, a fear of which could propel unionists into negotiation with historic enemies.

From Hotspot to Lukewarm Area? Is the Conflict Over?

The conflict in Northern Ireland has subsided, even though it has not entirely vanished. The fluctuating pace of progress is unsurprising given the tendency of peace processes to be a 'complex succession of transformations, punctuated by several turning points and sticking points' (Miall, Ramsbotham and Woodhouse 1999: 183). As in peace processes elsewhere, paramilitary cease-fires can be followed by 'new mountains', in this case the issues of the transparency of the decommissioning of IRA weapons and the permanency of political arrangements (Darby and MacGinty 2003: 272). However, the main paramilitary actor, the Provisional IRA, abandoned its campaign in 2005, eight years after its final armed actions against British rule had ceased and there appeared to be no prospect of a return to major violence. Global terrorism eclipsed the PIRA.

Only die-hard republicans rely upon historical determinism and a currently unforeseeable crisis in the northern state to revive an armed campaign. The durability of the republican physical force tradition should not be underestimated; nor should the extent of ethnic hostility in sectarian interface areas. Moreover, Northern Ireland exists as a fragile and unstable product of an arguably sectarian head count, this status exacerbated by the legislation arising from the 1998 GFA, which made its place in the United Kingdom explicitly conditional. None the less, it is difficult to envisage circumstances which would marry orthodox republican doctrine with particular events to mobilize the nationalist population, as occurred in 1969–70, to reignite widespread violence. The presence of republican ultra prisoners in jails is a reminder to the British and Irish governments (and to Sinn Fein) that republican militants still exist, but the routing of Sinn Fein and the PIRA into at least semi-constitutional *modus operandi* in the immediate post-GFA years has neutralized armed republicanism as a threat. Governmental tactics of prisoner releases for those on cease-fire and no compromise for the ultras who wished to continue the struggle have squashed most of the 'dissidents' and discouraged others disaffected with the Provisionals from following their path.

It was not merely republican ultras who were unwilling to let go of the war. Although the label 'securocrats' was classic Sinn Fein-speak, there was evidence of reluctance to let go of the certainties of 'war' among sections of the security services. The much-trumpeted IRA 'spy ring' at Stormont, which led to the collapse of the 1999–2002 Northern Ireland Assembly, did not result in a single prosecution. Similarly, the mysterious break-in at Castlereagh police station, blamed on republicans, failed to yield anything in the courts. Its main activities consisted of dealing with 'dissident' republicans or local suspected criminals, neither of which posed particular problems for the British government.

The peace 'dividend' after the GFA was considerable, a process which accelerated rapidly after the IRA stood down in 2005. Two-thirds of British Army bases were to be abandoned. The disbandment of the Northern Ireland-based battalions of the Royal Irish Regiment was announced and troop reductions, from 10,500 to a normal peacetime garrison of 5,000, were envisaged. Army back-up for the police service was to be ended, other than in exceptional circumstances. Remaining watch-towers were to be demolished, a process begun within days of the IRA standing down.

Meanwhile loyalist paramilitary groups oscillated between provocative violence and periods of quiet. The UDA and the UFF, sometimes operating under the pseudonym the 'Red

Hand Defenders', were responsible for the majority of violent incidents in the first five years after the GFA, although the removal of Johnny Adair's 'C Company' in the loyalist feud of 2002 quietened the UDA's violent instincts. Far less wedded to the GFA than their counterparts in the UVF, and lacking that organization's central control, the UDA's intention was clear if unsubtle in the early post-GFA years: to provoke the PIRA back into violence. After the failure of this tactic, the UDA showed signs of movement away from residual violence, and its cease-fire was reinstated. Its political outlet, the Ulster Political Research Group, began to emerge as an organization willing to shift loyalism towards community-oriented projects rather than low-level violence, even though transformation was incomplete. The Protestant working class remained sceptical of the GFA, and loyalist paramilitaries proved capable of organizing serious rioting, linked to the re-routing of Orange parades.

Who Won 'the War'?

The British and Irish governments, along with most of the political parties, were anxious to portray a power-sharing deal as an honourable compromise. Only ultra groups on both sides, plus the DUP, which supported merely a 're-negotiated' deal, opposed the GFA initially, even though many unionists were hostile to its conflict-resolution aspects. Unionists were defending merely the constitutional *status quo*. It was natural, therefore, that other measures within the package were seen as concessions to nationalists. In their support for the GFA and power sharing, it was evident that Sinn Fein had travelled furthest ideologically, given the rejection in previous decades by republicans of a deal which preserved Northern Ireland and offered a mere Irish dimension. Fearing continued marginalization, Sinn Fein dropped its 'Brits out' fundamentalism in favour of a deal which, whatever the claims of the party leadership, offered neither a time-scale nor a defined route (other than possible demographic change) to a united Ireland. As one commentator astutely put it:

By claiming that the GFA will lead to Irish unity, Adams et al are providing a fig leaf for an ideological retreat unequalled in Irish history. What they [Sinn Fein] have done, and are anxious to conceal from their supporters, is to accept a reformed Northern Ireland that, in accordance with the consent principle, will remain British as long as one can see. In return they have avoided political extinction, kept their skins and attained respectability and access to power.

The Agreement is indeed 'transformative', but not in the way 'Provo' spinmeisters suggest. By guaranteeing Catholics their place in the Northern Ireland sun, it has the potential to erode nationalist alienation from the constitutional status quo and, by so doing, dismantle the *raison d'être* of the Provisional IRA.

(Ed Moloney, *Sunday Independent*, 5 September 2004)

The ideological changes of the Provisionals have, for the first time, facilitated acceptance of Northern Ireland by nationalists. The traditional bases of Irish republican politics, the reunification of Ireland and the assertion of undivided national sovereignty, have been eroded by the willingness of Sinn Fein to enter a Northern Ireland Assembly under British jurisdiction. Whilst Sinn Fein may aspire to 'capture' such an institution and deliver it, and Northern Ireland's population, into a united Ireland, the demographic balance in the North precludes such a possibility for generations. The Northern Ireland peace process involved pacification of republicans, in which traditional demands were neutered amid obfuscation (Gilligan 1997). Republicans could also use the apparent impermanence of the GFA as a settlement to promote the impression, however illusory, of transformation. It was a deal on which there was 'no agreement on a common national identity or on the final borders or issue of sovereignty' (Bell 2003: 171). None the less, by default, it was the unionist position which held, as Northern Ireland remained what it had always been: a conditional, non-integrated part of the United Kingdom.

For all bar the most militant republicans, the transformation of Sinn Fein and the PIRA was acceptable, as the republican armed struggle had been long and unproductive. The Sinn Fein leadership could not openly state that reformism would replace rebellion, or that a rewriting of republicanism was on the agenda; yet, within a few years, it was apparent that this was the case. The fear of republicans was that another campaign would end with nothing. In this respect, 10 April 1992 can be seen as a landmark date in the peace process as much as 31 August 1994, the date of the PIRA cease-fire. On that April date, Gerry Adams lost his West Belfast Westminster seat, stark evidence of how Sinn Fein's electoral support had peaked as the IRA's violence continued. Although the IRA could respond – and did so that very evening with a huge bomb in London – it could not win its war, and with Sinn Fein's support checked, the lack of political strength of republicans was a serious weakness. Whilst republicans could have retreated into the cul-de-sac of further militarism at the expense of politics, Adams instead convinced doubters of the value of political routes, and the PIRA continued for some time to engage in sufficient, mainly low-level activity, to prevent defections to ultra groups, prior to its eventual anticipated standing down.

Despite all the changes within republicanism, unionists were far more sceptical of the GFA. This was understandable, given the defensiveness of the unionist position. Northern Ireland was already within the United Kingdom; the police service was adequate in the view of unionists, and there was little inequality between unionists and nationalists. Given this outlook, opposition to the reformism of the GFA was inevitable, as such a deal would be seen as a process of concessions, many yielded through the threat of armed republicanism. Such 'concessions' were seen as worthwhile only if accompanied by the demise of the IRA and the arrival of permanent peace. As these rewards could not be granted immediately, partly due to the process of management of the republican constituency by the Sinn Fein leadership, disillusionment was not surprising. The result of unionist disaffection was the switch in support to the DUP, pledged to remove obfuscations and ambiguities, particularly on IRA decommissioning, in a re-negotiated deal, even though its constitutional framework would be similar and its controversial measures on prisoners and policing already irreversible.

Continuing Community Conflict and Future Northern Ireland Politics

The gradual subsiding of the constitutional conflict in Northern Ireland (even if the status of the province is not fully resolved) does not eliminate problems in the non-constitutional sphere. Low-level inter-community tensions remain, particularly where unionist and nationalist communities live adjacent and are separated by so-called peace walls. There has been an expansion in the number and size of such walls since the GFA, part of a process of 'Balkanization' feared by critics of the deal. A top-down deal predicated upon the idea of a consociational grand coalition of rival forces, the GFA assumed a beneficial spill-over of institutional co-operation into societal reconciliation, but this may have been a somewhat optimistic scenario. A sceptical view of 'grandstanding' political deals suggests that 'to leave the problem of community relations until one has finally solved the constitutional issue may merely exacerbate not only the problem of relationships between the communities but also the task of finding an acceptable constitutional settlement' (Bloomfield 1997: 134).

Indeed, there are those who doubt whether the consociational approach of the GFA can survive, as such a deal institutionalizes division by recognizing and formalizing unionist–nationalist divisions rather than promoting a common humanity and ideology (Wilford 2001; Dixon 2001). The consequences of this have been greater electoral polarization, institutional chaos and increased communal segregation. Whilst the means to societal reconciliation are indeed implicit rather than explicit under consociationalism, criticisms of a GFA-type deal ignore the extent of change elicited within parties, as Sinn Fein and, to a lesser extent, the DUP have moderated their agendas and indicated a willingness to share power in a Northern Ireland Assembly, as they did, albeit

unsatisfactorily and briefly, from 1999 to 2002 in the immediate post-GFA era.

With the PIRA's war against the British over, the question
remains of how future Northern Ireland politics are conducted. Many problems remain regarding the government and
economy of Northern Ireland, a legacy of the rejection of the
state by the minority community, misrule by its majority,
emergency-oriented direct rule and unsatisfactory executive
power sharing. The inability of Northern Ireland to function
as a proper democracy created a need for the Westminster
government to manage the province, ensuring a dependency
culture that the peace and political processes have not lifted.
Northern Ireland remains bereft of productive industry. It has
been described as having 'an economy more collectivized than
Stalin's Russia, more corporatist than Mussolini's and more
quangoised than Wilson and Heath's United Kingdom governments' (Lord Trevor Smith of Clifton, *Hansard*, 20 July,
2004, c152). In 2004, the Northern Ireland Office announced
proposals to reduce the number of councils from twenty-six
to eight, but the new, larger councils would not acquire new
powers.

Perhaps the most important political development would be
the move from a dual party bloc system towards a single party
bloc formation, with the DUP and Sinn Fein the effective
parties within their respective blocs. Assuming continued
moderation of their agendas, this would allow these parties to
construct a deal offering greater permanence than one subject
to destabilizing intra-bloc criticisms. With the PIRA reduced
to a mere 'comrades club', a deal appeared possible, but the
longstanding hostility between unionist and republican representatives meant that few saw Northern Ireland as a stable
political entity. Obituaries have of course been written prema-
turely for the IRA in earlier decades, and 'armed resistance' to
British rule has endured at various levels for centuries, but it
would take a remarkable event to transform the RIRA or CIRA
into large-scale organizations. The most likely eventuality,
therefore, is for power sharing attached to modest all-Ireland
bodies, accompanied by a slow thaw in inter-community relations. Default positions remain direct rule from Westminster or,

more radically and perhaps usefully given the long-term Irish aspiration for unity, joint British–Irish authority, either permanently or as a transition to a united Ireland. Until a settlement embeds, Northern Ireland, although largely peaceful, remains a failed political entity.

Chronology of Events

1800   Act of Union between Great Britain and Ireland.

1886   First Home Rule bill, offering Ireland limited self-government, is defeated.

1905   Sinn Fein is formed, as is the Ulster Unionist Council.

1912   Ulster Volunteer Force formed by Protestants opposed to Home Rule.

1916   Easter Rising launched against British rule by Irish republicans.

1918   Sinn Fein, campaigning for an independent Ireland, wins 73 of 105 seats at the (final) all-Ireland general election. Forms a government not recognized by the British government.

1920   Ireland is partitioned under the Government of Ireland Act. A six-county state, with a devolved parliament, is created in the north-east of the country. The remaining twenty-six counties of Ireland are to be governed by a parliament in Dublin with limited powers.

1921   Anglo-Irish Treaty gives greater powers to the Dublin parliament, following the IRA's war of independence.

1922–3   The Irish civil war is fought between pro- and anti-Treaty IRAs. The pro-Treaty side wins.

1956–62   The IRA stages a border campaign of violence against British rule in Northern Ireland.

1967	Northern Ireland Civil Rights Association formed, demanding equal treatment of all in respect of jobs, votes, houses and policing.
1969	The British Army is sent to Northern Ireland to quell widespread disturbances arising in response to civil rights demands.
1969–70	Provisional IRA and Provisional Sinn Fein are formed, pledging allegiance to the Irish Republic proclaimed in the 1916 Easter Rising. IRA begins campaign of violence aimed at ending British rule in Northern Ireland. The SDLP and Alliance parties are formed.
1971	The Democratic Unionist Party is founded.
1972	Worst year of the 'Troubles', with nearly 500 deaths from political violence. The British Army kills fourteen unarmed civilians in Derry; the IRA campaign includes 'Bloody Friday' in July, when twenty bombs in a single afternoon in Belfast kill nine civilians.
1973	IRA extends its campaign from Northern Ireland to England.
1974	Power-sharing devolved government created under the Sunningdale Agreement, but collapses after 5 months amid a loyalist strike. IRA pub bombings in Birmingham kill twenty-two.
1976	The British ambassador to Ireland, Christopher Ewart-Biggs, is killed by the IRA.
1979	The IRA kills eighteen British soldiers and Lord Mountbatten on the same day in August.
1981	Ten republican prisoners die on hunger strike in a protest for political status.
1982	The British government attempts to 'roll' back devolution to Northern Ireland, but the initiative fails as the new Assembly is boycotted by nationalists.
1985	Anglo-Irish Agreement gives the government of the Irish Republic consultative rights in respect of British policy in Northern Ireland.
1987	IRA bombing of a Remembrance Sunday parade at Enniskillen causes outrage.

1988   Dialogue between the nationalist parties, the SDLP and Sinn Fein, begins.

1989   The Secretary of State for Northern Ireland insists he has 'no selfish strategic or economic interest in Northern Ireland'.

1993   The Downing Street Declaration issued by the British and Irish governments talks of the need for 'Irish self-determination', to be exercised concurrently on a North and South basis.

1994   The IRA declares a cease-fire, reciprocated six weeks later by the loyalist paramilitaries.

1996   The IRA cease-fire breaks down due to Sinn Fein's exclusion from direct negotiations with the British government. The IRA bombs Canary Wharf in London and destroys much of Manchester city centre with the biggest bomb of its entire campaign.

1997   The IRA cease-fire is restored following Labour's election victory in the UK and Fianna Fail's victory in Ireland. The Real IRA is formed by hard-liners angered by the restoration of the Provisional IRA's cease-fire.

1998   The Good Friday Agreement is reached by all the main parties except Ian Paisley's Democratic Unionist Party. It establishes a cross-community executive, a devolved 108-member Northern Ireland Assembly and cross-border bodies. The deal is supported overwhelmingly by voters in the Irish Republic and by a large overall majority in Northern Ireland, although there, the majority of backers amongst Protestants is slight. The Real IRA kills twenty-nine by bombing Omagh, the worst atrocity of the Troubles in Northern Ireland.

1999   Northern Ireland Executive is formed, headed by the Ulster Unionist Party's David Trimble as First Minister and the SDLP's Seamus Mallon as Deputy First Minister. The Patten Report advocates 50/50 Catholic/non-Catholic recruitment to the police service, which is to be renamed.

2000   Devolved government is suspended temporarily, amid unionist concern over the slow pace of IRA decommissioning of weapons.

2001   Westminster and local elections indicate increased support for the DUP and Sinn Fein.

2002   Devolved government collapses after the Police Service of Northern Ireland raids Sinn Fein's office at the Northern Ireland Assembly, claiming the existence of a republican 'spy ring'.

2003   Elections to the moth-balled Assembly confirm big rise in support for the DUP and Sinn Fein, now clearly the main representatives of their ethnic blocs.

2004   The IRA is accused of carrying out the largest bank raid in British and Irish history.

2005   The UUP loses all but one of its Westminster seats in the general election, and its leader, David Trimble, resigns. The IRA formally abandons its armed campaign.

Glossary

Alliance Party Centrist, cross-community party formed in 1970, arguing that Northern Ireland should remain in the United Kingdom for as long as its citizens so choose. Support has dwindled, but is drawn from both communities, albeit mainly from Protestants.

Anglo-Irish Agreement A deal struck between the British and Irish governments in 1985, giving the Irish government consultative rights on Northern Ireland.

Collusion Term used to describe systematic passing of information from the security forces to loyalist paramilitaries to help them target suspected republicans.

Confederalism The establishment of linkages between states under a loose 'umbrella' arrangement, such as the British–Irish Council established in 1998.

Consent principle The view held by the British and Irish governments and most political parties that the decision of whether Northern Ireland should remain under British sovereignty or be placed within a united Ireland should rest with the people of Northern Ireland.

Consociation Power sharing in a divided society between representatives of ethnic blocs, based upon shared government, proportionality, veto rights and community autonomy.

Continuity IRA Tiny IRA splinter group which emerged in the 1990s, committed to physical force to end British rule in Northern Ireland. Linked to Republican Sinn Fein.

Democratic Unionist Party Formed in 1971 from the old Protestant Unionist Party, the DUP was led from the outset by the Reverend Ian Paisley. It offers a staunch defence of the Union and Protestant interests. Support base is exclusively Protestant.

Devolution The transfer of power from a superior parliament to a subordinate body.

Fenian Irish nationalist, although the term is used in a derogatory sense by some Protestants.

Fianna Fail Republican party in the Irish Republic.

Good Friday Agreement 'Peace deal' of 1998, which created devolved government in Northern Ireland, on the basis of power sharing between representatives of the unionist and nationalist communities. The agreement established a cross-community ruling executive, a 108-member Northern Ireland Assembly, cross-border bodies and a British–Irish council. The deal was ratified in referendums north and south of the border.

Integration The belief held by some unionists that Northern Ireland should be fully incorporated into the United Kingdom to prevent uncertainty over its constitutional future.

Irish National Liberation Army Left-wing offshoot of the IRA, formed partly by disaffected members of the old 'Official IRA' of the 1960s. Highly active from the mid-1970s to the late 1980s, but less prominent since.

Loyalist Volunteer Force Tiny Protestant paramilitary group which split from the Ulster Volunteer Force in opposition to its 1994 cease-fire. Based mainly in mid-Ulster.

Nationalist Advocate of a united Ireland.

Orange Order Protestant religious, cultural and political organization, dedicated to upholding the Protestant faith and keeping Northern Ireland within the United Kingdom. Severed its link with the Ulster Unionist Party in 2005 after a century of affiliation.

Progressive Unionist Party Small loyalist political party linked to the Ulster Volunteer Force and supported by some working-class Protestants.

Provisional IRA The main paramilitary actor since its foundation in late 1969, the Provisional IRA killed more than

2,000 people in its quest for a united, independent Ireland. On cease-fire from 1997, the Provisional IRA abandoned its campaign in 2005.

Real IRA Tiny IRA splinter group which rejected the Provisional IRA's second cease-fire in 1997 and remains committed to the use of violence against British rule in Northern Ireland. The Real IRA killed twenty-nine people in its bombing of Omagh in 1998. Linked to the 32 County Sovereignty Committee.

Red Hand Commando Tiny Protestant paramilitary group linked to the Ulster Volunteer Force.

Republican Advocate of a united Ireland and the severing of the British connection with Ireland.

Republican Sinn Fein Tiny political party which split with Provisional Sinn Fein in 1986 on the issue of whether to end abstention from the Dublin parliament. Republican Sinn Fein takes a fundamentalist view, rejecting both 'partitionist' states in Ireland. It argues for a united, independent Ireland.

Self-determination The belief that the Irish people should determine their own future. The difficulty has lain with the unit of self-determination – all of an indivisible Ireland, or both parts of Ireland separately.

Sinn Fein A party that has endured in various forms and survived splits since 1905, and was briefly the largest party in Ireland, from 1918 to 1920. Most people now associate the name 'Sinn Fein' with the party formed in 1970 as Provisional Sinn Fein. Initially a welfare adjunct of the IRA, the party has risen since contesting elections in 1982 to become the majority choice of nationalists in Northern Ireland and now a significant party in the Irish Republic. The party advocates a united, independent Ireland, but has become more pragmatic on the means of its attainment.

Social Democratic and Labour Party Formed in 1970 as a constitutional party arising from the civil rights campaigns. Originally claimed socialist credentials, but supported almost exclusively from the outset by Catholic nationalists.

32 County Sovereignty Committee The political arm of the Real IRA, this committee rejects British rule in Northern Ireland, and believes that Sinn Fein has 'sold out' by entering a Northern Ireland Assembly and ending support for armed struggle.

Ulster Nine-county ancient province, six counties of which form Northern Ireland.

Ulster Defence Association Large paramilitary group formed in the 1970s from local Protestant defence forces. Made illegal in 1992, after involvement in the murder of hundreds of Catholics. Avowedly on cease-fire since 1994, but internal splits mean that the cease-fire has not always been observed.

Ulster Freedom Fighters Cover name for the Ulster Defence Association when involved in killings.

Ulster Political Research Group Political associates of the Ulster Defence Association.

Ulster Unionist Party Formed in 1905 via the Ulster Unionist Council, the UUP was the dominant unionist party of the twentieth century, dedicated to preserving Northern Ireland's place in the United Kingdom. It has been outflanked by the ostensibly more hard-line DUP in recent years.

Ulster Volunteer Force Mass paramilitary organization of 1913–20, formed to oppose Home Rule for Ireland. Reborn as a tiny force in 1966 to oppose supposed revival of Irish republicanism, and active throughout the next three decades in killing Catholics as a supposed deterrent to that community supporting the IRA.

Unionist Supporter of the Union between Great Britain and Northern Ireland and the retention of Northern Ireland's place in the United Kingdom.

United Kingdom Unionist Party Tiny unionist party which supports the integration of Northern Ireland into the United Kingdom.

Internet Links

Alliance Party of Northern Ireland	<www.allianceparty.org>
An Phoblacht	<www.anphoblacht.com>
BBC Northern Ireland	<http://news.bbc.co.uk/northern_ireland>
Belfast Telegraph	<www.belfasttelegraph.co.uk>
Conflict Archive on the Internet (CAIN)	<http://cain.ulst.ac.uk>
Daily Ireland	<www.dailyireland.com>
Democratic Unionist Party	<www.dup.org>
Irish News	<www.irishnews.com>
Linenhall Library, Belfast	<www.linenhall.com>
Newsletter	<www.newsletter.co.uk>
Northern Ireland Assembly	<www.niassembly.gov.uk>
Northern Ireland Life and Times Survey	<www.ark.ac.uk>
Orange Order	<www.grandorange.uk>
Police Service of Northern Ireland	<www.psni.police.uk>
Progressive Unionist Party	<www.pup.org.uk>
Republican Sinn Fein	<http://rsf.ie>
Sinn Fein	<http://sinnfein.ie>
Slugger O'Toole (politics and culture)	<www.sluggerotoole.com>
Social Democratic and Labour Party	<www.sdlp.ie>
Ulster Unionist Party	<www.uup.org>
United Kingdom Unionist Party	<www.welcome.to/ukup>

References

Adams, G. 1995: *Free Ireland: Towards a Lasting Peace*. Dingle: Brandon.

Adamson, I. 1982: *The Identity of Ulster: The Land, the Language and the People*. Belfast: Nosmada.

Anderson, E. 1993: Who's influencing whom? *Irish Freedom*, 24, 14–15.

Anderson, J. and Goodman, J. (eds) 1998: *Dis/Agreeing Ireland*. London: Pluto.

Ardoyne Commemoration Project 2002: *Ardoyne: The Untold Truth*. Belfast: Beyond the Pale.

Arthur, P. 2000: *Special Relationships: Britain, Ireland and the Northern Ireland Problem*. Belfast: Blackstaff.

Aughey, A. 1989: *Under Siege: Ulster Unionism and the Anglo-Irish Agreement*. London: Hurst.

Aughey, A. 2005: *The Politics of Northern Ireland: Beyond the Belfast Agreement*. London: Routledge.

Baldy, T. 1987: *Battle for Ulster: A Study in Internal Conflict*. Washington: National Defense Security Press.

Bean, K. 1995: The new departure? Recent developments in Republican strategy and ideology. *Irish Studies Review*, 10, 2–6.

Bean, K. 2001: Defining Republicanism: shifting discourses of new nationalism and post-republicanism. In M. Elliott (ed.), *The Long Road to Peace in Northern Ireland*, Liverpool: Liverpool University Press, 129–42.

Bell, C. 2003: Human rights and minority protection. In J. Darby and R. MacGinty (eds), *Contemporary Peacemaking: Conflict, Violence and Peace Processes*, Basingstoke: Palgrave, 161–73.

Bennett Report 1979: *Committee of Inquiry into Police Interrogation Procedures in Northern Ireland.* London: HMSO, Cmnd 7497.

Beresford, D. 1987: *Ten Men Dead: The Story of the 1981 Irish Hunger Strike.* London: HarperCollins.

Bew, P., Gibbon, P. and Patterson, H. 2002: *Northern Ireland 1921–2001: Political Forces and Social Classes.* London: Serif.

Bishop, P. and Mallie, E. 1988: *The Provisional IRA.* London: Corgi.

Black, B. 2004: The changing world of work. In K. Lloyd, P. Devine, A. Gray and D. Heenan (eds), *Social Attitudes in Northern Ireland: The Ninth Report.* London: Pluto, 67–80.

Bloomfield, D. 1997: *Peacemaking Strategies in Northern Ireland: Building Complementarity in Conflict Management Theory.* London: Macmillan.

Bowyer Bell, J. 2000: *The Dynamic of Armed Struggle.* London: Frank Cass.

Boyce, D. G. 1991: *Nationalism in Ireland.* London: Routledge.

Boyle, K., Hadden, T. and Hillyard, P. 1980: *Ten Years on in Northern Ireland: The Level and Control of Political Violence.* London: Cobden Trust.

Brewer, J. 1998: *Anti-Catholicism in Northern Ireland 1600–1998.* London: Macmillan.

Bric, M. and Coakley, J. (eds) 2004a: *From Political Violence to Negotiated Settlement: The Winding Path to Peace in Twentieth-Century Ireland.* Dublin: UCD Press.

Bric, M. and Coakley, J. 2004b: The roots of militant politics in Ireland. In M. Bric and J. Coakley (eds), *From Political Violence to Negotiated Settlement.* Dublin: UCD Press, 1–12.

British-Irish Rights Watch 1999: *Deadly Intelligence: State Involvement in Loyalist Murder in Northern Ireland.* London: n.p.

Bruce, S. 1986: *God Save Ulster! The Religion and Politics of Paisleyism.* Oxford: Oxford University Press.

Bruce, S. 1989: Protestantism and terrorism. In Y. Alexander and A. O'Day (eds), *Ireland's Terrorist Trauma.* London: Harvester Wheatsheaf, 52–75.

Bruce, S. 1992: *The Red Hand: Protestant Paramilitaries in Northern Ireland.* Oxford: Oxford University Press.

Buckland, P. 1981: *A History of Northern Ireland.* Dublin: Gill and Macmillan.

Clayton, P. 1996: *Enemies and Passing Friends: Settler Ideologies in Twentieth Century Ulster.* London: Pluto.

Clinton, B. 2004: *My Life.* London: Hutchinson.

Coakley, J. (ed.) 2002: *Changing Shades of Orange and Green.* Dublin: UCD Press.

Cochrane, F. 2001: *Unionist Politics and the Politics of Unionism since the Anglo-Irish Agreement.* Cork: Cork University Press.

Colville Report 1989: *Report on the Operation in 1988 of the Prevention of Terrorism (Temporary Provision) Act 1984.* London: Home Office.

Coogan, T. P. 1989: *The IRA.* London: Fontana.

Coogan, T. P. 1996: *The Troubles: Ireland's Ordeal 1966–1996 and the Search for Peace,* London: Arrow.

Cooke, D. 1996: *Persecuting Zeal: A Portrait of Ian Paisley.* Dingle: Brandon.

Cory Collusion Inquiry Report, 2004a: *Patrick Finucane.* London: HMSO, HC470.

Cory Collusion Inquiry Report, 2004b: *Robert Hamill.* London: HMSO, HC471.

Cory Collusion Inquiry Report, 2004c: *Rosemary Nelson.* London: HMSO, HC473.

Coulter, C. 1999: *Contemporary Northern Irish Society.* London: Pluto.

Cox, M. 1998: Northern Ireland: the war that came in from the cold. *Irish Studies in International Affairs,* 9, 73–84.

Cox, M., Stephens, F. and Guelke, A. (eds) 2001: *A Farewell to Arms? From 'Long War' to Long Peace in Northern Ireland.* Manchester: Manchester University Press.

Cox, W. H. 1985: Who wants a united Ireland? *Government and Opposition,* 20, 29–47.

Crawford, R. 1987: *Loyal to King Billy: A Portrait of the Ulster Protestants.* London: Hurst.

Cronin, S. 1980: *Irish nationalism: A History of its Roots and Ideology.* Dublin: Academy Press.

Cunningham, M. 2001: *British Government Policy in Northern Ireland.* Manchester: Manchester University Press.

Cusack, J. and McDonald, H. 2000: *The UVF.* Dublin: Poolbeg.

Darby, J. and MacGinty, R. (eds) 2003: *Contemporary Peacemaking: Conflict, Violence and Peace Processes.* Basingstoke: Palgrave.

De Chastelain, J. 2004: The Northern Ireland peace process and the impact of decommissioning. In M. Bric and J. Coakley (eds), *From Political Violence to Negotiated Settlement.* Dublin: UCD Press, 154–78.

Democratic Unionist Party 1996: *Silver Jubilee Yearbook 1971–1996.* Belfast: DUP.

Democratic Unionist Party 2001: *Leadership to Put Things Right: Election Manifesto 2001*. Belfast: DUP.

Democratic Unionist Party 2003: *Towards a New Agreement*. Belfast: DUP.

Democratic Unionist Party 2005: *Leadership to Put Things Right: Election Manifesto 2005*. Belfast: DUP.

Dillon, M. 1988: *The Dirty War*. London: Hutchinson.

Dillon, M. 1994: *25 Years of Terror: The IRA's War against the British*. London: Bantam.

Diplock Report 1972: *Report of the Commission to Consider Legal Procedures to Deal with Terrorist Activities in Northern Ireland*. London: HMSO, Cmnd 5185.

Dixon, P. 2001: *Northern Ireland: The Politics of War and Peace*. Basingstoke: Palgrave.

Elliott, S. and Flackes, W. 1999: *Northern Ireland: A Political Directory 1968–1999*. Belfast: Blackstaff.

Ellison, G. and Smyth, J. 1999: *The Crowned Harp: Policing in Northern Ireland*. London: Pluto.

English, R. 2003: *Armed Struggle: The History of the IRA*. London: Macmillan.

Evans, J. and Tonge, J. 2003: The future of the 'radical centre' in Northern Ireland after the Good Friday Agreement. *Political Studies*, 51 (1), 26–50.

Evans, J., Tonge, J. and Murray, G. 2000: Constitutional nationalism and socialism in Northern Ireland: the greening of the Social Democratic and Labour Party. In P. Cowley, D. Denver, A. Russell and L. Harrison (eds), *British Elections and Parties Review*, 10, London: Frank Cass, 117–32.

Eveleigh, R. 1978: *Peace-Keeping in a Democratic Society*. London: Hurst.

Fahey, T., Hayes, B. and Sinnott, R. 2005: *Conflict and Consensus: A Study of Values and Attitudes in the Republic of Ireland and Northern Ireland*. Dublin: ESRI.

Farrell, M. 1976: *Northern Ireland: The Orange State*. London: Pluto.

Farrington, C. 2004: Watch Paisley: he's moving. *Fortnight*, 428, 9.

Farry, S. and Neeson, S. 1999: Beyond the band-aid approach: an Alliance Party perspective on the Belfast Agreement. *Fordham International Law Journal*, 22 (4), 1221–49.

Fay, M., Morrisey, M. and Smyth, M. 1999: *Northern Ireland's Troubles: The Human Costs*. London: Pluto.

Feeney, B. 2002: *Sinn Fein: A Hundred Turbulent Years*. Dublin: O'Brien.

Fields, R. 1989: Terrorised into terrorist: 'Pete the Para strikes again'. In Y. Alexander and A. O'Day (eds), *Ireland's Terrorist Trauma*. London: Harvester Wheatsheaf, 102–38.

Flynn, I. 2003: Rights, equality and the middle ground. *Fortnight*, 416, 9.

Gafikin, F. and Morrisey, M. 1990: *Northern Ireland: The Thatcher Years*. London: Zed.

Gardiner Report 1975: *Report of a Committee to Consider in the Context of Civil Liberties and Human Rights, Measures to Deal with Terrorism in Northern Ireland*. London: HMSO, Cmnd 5847.

Garry, J., Kennedy, F., Marsh, M. and Sinnott, R. 2003: What decided the election. In M. Gallagher, M. Marsh and P. Mitchell (eds), *How Ireland Voted 2002*. Basingstoke: Palgrave Macmillan, 119–42.

Gillespie, G. 1998: The Sunningdale Agreement: lost opportunity or an agreement too far? *Irish Political Studies*, 13, 100–14.

Gilligan, C. 1997: Peace or pacification process? A brief critique of the peace process. In C. Gilligan and J. Tonge (eds), *Peace or War? Understanding the Peace Process in Northern Ireland*. Aldershot: Ashgate, 19–34.

Graham, B. 1997: A representation of place yet to be imagined. In P. Shirlow and M. McGovern (eds), *Who are 'the People'? Unionism, Protestantism and Loyalism in Northern Ireland*. London: Pluto, 34–54.

Haagerup, N. 1984: *Report Drawn up on Behalf of the Political Affairs Committee on the Situation in Northern Ireland*. European Parliament working documents, 1–1526/83.

Harnden, T. 1999: *Bandit Country: The IRA and South Armagh*. London: Hodder & Stoughton.

Harris, R. 1972: *Prejudice and Tolerance in Ulster*. Manchester: University of Manchester Press.

Hayes, B. and McAllister, I. 1996: British and Irish public opinion towards the Northern Ireland problem. *Irish Political Studies*, 11, 61–82.

Hayes, B. and McAllister, I. 2001: Who voted for peace? Public support for the 1998 Northern Ireland Agreement. *Irish Political Studies*, 16, 73–84.

Hayes, B. and McAllister, I. 2004: The erosion of consent: Protestant disillusionment with the 1998 Northern Ireland Agreement. Paper presented to the Elections, Public Opinion and Parties Annual Conference, Nuffield College, Oxford University, September.

Hennessey, T. 2000: *The Northern Ireland Peace Process: Ending the Troubles?* Dublin: Gill and Macmillan.

Hickey, J. 1984: *Religion and the Northern Ireland Problem.* Dublin: Gill and Macmillan.

Hillyard, P. 1997: Security strategies in Northern Ireland: consolidation or reform? In C. Gilligan and J. Tonge (eds), *Peace or War? Understanding the Peace Process in Northern Ireland.* Aldershot: Ashgate, 103–18.

HM Government 1998: *The Agreement.* Belfast: HMSO.

HM Government 2003: *Joint Declaration on The Way Forward.* London, n.p.

Holland, J. and McDonald, H. 1994: *INLA: Deadly Divisions.* Dublin: Torc.

Horgan, J. and Taylor, M. 1997: Proceedings of the Irish Republican Army General Army Convention, December 1969. *Terrorism and Political Violence*, 9 (4), 151–8.

Horowitz, D. 2001: The Northern Ireland Agreement: clear, consociational, and risky. In J. McGarry (ed.), *Northern Ireland, Civic Nationalism and the Good Friday Agreement.* Oxford: Oxford University Press, pp. 89–108.

Hume, D. 1996: *The Ulster Unionist Party.* Belfast: Lurgan.

Hunt Report 1969: *Report of the Advisory Committee on Police in Northern Ireland.* Belfast: HMSO, Cmnd. 535.

Independent Monitoring Commission 2004: *Second Report.* London: HMSO.

Independent Study Group 1984: *Britain's Undefended Frontier.* London: n.p.

Irish Independence Party 1977: *Irish Dialogue – The First Step.* Armagh: IIP.

Irwin, C. 2002: *The People's Peace Process in Northern Ireland.* Basingstoke: Palgrave.

Irwin, C. 2003: Devolution and the state of the Northern Ireland Peace Process. *Global Review of Ethnopolitics*, 2 (3–4), 71–91.

Irvin, C. and Byrne, S. 2002: Economic aid and its role in the peace process. In J. Neuheiser and S. Wolff (eds), *Peace at Last? The Impact of the Good Friday Agreement on Northern Ireland.* Oxford: Berghahn, 132–52.

Kelly, M. and Doyle, J. 2000: The Good Friday Agreement and electoral behaviour – an analysis of transfers under PRSTV in the Northern Ireland Assembly elections of 1982 and 1998. Paper presented to the Political Studies Association of Ireland Annual Conference, University College Cork, October.

Kennedy, F. and Farrington, C. (eds) 2005: *Northern Ireland. Irish Political Studies Data Yearbook 2004*, 20 (1), 77–106.

Kennedy-Pipe, C. 1997: *The Origins of the Present Troubles in Northern Ireland*. Harlow: Longman.

Laffan, M. 1999: *The Resurrection of Ireland: The Sinn Fein Party 1916–1923*. Cambridge: Cambridge University Press.

Lawyers Committee for Human Rights 2002: *Beyond Collusion: The UK Security Forces and the Murder of Patrick Finucane*. London: n.p.

Lijphart, A. 1975: *Democracy in Plural Societies: A Comparative Exploration*. New Haven: Yale University Press.

Little, A. 2004: *Democracy and Northern Ireland*. Basingstoke: Palgrave.

Livingstone, S. 2000: The Northern Ireland Human Rights Commission. *Irish Political Studies*, 15, 163–71.

McAllister, I. 2004: The Armalite and the ballot box: Sinn Fein's electoral strategy in Northern Ireland. *Electoral Studies*, 21 (1), 123–42.

McAllister, I. and Wilson, B. 1978: Bi-confessionalism in a confessional party system: the Northern Ireland Alliance Party. *Economic and Social Review*, 9 (3), 207–25.

McAuley, J. 2002: The emergence of new loyalism. In J. Coakley (ed.), *Beyond Orange and Green*, Dublin: UCD Press, 106–22.

McCall, C. 1999: *Identity in Northern Ireland*. London: Macmillan.

McCann, E. 1980: *War and an Irish Town*. London: Pluto.

McDonald, H. and Cusack, J. 2004: *UDA*. Harmondsworth: Penguin.

McGarry, J. 2004: Globalization, European integration and the Northern Ireland conflict. In J. McGarry and B. O'Leary, *Consociational Engagements*, Oxford: Oxford University Press, 294–322.

McGarry, J. and O'Leary, B. 1995: *Explaining Northern Ireland*. Oxford: Blackwell.

McGarry, J. and O'Leary, B. 1999: *Policing Northern Ireland: Proposals for a Fresh Start*. Belfast: Blackstaff.

McGarry, J. and O'Leary, B. 2004: *Consociational Engagements*. Oxford: Oxford University Press.

McGladdery, G. 2004: Terrorising the heartland? The Provisional IRA bombing campaign in England 1973–97. Unpublished Ph.D. thesis, University of Ulster.

McGowan, L. and O'Connor, J. 2004: Exploring Eurovisions: awareness and knowledge of the European Union in Northern Ireland. *Irish Political Studies*, 19 (2), 21–42.

McGuire, M. 1973: *To Take Arms: A Year in the Provisional IRA.* London: Macmillan.

McIntyre, A. 1995: Modern Irish Republicanism: the product of British state strategies. *Irish Political Studies,* 10, 97–121.

McIntyre, A. 2001: Modern Irish Republicanism and the Belfast Agreement: chickens coming home to roost or turkeys celebrating Christmas? In R. Wilford (ed.), *Aspects of the Belfast Agreement,* Oxford: Oxford University Press, 202–22.

McIntyre, A. 2004: Ultimate deadline by endless postponement. *Fortnight,* 429, 7.

McKittrick, D. and McVea, D. 2001: *Making Sense of the Troubles.* Harmondsworth: Penguin.

McKittrick, D., Kelters, S., Feeney, B., and Thornton, C. 1999: *Lost Lives: The Stories of the Men, Women and Children who Died as a Result of the Northern Ireland Troubles.* Edinburgh: Mainstream.

McStiofain, S. 1975: *Memoirs of a Revolutionary.* Edinburgh: Gordon Cremonesi.

MacGinty, R. 2003: What our politicians should know. *Research Update, Ark. Northern Ireland Social and Political Archive,* April.

Maillot, A. 2005: *New Sinn Fein: Irish Republicanism in the Twenty-first Century.* London: Routledge.

Mallie, E. and McKittrick, D. 1996: *The Fight for Peace: The Secret Story behind the Irish Peace Process.* London: Heinemann.

Mallie, E. and McKittrick, D. 2001: *Endgame in Ireland.* London: Hodder & Stoughton.

Miall, H., Ramsbotham, O. and Woodhouse, T. 1999: *Contemporary Conflict Resolution.* Cambridge: Polity.

Miller, D. 1978: *Queen's Rebels: Ulster Loyalism in Historical Perspective.* Dublin: Gill and Macmillan.

Miller, D. (ed.) 1998: *Rethinking Northern Ireland.* Harlow: Longman.

Mitchell, P. 1999: The party system and party competition. In P. Mitchell and R. Wilford (eds), *Politics in Northern Ireland.* Oxford: Westview, 91–116.

Moloney, E. 2002: *A Secret History of the IRA.* Harmondsworth: Penguin.

Mooney, J. and O'Toole, M. 2003: *Black Operations: The Secret War against the Real IRA.* Ashbourne: Maverick House.

Morgan, A. 2004: This isn't civil rights, this is an equality industry. *Fortnight,* 431, 10–11.

Morrisey, M. and Smyth, M. 2002: *Northern Ireland after the Good Friday Agreement.* London: Pluto.

Mulholland, M. 2000: *Northern Ireland at the Crossroads*. London: Macmillan.

Murray, R. 1990: *The SAS in Ireland*. Dublin: Mercier.

Needham, R. 1998: *Battling for Peace*. Belfast: Blackstaff.

Neuheiser, J. and Wolff, S. (eds) 2002: *Peace at Last? The Impact of the Good Friday Agreement on Northern Ireland*. Oxford: Berghahn.

Ni Aolain, F. 2000: *The Politics of Force: Conflict Management and State Violence in Northern Ireland*. Belfast: Blackstaff.

Northern Ireland Life and Times Survey, various, <www.ark.ac.uk>

Northern Ireland Office 2000: *Report of the Independent Commission on Policing, Implementation Plan*. London: HMSO.

O'Brien, B. 2000: *The Long War: The IRA and Sinn Fein*. Dublin: O'Brien.

O'Clary, C. 1997: *The Greening of the White House*. Dublin: Gill and Macmillan.

O'Dochartaigh, N. 1997: *From Civil Rights to Armalites: Derry and the Birth of the Irish Troubles*. Cork: Cork University Press.

O'Duffy, B. 1993: Containment or regulation? The British approach to ethnic conflict in Northern Ireland. In J. McGarry and B. O'Leary (eds), *The Politics of Ethnic Conflict Regulation*. London: Routledge, 51–76.

O'Leary, B. 1997: The Conservative stewardship of Northern Ireland 1979–97: sound-bottomed contradictions or slow learning? *Political Studies*, 45 (4), 663–76.

O'Leary, B. 1999: The nature of the British-Irish Agreement. *New Left Review*, 233, 66–96.

O'Leary, B. 2001: The Belfast Agreement and the Labour Government. In A. Seldon (ed.), *The Blair Effect*, London: Little, Brown, 449–88.

O'Leary, B. and McGarry, J. 1996: *The Politics of Antagonism: Understanding Northern Ireland*. London: Athlone.

O'Malley, P. 1983: *The Uncivil Wars*. Belfast: Blackstaff.

O'Muilleoir, M. 2000: *Belfast's Dome of Delight: City Hall Politics 1981–2000*. Belfast: Beyond the Pale.

O'Rawe, R. 2005: *Blanketmen, An Untold Story of the H-Block Hunger Strike*. Dublin: New Island.

Pardoe, P. 1998: The nature of change in the Provisional Movement from 1970 until 1998: a question of strategy. Unpublished M.A. thesis, University of Salford.

Patten Report 1999: The Independent Commission on Policing for

Northern Ireland. *A New Beginning. Policing in Northern Ireland*. Belfast: HMSO.

Patterson, H. 1997: *The Politics of Illusion: A Political History of the IRA*. London: Serif.

Patterson, H. 2002: *Ireland since 1939*. Oxford: Oxford University Press.

Police Service of Northern Ireland 2003: *Report of the Chief Constable 2003*. Belfast: PSNI.

Porter, N. 1996: *Rethinking Unionism*. Belfast: Blackstaff.

Republican Sinn Fein 2001: *Towards a Peaceful Ireland*. Dublin: RSF.

Riddell, P. 2003: *Hug them Close: Blair, Clinton, Bush and the 'Special Relationship'*. London: Politicos.

Rolston, B. 1991: The British state and Northern Ireland. In A. George (ed.), *Western State Terrorism*. Cambridge: Polity, 102–25.

Rooney, K. 1997: Education: a panacea for our sectarian ills? In C. Gilligan and J. Tonge (eds), *Peace or War? Understanding the Peace Process in Northern Ireland*. Aldershot: Ashgate, 119–32.

Rose, R. 1971: *Governing without Consensus*. London: Faber.

Rose, R. 1976: *Northern Ireland: A Time of Choice*. Washington: American Enterprise Institute for Public Policy Research.

Rowan, B. 1995: *Behind the Lines: The Story of the IRA and Loyalist Ceasefires*. Belfast: Blackstaff.

Ryan, M. 1994: *War and Peace in Ireland: Britain and the IRA in the New World Order*. London: Pluto.

Ryan, M. 1997: From the centre to the margins: the slow death of Irish Republicanism. In C. Gilligan and J. Tonge (eds), *Peace or War? Understanding the Peace Process in Northern Ireland*. Aldershot: Ashgate, 72–84.

Ryder, C. and Kearney, V. 2001: *Drumcree: The Orange Order's Last Stand*. London: Methuen.

Scorer, C. and Hewitt, P. 1981: *The Prevention of Terrorism Act: The Case for Repeal*. London: National Council for Civil Liberties.

Shirlow, P. 2002: Sinn Fein: beyond and within containment. In J. Neuheiser and S. Wolff (eds), *Peace at Last? The Impact of the Good Friday Agreement on Northern Ireland*. Oxford: Berghahn, 60–75.

Shirlow, P. and McGovern, M. (eds) 1997: *Who are 'the People'? Unionism, Protestantism and Loyalism in Northern Ireland*. London: Pluto.

Sinn Fein 1987: *A Scenario for Peace: Sinn Fein Discussion Document*. Dublin: Sinn Fein.

Sinn Fein 1992: *Towards a Lasting Peace in Ireland*. Dublin: Sinn Fein.

Sinn Fein 1999: *Sinn Fein and the European Union: Draft Discussion Document*. Dublin: Sinn Fein.

Sinn Fein 2003: *Sinn Fein and the European Union: Draft Discussion Document*. Dublin: Sinn Fein.

Smith, M. 1995: *Fighting for Ireland? The Military Strategy of the Irish Republican Movement*. London: Routledge.

Social Democratic and Labour Party 2005: *The Better Way*. Belfast: SDLP.

Stalker, J. 1988: *Stalker*. London: Harrap.

Stevens Report 1990: *The Report of the Deputy Chief Constable of Cambridgeshire into Allegations of Collusion between Members of the Security Forces and Loyalist Paramilitaries*. London: HMSO.

Stevens Report 1994: *Second Report of Inquiry into Allegations of Collusion between Members of the Security Forces and Loyalist Paramilitaries*. London: HMSO.

Stevens Report 2003: *Third Report of Inquiry into allegations of Collusion between Members of the Security Forces and Loyalist Paramilitaries*. London: HMSO.

Sunday Times Insight Team 1972: *Ulster*. London: Penguin.

Taylor, P. 1997: *Provos: The IRA and Sinn Fein*. London: Bloomsbury.

Taylor, P. 2000: *Loyalists*. London: Bloomsbury.

Taylor, P. 2001: *Brits: The War Against the IRA*. London: Bloomsbury.

Thatcher, M. 1993: *The Downing Street Years*. London: HarperCollins.

Tonge, J. 2000a: The Formation of the Northern Ireland Executive, *Irish Political Studies*, 15, pp. 153–61.

Tonge, J. 2000b: From Sunningdale to the Good Friday Agreement: creating devolved government in Northern Ireland. *Contemporary British History*, 14 (3), 39–60.

Tonge, J. 2002: *Northern Ireland: Conflict and Change*. London: Pearson.

Tonge, J. 2003: Victims of their own success? Post-Agreement dilemmas of political moderates in Northern Ireland. *Global Review of Ethnopolitics*, 3 (1), 39–59.

Tonge, J. 2004: They haven't gone away, you know: Irish Republican 'dissidents' and 'armed struggle'. *Terrorism and Political Violence*, 16 (3), 671–93.

Tonge, J. 2005: *The New Northern Irish Politics?* Basingstoke: Palgrave Macmillan.

Tonge, J. and Evans, J. 2001: Faultlines in Unionism: division and dissent within the Ulster Unionist Council. *Irish Political Studies*, 16, 111–32.

Tonge, J. and Evans, J. 2002: Party Members and the Good Friday Agreement. *Irish Political Studies*, 17 (2), 59–73.

Ulster Unionist Party 2003: *Simply British: Northern Ireland Assembly Election Manifesto 2003*. Belfast: UUP.

Walker, G. 2004a: *A History of the Ulster Unionist Party: Protest, Pragmatism and Pessimism*. Manchester: Manchester University Press.

Walker, G. 2004b: The Ulster Unionist Party and the Bannside by-election 1970. *Irish Political Studies*, 19 (1), 59–73.

Walsh, P. 1994: *Irish Republicanism and Socialism: The Politics of the Republican Movement 1905 to 1994*. Belfast: Athol.

Ware, J. 1998: Time to come clean over the Army's role in the dirty war. *New Statesman*, 24 April, 10–11.

Whyte, J. 1991: *Interpreting Northern Ireland*. Oxford: Clarendon Press.

Wichert, S. 1999: *Northern Ireland since 1945*. Harlow: Longman.

Widgery Report 1972: *Report of the Tribunal Appointed to Inquire into the Events of Sunday January 30 1972 which Led to the Loss of Life in Connection with the Procession in Londonderry on that Day*. London: HMSO, Cmnd. 220.

Wilford, R. (ed.) 2001: *Aspects of the Belfast Agreement*. Oxford: Oxford University Press.

Wilson, T. (ed.) 1955: *Ulster under Home Rule*. Oxford: Oxford University Press.

Wilson, T. 1989: *Ulster: Conflict and Consent*. Oxford: Blackwell.

Note: page references in **bold** type indicate Glossary entries.